The
Mighty
Continent

„Der junge General"
Kaisersgeburtstagfeier
27. Januar 1915

John Terraine

The Mighty Continent

a view of
Europe in the
twentieth
century

British Broadcasting Corporation
and Hutchinson of London

Title page:
Cologne high-school boys celebrate the
Kaiser's birthday in 1915 (August Sander)

Published by the
British Broadcasting Corporation
35 Marylebone High Street, London W1M 4AA

ISBN 0 563 12656 6

and

Hutchinson & Co (Publishers) Ltd
3 Fitzroy Square, London W1P 6JD
London Melbourne Sydney Auckland
Wellington Johannesburg Cape Town
and agencies throughout the world

ISBN 0 09 122260 5

First published 1974

Printed in England by
Jolly and Barber Ltd, Rugby

Contents

Preface 7

Prologue 11

1 Hey-day Fever 17

2 The Day of Empires 43

3 A World to Win 79

4 When the drums begin to roll 107

5 This generation has no future 127

6 Are we making a good peace? Are we? 157

7 The Hope of Mankind 177

8 Form! Riflemen form! 201

9 With hardship their garment 227

10 Human rights and fundamental freedoms 251

11 The Mighty fallen 277

12 A certain amount of violence 297

13 A European idea 317

References 342

Index 346

Acknowledgements

Most historians acknowledge the services rendered to their books by learned colleagues, careful proof-readers and well-disposed associates of various descriptions. This book, as much as any other, owes a debt to such helpers; being a television history, it should also acknowledge certain other contributions. But first, on the academic side, I must thank Professor Donald Watt of the London School of Economics, who was the historical adviser to the television series from start to finish; Dr Guy Métraux of UNESCO for his stimulating and corrective comments; and Professor Martin Greiffenhagen of Stuttgart University who held the advisory brief for our German partners, Süddeutscher Rundfunk. On the television side of the project, Miss Jane Ades performed miracles in the research of paintings, drawings, cartoons, still photographs and similar material; Miss Maxine Baker unearthed film to frequently exacting specifications; Mr Colin Reid burrowed industriously for diverse and unlikely facts; Mr Allan Tyrer, as chief film editor, was a doughty fighter for clarity in obscure areas.

The series was produced by Peter Morley, in collaboration with whom I first worked out the whole idea. Brian Lewis was the associate producer, coming rather later to the project, but bringing an invaluable experience of documentary film-making. It was a particular satisfaction to be able to call on the help of the BBC's European Service on various occasions; the BBC Television Service gave its steady support through bad times as well as good.

Preface

This book is another sample of television history; that is to say, it is complementary to a series of television programmes of the same title. It requires to be judged alongside Alistair Cooke's *America* (BBC tv 1972), Mark Arnold-Forster's *The World at War* (Thames tv 1974), or my own *Life and Times of Lord Mountbatten* (Thames tv 1969). I feel sure that it is better to describe all such works as 'television history' rather than as 'books of the film', which is an inexact, misleading and vulgar phrase at best.

The relationship between book and film in television history can, of course, vary enormously; they are linked to each other, not shackled. In all three cases mentioned above, and in the case of *The Mighty Continent* also, the subject is very large, the interpretation is in no way 'definitive', but the act of selection – the editorial discretion – is all-important. What separates television history from printed history is that this act of selection is necessarily greatly influenced by what it is possible to put on the screen – and even more, perhaps, by what is impossible. And this influence, not always agreeable to the historian, is itself determined by the style of the television programmes themselves.

When the BBC made its 26-programme series *The Great War* (1964), the chosen style was a mixture of a very large amount of archive film from many sources and a number of eye-witnesses. Thames Television adopted the same formula for World War II in *The World at War*. In each case an immensely successful series resulted, because of the great strength of the visual material screened. But in each case there was a weakness: the difficulty of presenting on television the intellectual background of the events shown, the thinking behind them – their motivations, in other words. For instance, the strategic dispute between 'Easterners' and 'Westerners' profoundly affected the conduct of the First World War, and is unresolved among historians to this day. But there is no film of such disputes, and so this vast question was lucky to receive a 30-second treatment in a series lasting for over seventeen hours of screen-time. The great wrangles of the Second World War have fared a little better at the hands of Thames TV, because some of the protagonists are still alive; but the fact remains that this style of production is not suited to the reflection of significant debate.

There are stylistic answers to this particular problem. One was provided in the BBC's *Grand Strategy* series (1970), where Professor Michael Howard supplied the intellectual 'frame' for the archive material. In *The Life and Times of Lord Mountbatten*, Lord Mountbatten could speak for himself and explain the motives for his own actions: the necessity for the Dieppe Raid in 1942, his response to rising Asian nationalism in 1945, his reasons for bringing forward the date of Indian Independence in 1947. In *America* Alistair Cooke was able to explore unfamiliar personalities and institutions by the exercise of his own erudite and persuasive charm on the screen.

In the case of *The Mighty Continent*, the BBC Documentary Department experimented with another mixture. The breakdown of seventy-five years of European history into thirteen television programmes, the deciding of the contents of each one of those programmes (and thus of each of the chapters of this book) was my task, in close collaboration with the producer of the series, Peter Morley; consequently, it also became my task to tell the resulting story on the television sound-track. But the BBC provided an additional element; our narrative was, in his own words, 'embellished by comments from a mongrel with antecedents in most of the countries described' – Peter Ustinov.

It was desirable, we thought, in telling the story of Europe, to have the services of a truly 'European man', if such a person could be found; and no sooner was the question posed than Peter Ustinov's name sprang to mind. His ancestry is part Russian, part French; one of his grandmothers was part Swiss, part Ethiopian; she and his grandfather lived in Italy; his father served in the Imperial German Army; he himself served in the British Army; his wife is French; he lives in Switzerland and Paris and has a villa in Spain, but went to school in England. His contribution, in other words (once more, his own) was to 'add a little condiment born of mixed blood to the meal of erudition and fact'.

It is in such areas that television can provide an extra factor in the presentation of history; the books score in other ways – by developing themes which television must necessarily cut short, by filling distressing gaps, offering supporting detail and documentation, and finally by erecting the defence of hard covers against the ephemerality of the visual medium. And this, from the historian's point of view, is important, because although television history cannot pretend to be 'definitive', it does require a long time to prepare, it does absorb a great deal of research and demand a great deal of thought. It would be a pity if all that faded to nothing with the end titles of the last programme in the series.

John Terraine

The
Mighty
Continent

The Moulin Rouge about 1900

Prologue

In 1900 Europe dominated the world. This is not just a figure of speech, nor is it simply a way of saying that Europeans exercised direct rule, though Europe did, in fact, exercise direct rule over a very large part of the world. European Asia included French Indo-China, the Dutch East Indies, German New Guinea and the great British Raj in India, Burma and Malaya. Africa was almost entirely divided between seven European nations: Britain, France, Germany, Belgium, Portugal, Spain and Italy. Britain, France and Holland also had colonies in the Western hemisphere. But there was more besides: there was also indirect domination in various forms. European culture, for instance, expressed through the medium of European languages, ran right through the Americas, North and South, through New Zealand and the continent of Australia. European economic penetration thrust deep into the independent states of Latin America and gnawed at the Chinese Empire. The Empire of Japan was an unashamed imitator of European technology. That is how it was in 1900. Europe was a mighty continent.

It was also an imperial continent. In 1900, the Emperor Franz Josef had been on the throne of the Austro-Hungarian Empire for fifty-two years. The Emperor Wilhelm II had been on the throne of the German Empire for twelve years. The Emperor Nicholas II had been on the throne of the Russian Empire for six years. Queen Victoria, 'of the United Kingdom of Great Britain and Ireland and the British Dominions across the seas, Queen, Empress of India', had ruled for sixty-three years. She was a very old lady now, very near death. Her world, also, was about to die.

A new century was beginning, brand-new, brash and boastful. The twentieth century came in believing that it had a lot to boast about, more than any of its predecessors. The nineteenth century had opened in Europe to the sound of Industrial Revolution and had been alarmed by the noises of other revolutions at intervals ever since. The eighteenth century had been called the Age of Reason – but it had also been the age of despotism and dynastic wars. The seventeenth century had been an age of plague – and merciless religious wars. After that one was back in the Middle Ages, a deplorable time only to be admired by hopeless romantics in quest of

11

The Palace of Electricity
at the Paris International Fair, 1900

mythical grails. And always, in every century, there were the wars; always the wars.

The twentieth century was going to be different from all that. The twentieth century would know better. In Europe there had now been two decades of peace among the great powers, twenty years during which Austria-Hungary had not been at war, Germany had not been at war, Russia and France had not been at war – at any rate in Europe. Britain had been at war, of course – still was – but Britain's wars nowadays were never in Europe, and this was no exception. Britain's wars were to do with her Empire, and now she was fully occupied amid the kopjes and dorps of South Africa. But Europe had better things to do.

Europe's historic centre might be Vienna; her religious centre – if one could talk of such a thing – might be Rome; her military/economic centre might be Berlin; her trade/financial centre might be London. Paris still stole the show. It was Paris, in 1900, that put this new century, dominated by European political and military power, by European technology and economic strength, by European culture, on display.

The 1900 World Fair is destined to incarnate the philosophy and the sympathy of the century, as well as its grandeur, grace and beauty; it will reflect the clear genius of France, and it will show our fair country to be, today as yesterday, in the very vanguard of Progress.[91]*

Thus the Prospectus of the great International Fair which Paris offered, as host, to the world. To this extraordinary exhibition all could come and admire . . . themselves. There was a Spanish Esplanade, a street of Imperial Russia, a Chinese Pavilion. Under the slopes of the Trocadero, where today we look up to the crisp, modern outlines of the Palais de Chaillot, stood a full-blown Arab city – full-blown, but happily less fly-blown than those in whose conquest the French at that time took such pride. These were the splendours of pomp and power, but the real message of 1900 lay else-where: in the pavilions where the miracles of mechanics, engineering, chemistry, industry, aviation and electricity were revealed.

The Palace of Electricity glows nightly with dazzling lights, and there written, as it were, in letters of fire, will be found the history of electricity from its most primitive manifestations to its latest application: the telephone, bearer of winged words and herald of the television of the future which will transmit over long distances the living image of the person speaking . . . the fairy goddess of elec-tricity has become a mighty sovereign, endowed, thanks to the genius of man, with infinite powers. . . .[91]

This is the authentic language of the twentieth century, the century which

*The figures refer to the bibliographical references on p. 342.

14

lost no time in transferring 'infinite powers' from the province of God to 'the genius of man'.

None would be quicker to assert that transfer than the French, and whatever else Paris may display, she never fails to display herself and France. It was not at all difficult for admiring visitors, carried along perhaps by the moving pavements which provided one more proof of technology's triumph in 1900, to find France's tributes to herself. Somewhat ludicrous now, possibly, but far from ludicrous then, was her warm approval of the empire-building in which she was vigorously engaged:

An entire pavilion has been taken to illustrate the work of material and moral improvement undertaken in the colonies. The results so far obtained amply justify the necessity of colonial expansion so pressingly felt by the civilised nations.[91]

In the Europe of 1900 few would challenge these sentiments, even if they queried the right of the French to express them so forcefully. The French Empire was, after all, a very young institution compared with some. Nevertheless, this was a message that most of Europe would understand. And France had another message too, which she hoped that certain parts of Europe in particular would understand. The Army and Navy pavilion reflected French pride in what was hoped to be a military revival after the disastrous defeat by Germany in 1871. But this pride was even better reflected in the prolific output of a school of painters, headed by Edouard Detaille and Alfred de Neuville, who truly expressed the latest renewal of France's long love affair with her Army. Some such expression was needed, after the venoms and squalors of the Dreyfus Case. Whatever the rights and wrongs of that case might be, whether the Jewish Captain Dreyfus was really a spy or not, whether he was a victim of Army anti-Semitism or not, France had been bitterly divided on this issue. Yet most Frenchmen recognised that it was the Army which would have to protect France from fresh invasions like 1870, it was the Army which had made her a great imperial power, and it was the Army which was the symbol of her astonishing recovery from defeat.

All in all, the great Exhibition of 1900, with its marvels, its mysteries and its vulgarities, had a lot to say – about France, about Europe, and in particular about the twentieth century which it heralded.

A lady photographed in the Bois de Boulogne
in 1910 by the fifteen-year-old Lartigue

1   Hey-day Fever

It was Paris, at her most self-confident, that gave to the first years of Europe's new century the name by which, rightly or wrongly, we remember them: 'La Belle Epoque'. France now felt herself once again to be the 'grande nation', and Paris could preen herself as a major world capital. Her evident wealth and her impressive ceremonials compelled respect, her artistic brilliancies and outward glitter compelled admiration, even among the envious. This, after all, was the high summer of the Paris we know: Baron Haussmann's Paris, begun at the behest of Napoleon III, with long, open vistas replacing the complex of old, narrow streets, so that well-placed artillery could keep the mob at bay and protect the usurper from would-be imitators. Now the fields of fire of the cannon had turned into elegant boulevards, where dandies and stylish ladies strolled before the admiring audience of the cafés.

The boulevards and buildings of Paris provided the backdrop to a continuous succession of tableaux presented to an applauding world. There was the tableau of political notables. The President of France in 1900 was Emile Loubet and the Prime Minister was René Waldeck-Rousseau. Neither of them has left any deep impression on the tablets of European history, though each had a precise niche in French politics. And around both circulated the interchangeable, hairy procession of the Third Republic, names that men would later conjure with, names they might prefer to forget: Alexandre Ribot, Joseph Caillaux, Georges Clemenceau, Aristide Briand, Raymond Poincaré. All were now reaching towards the peaks of their careers. By 1900 there had already been thirty-seven changes of government in France in twenty-nine years, without making any noticeable difference to French society or French policy.

Mingling with, but quite separate from, the political tableau was the Beau Monde. In this rarefied air such legendary eccentrics as Bony de Castellane found a thousand sensational ways of parting with a fortune. Eccentrics of another kind, like Lord Alfred Douglas, caused a different sort of sensation in those days when homosexuality quite often happened, but was regarded as too shameful to admit, even in the Beau Monde. This was the world of brilliant ladies and gentlemen who liked to think themselves abreast of modern thinking, who raced at Longchamps, rode and drove in the Bois de Boulogne, dined at Maxim's, and entertained each other in houses whose doors were impenetrable to those who did not 'belong'. And thanks to the immense vanity of this aristocracy and its followers, the determination of both its male and female members never to be out-done in the competition of fashion, Paris had become the capital of that world too – that gilded world in which the latest couturier was king.

And then there was the Demi-Monde, whose tableau mingled with that of the Beau Monde sometimes quite blatantly, but usually only by the discreetest assignation. The Demi-Monde was a race apart of beautiful ladies whose profession it was to be intimately acquainted with rich men. There were various disrespectful names for them: 'coquettes', 'horizontales', 'dégrafées' (we would have to translate that now as 'unzipped'), but these roses, by any name, were always recognisable – and recognised wherever they went: Liane de Pougy, Polaire, Emilienne d'Alençon, Lina Cavalieri, Manon Loti. Their rivalries were news; their progresses, down the Champs Elysées or in the Bois, were regal; their fame was international.

The spirit of the new century was everywhere restless, inquisitive, prone to excitements that were often unashamedly vulgar. The quest for novelties had never been more relentless – nor so readily satisfied. In Paris the new motor-buses and electric trams advertised the century's new power-sources. There were motor-cycles – and there were even women who dared to mount them, thus making a large stride towards future Liberation. Motor-racing was already an established sport. All the new century's favourite toys were now to be seen, not so numerous, not so dangerous as they would soon become, but already capable of disconcerting.

Flying was the newest thing of all. Parallel with the Wright brothers in America, France was pioneering the aeroplane while Germany pioneered the airship, and no one yet knew with which of the two the future would lie. The first heavier-than-air machines looked fragile and puny by comparison with the big airships. But experiment was going on all the time. It was the Frenchman, Captain Ferber, who said: 'To design a flying machine is nothing; to build one is nothing much; to try it in the air is everything.' And so it was: Ferber gave his life, 'trying it in the air', but his work was carried on by the Voisin brothers, the Brazilian Santos Dumont, Esnault-Pelterie, Farman and Blériot. France and Paris applauded their successes with enthusiasm: all novelty was good; successful novelty was superb!

Haute Couture, Haute Cuisine . . . Paris had no rivals in these fields, and few rivals in the variegated world of Art. At the turn of the century Paris herself was dominated by one extraordinary artiste: Sarah Bernhardt.

The actor's art dies with him; but the rumour of it, when it is very great, lives on the tongue and sometimes in the soul of man, and forms part of his dreams and visions . . . There will, it is to be hoped, be great actresses in the future – actresses filled with the Muses' madness and constrained to enlarge rather than to interpret the masterpieces of the world; but Providence (so economical, so generous!) never repeats an effect; and there will never be another Sarah Bernhardt . . .[6]

Indeed there will not. Bernhardt the actress could reduce a theatre audience to tears with her stage passions. The passions of Bernhardt the woman produced scandal after scandal for Paris to gasp at and revel in; for thirty-five years she lived 'at the centre of scandal and publicity'. A 'Journée Sarah Bernhardt' offered her by Paris in 1896 began with a banquet for six hundred; then two hundred carriages followed her to her own Théâtre de la Renaissance, where she performed the third act of *Phèdre*, after which half a dozen poets, including the dramatist Edmond Rostand who was now her lover, 'recited verses to her on a stage banked with flowers.'[99] In 1900 she made an entirely characteristic gesture of contempt for the ordinary rules of possibility by playing Hamlet. Paris was delighted, London was outraged; neither had heard the last of Bernhardt by any means.

'The divine Sarah' ruled the grand stage, but the truth was that Paris was full of stages. Theatre was flourishing, but so was Music Hall, those boisterous, gay, strenuous performances of the Moulin Rouge and other cafés chantants which have been immortalised by Toulouse Lautrec, and whose divinities were La Goulue, Yvette Guilbert, and not long afterwards Mistinguett, queen of them all, whose legs were as famous as Marlene Dietrich's or Betty Grable's in later generations. And yet all this – theatre, opera, ballet, music hall – was, as someone said, 'a show within a show'. All the frenzy on a hundred stages all over Paris merely reflected the gala life going on around them.

Paris has never been short of painters. Left Bank and Right have throbbed with the activity of the ateliers, the masters of the Classical School, the Romantics, the Academicians, and the rebels of every denomination. The Impressionists, by now, had arrived; they were no longer fighting for recognition – they could even think of making a little money, with luck a modest competence. If they had known what prices their pictures were going to fetch in the 1960s and 70s, they would probably have broken blood-vessels! But in 1900 Paul Cézanne could produce *Still Life with Onions*, Claude Monet could paint *Water Lilies* and *Harmony in Rose*, and Auguste Renoir *Nude in the Sun* without uproar, even if none of these works led the artists themselves to a crock of gold.

The Impressionists brought the bright light of Provence and the clean air of the Ile de France into the exhibition rooms of Paris, and there we may still see them, offering their own reminders of the Belle Epoque. There was also music – the haunting or stirring music of Debussy and Ravel – and sculpture. In the Place de l'Alma, right beside the World Fair, there was a special exhibition of the works of Auguste Rodin. These essays in crystallised sensuality, which have the power of transferring to stone or bronze the tactile qualities of human flesh and skin, have now found another home. They are lodged in one of those splendid mansions of the Faubourg St Germain, whose select society was soon to find its own crystallisation in Marcel Proust's vast novel *Remembrance of Things Past*. Proust was the great recorder of the Belle Epoque, its morals and manners, its culture, its wit, its assorted snobberies. But France was full of writers at the turn of the century: Emile Zola, André Gide, Edmond Rostand, Charles Péguy, Maurice Barrès, Colette . . . these are just a few of the names on the counters of the bookshops.

All in all, it was an amazing time. Looking back at it, with the hindsight of over seventy years, it is not altogether easy to understand why the French felt so exuberant at that time. One cannot help feeling that there was more than a touch of hysteria in this tremendous activity of Paris. It certainly did not correspond to the hard realities of a backward French economy, in which coal production was only 33,400,000 metric tons compared with Germany's 149,000,000, while steel was 1,565,000 metric tons compared with 6,461,000, and the gaps were increasing every year. Worse still was the daunting fact of a declining population: just under thirty-nine million Frenchmen in 1900 compared with Germany's fifty-six million, and just under thirty-eight million in 1913 compared with nearly sixty-seven million. Even Britain, outnumbered for centuries by her neighbour across the Channel, had caught up with and passed the French figure, with a population of forty-one million in 1900. These were ominous truths, which could not always be pushed out of sight. Did the French of the Belle Epoque perhaps have a sense of things being too good to last, of time running out? It was thirty years since they had last faced catastrophe. Dared they hope for another thirty years?

And yet to some extent all Europe shared this hey-day fever, this feeling of high summer in the century's first year. For where Paris unquestionably led, others were not far behind. London also was enjoying a festival of diversified arts: listening to Elgar's *Dream of Gerontius*, admiring Sargent's portraits and the classical fantasies of Alma-Tadema, digesting – possibly with hiccups – the doctrines of *The Yellow Book* and the drawings of Aubrey Beardsley, reading Joseph Conrad's *Lord Jim*, Bernard Shaw's *Plays and Prefaces* and the philosophy of Bertrand Russell. Elsewhere in Europe, Puccini was producing *Tosca*, Sibelius the *Finlandia* overture, and

Young peasants on
their way to a dance,
Westwerwald,
Germany
(August Sander)

Strindberg was writing *The Dance of Death*. In Russia the revered Count
Tolstoy, now seventy-two years old, was in the midst of a sensational
quarrel with the Holy Synod of the Orthodox Church over *Resurrection*,
while Chekhov was producing *Uncle Vanya* and Maxim Gorky *Three
People*.

Never had a new century proclaimed itself like this. Never had the cities
of Europe – Paris, Vienna, Milan, Berlin, London – put on such a show of
arts for those who cared, and could afford it. But all this intellectual glitter
and talent is misleading: it reveals only a part of the truth about the
continent at that time. If the saying is true that Paris is not France, it is
certainly equally true that Europe was not just cities, no matter how
artistic or how grand. Thomas Hardy's poem, 'In Time of the Breaking of
Nations', reminds us of an important truth:

> Only a man harrowing clods
> In a slow silent walk
> With an old horse that stumbles and nods
> Half asleep as they stalk.
> Only thin smoke without flame
> From the heaps of couch-grass;
> Yet this will go onward the same
> Though Dynasties pass.

Hardy perceived an enduring element, less obvious now in the 1970s,
sometimes hard to grasp: that at the opening of the twentieth century
Europe was predominantly a continent of peasants. It was only in a few
highly industrialised countries that town-dwellers outnumbered them;
the majority of Europeans lived by the soil and with the soil.

Then – as now, as always – the peasants of Europe were accustomed to
rise before first light, to begin work as the sun rose, and continue until it
went down. They worked with their hands, their legs, their feet, and on
their knees. They worked by instinct and experience, distilled down the
years into shrewd knowledge. They worked from the time they were old
enough to watch a flock or lift a hoe, until old age dimmed their sight,
stiffened their joints, and brought them to unaccustomed, undesired idle-
ness for a few years before they died. For most Europeans, life was work,
sometimes rewarding as only a fine harvest can be, sometimes – at the
caprice of a season, or a war – heartbreakingly thrown away. In some
countries, like Ireland or Russia, the word 'peasant' denoted poverty and
wretchedness; in others, like France or Germany, it denoted unremitting
toil, but also thrift and substance, a certain affluence no less real because it
was concealed.

In the villages and the countryside, even Sunday was a day of only

23

partial rest. There were cows to be milked seven days a week, pigs to be fed, crops to be sown, tended and reaped. These were facts of life as man had known them since the beginning of civilisation, and the Churches of Europe, like everyone else, naturally accepted them. And it was in the peasantry of Europe – with certain crushed exceptions – that the Churches, Catholic, Protestant, Orthodox, found their most constant support. A country-dweller wrote: 'For us God was fact. The Town accepted Him, slightly supercilious and doubting. God did not live in the town house. He lived in the cottage and even in the manor house.'[34]

The most familiar sound in Europe in 1900 was the sound of bells – church bells of infinite variety: the single bell in the lonely steeple, the village chime that was the pride of the ringers, the elaborate carillon of cathedral belfries summoning the citizens of sleepy towns to worship. Church bells signalled birth and rejoicing, sorrow, alarm and death. But whatever their purpose, the bells called people together to receive their message mutually. Theirs was a centripetal sound, not centrifugal, and it was not yet blotted out by factory hooters, or air-raid sirens.

Machines, after all, had not yet won all their battles. The real motive power of Europe in 1900 was still the horse – and in some substantial areas this was going to remain true for at least another fifty years. Horse breeding was an essential industry, breeding for strength and endurance as well as for speed. In the words of the poet Laurie Lee:

. . . the horse was king, and almost everything grew around him: fodder, smithies, stables, paddocks, distances, and the rhythm of our days. His eight miles an hour was the limit of our movements, as it had been since the days of the Romans. That eight miles an hour was life and death, the size of our world, our prison.[63]

It was not merely Europe's peasant economies that depended on horses. They were a power factor, too. Armies needed horses, vast numbers of horses, for mobility and for transportation. After the Haldane Reforms (which began in 1906) a British *infantry* division of 18,000 men required nearly 6000 horses. At the same period, a German cavalry division contained 5200 men – and 5600 horses. The Imperial Russian Army, fully mobilised, could put thirty-six cavalry divisions into the field, or a grand total of about 400,000 men on horseback.

The streets of Europe's cities were full of horses. The great thoroughfares – the Champs Elysées, Unter den Linden, the Corso, the avenidas of Madrid, Piccadilly and the Strand – resounded to the clatter of hoofs, the crack of whips, and no doubt a great quantity of that appalling language which always seems to go with equestrian activities. But the horse was not merely a drudge, it was a mark of fashion. Sir Osbert Sitwell calls the hansom cab, now in its last days of splendour,

Degas. *At the races, before the start*

the very perfect expression of the wealth of London, its luxury and its particular understanding . . . of shining, clean surfaces, of gloss and nap . . . The whole equipage possessed a frail and brittle elegance, every single thing about it, from the top-hat and red buttonhole of the driver, down to the two sliding glass panes of the front, even down to the tail, shoes and hoofs of the horse, had polish, finish and ingenuity. This was essentially the vehicle that had been perfected, through more than a century or two, for – and by – a continuing line of fops, beaux, macaronis, dudes, blades, swells, bloods and mashers . . .[100]

As magically evocative as the names of the dandies in the hansoms are the names of the carriages in which the cream of Europe's society displayed itself; the very sound of broughams, landaus, drags, waggonettes, sociables and victorias conjures up a departed world, a departed style of life.

And yet, despite these horses which were to be seen on all sides, Europe was now well embarked on that process of terrifyingly rapid technological change which has been the distinguishing mark of this century. London's first Underground Railway was opened in 1890 – which was also the year of the opening of the first British electric power station, at Deptford. In 1900, the two innovations were wedded: an experimental train came into operation hauled by electric locomotives. The same year saw the opening of the Central London Railway, the famous 'Tuppenny Tube', because that was the price of its fares to anywhere on the line: two pence. Those were the days of First, Second and Third Class coaches on the London Underground. An old railwayman recalls:

The second-class male passenger was an oddity but generally a fine fellow. He smoked Guinea Gold, drank bottled beer, read Marie Corelli, bet on favourites, worshipped a fox terrier, believed Britain was a Democracy and held a commission in the Volunteers. On Saturday afternoons he fired at Wormwood Scrubs and gathered teaspoons as prizes.[71]

The same man – then fourteen years old and deeply in love with steam engines – says that he and his mates 'did not think much' of electrification. But it was there, its early drawbacks would be overcome, and only fanatics could deny that it was a lot better than the stink of steam and sulphur which filled the tunnels before.

At the beginning of the century Europe had a settled air, its great cities flourished with a look of permanence, and people, disregarding the evidence of their own eyes and ears, tended to speak and act as though this way of things would last for ever. Yet one object alone, says Sir Osbert Sitwell,

might have given them a vision of a civilisation falling to chaos, and of the cities they loved, laid waste: the motor which sometimes tinnily vibrated and steamed in the frost outside the door; for this was the first appearance of the internal combustion engine which was to destroy them. A few of the older generation, it is true, fought the very idea of their ultimate destroyer, but this was because of the novelty of the conveyance, not because of any instinct for their own protection: and perhaps, too, because their sons and daughters took to these machines as if born to them – which, in fact, they were.[100]

Sitwell records that he himself, as a boy and a young man, was one of those who loved the destructive motor-car.

The motor-car was still, nevertheless, a newcomer in 1900; this was the world of the First Industrial Revolution. Its prime mechanical motive power was steam, and its energy source was coal. Britain had a long lead over the rest of the world in terms of the First Industrial Revolution; it had come to her earlier and changed her drastically. In 1800 Britain and Ireland together had a population of $15\frac{1}{2}$ millions, the vast majority of them being country-dwellers, living in farms, villages and small country towns. London, then, had a population of 864,000, which was considered gigantic. A hundred years later the total population had risen to 41·4 millions, 71% of them living in cities and industrial areas. London's population was over four millions.

A considerable proportion of this new, urbanised population lived in the drab sprawl of the mining centres, the valleys of South Wales where the slag-heaps were already rising to heights rivalling the neighbouring hills, the grim, grey-brown mining villages of Durham and the North-east, and the Lowlands of Scotland. As recently as 1890 British coal production had been substantially the highest in the world: 184 million tons a year, with the United States next best at 143 million tons, and Germany third with 89 million. By 1900 there had been a significant change: Britain's production had risen to 219 million tons (Germany 149 million) – but America had swept into a staggering lead over her European competitors with 268 million tons. And in terms of the new motive power that would replace steam – the petrol engine and its energy source – America had the field almost to herself, producing 69·3 million barrels of crude petroleum a year.

It was a similar story with steel. Steel and coal were the twin foundations of First Industrial Revolution technology: railways and locomotives (the basic heavy transport of the age), ships, bridges, machinery, machine tools, armaments, all were made of steel – and in steel production America led the world, with 10·1 million tons a year. This was an ominous portent for Europe's vaunted economic supremacy. It was an especially serious matter for Britain, which by now had fallen back to third place in the vital competition of steel. But there will be more to say about that in a moment.

Officers and men of the Death's-head Hussars, 1910. Nearest camera their colonel, the German Crown Prince

So the lead which the First Industrial Revolution had given to Britain was slipping away. Nevertheless, partly as a legacy of the manufacturing and financial advantage which she had enjoyed throughout the previous century, and partly for solid present reasons, London – the City of London – remained the financial capital of the world. This was a consequence of trade: 29·4% of world trade in manufactured goods was British; imports amounted to £466 million a year, exports to nearly £283 million. Over nine million tons of merchant shipping sailed the oceans of the world under the Red Ensign. The City of London (with the great Port of London as its doorstep) was the focal point of this ceaseless commerce, and Lloyds of London insured it all.

It was hard for the British to feel seriously threatened by economic – or any other – rivalry. An expanding population, increasing production, new inventions and techniques, a long lead over most potential challengers and a worldwide empire brimming with raw materials and other riches tempted the British into complacency. In 1901 Queen Victoria died, and was succeeded by King Edward VII; the following year London, which only five years earlier had been savouring the Queen's Diamond Jubilee, enjoyed the lush spectacle of a coronation which inaugurated a new period: the Edwardian Age. Edward VII, says one historian,

represented, in a concentrated shape, those bourgeois kings whose florid forms and rather dubious escapades were all the industrialised world had left of an ancient divinity: his people saw in him the personification of something nameless, genial and phallic, the living excuse for their own little sins. . . . The blood of his ancestors, agitated by so many crises and so many loves, had taught him to combine duty with indulgence; every beat of it was a warning to constitutional behaviour. He was never tyrannical, he was never loud, or ill-mannered; he was just comfortably disreputable.[29]

The outward image of a glittering Edwardian decade does not stand probing; on the other hand, the period does not entirely deserve the strictures of Harold Nicolson:

Let us be frank about it. The Edwardians were vulgar to a degree. They lacked style. . . . Nor, when all is said and done, can one forgive the Edwardians for their fundamental illusion. For it never dawned upon them that intelligence was of any value.[87]

There was a great deal of intelligence at large when one year alone (1904) saw the foundation of such diverse institutions as the Workers' Educational Association, the Abbey Theatre in Dublin and the firm of Rolls-Royce. There was a lot of intelligence in public life, in the political leadership of the nation. And yet it is a fact that very few people – and they rather late

'Fritz', the hammer designed by Alfred Krupp,
forging a propeller shaft

in the day – perceived the dangerous national rivalry in which Britain was becoming unwittingly involved.

The rivalry was definitely there. The energy – and the direction – of German economic expansion were unmistakable. It was steel, that key material, that told the story: in 1890 Britain produced $3\frac{1}{2}$ million tons of steel a year, Germany just over two million; by 1901, Britain's output had risen to just under five million tons, but Germany's had leapt ahead to over six. And this was only a beginning: by 1908 Germany's steel production would more than double Britain's, by 1913 it would almost treble the British figure. And this was not all; other industries showed similar advances. Even Britain's long-cherished private preserves – shipping and world trade – were now being challenged by German intrusion. In 1900 Germany already held 20% of world trade in manufactures, and possessed nearly two million tons of merchant building. Under the presiding genius of Bismarck, Germany had discovered prosperity, unified in an empire under Prussian leadership. But Bismarck had understood the delicate internal balances of the European order; his successors did not. 'Bismarck, visiting Hamburg in 1896, saw the vast harbour crowded with ships, heard the deep murmur of German power, sensed the ruin of his system, and turned away in fear; "It is a new world, a new age." '[104]

A new world it certainly was, with new enterprises to fit it. Germany's rising position was not simply a matter of taking the lead in industries which were already fundamental to the economies of nations; she had also established a lead in new fields which would become increasingly important. The German electrical industry employed 26,000 men in 1895; twelve years later it was employing 107,000. Germany's chemical industry was exporting twice the amount of Britain's; in some sectors, Germany enjoyed a virtual monopoly; her exports of dyestuffs, for example, increased from 35,000 tons in 1897 to nearly 100,000 tons in 1912. The optical industry, with the famous firm of Zeiss setting the example, had a clear lead over almost every rival. In the new world of the motor-car, Gottlieb Daimler, Karl Benz and Rudolf Diesel had already ensured that Germany's position would be – and continue – strong.

New inventions, new industries – even a new dimension: on 2 July 1900, at Friedrichshaven on Lake Constance, a dream was fulfilled. Count Ferdinand von Zeppelin's new experimental airship, on which he had been working for two years, rose into the air and flew for three and a half miles above the surface of the lake. The Count was a Württemberg-born cavalry officer; he resented Prussian dominance of the army of his native state, and had been unwise enough to say so. At the age of fifty-two he had reached the rank of general, but his further career was clearly blocked,

Graf Zeppelin, the great airship of the 1920s named after the founder of the line who launched his prototype in 1900

The German Empire took on the Prussian image: a group of Prussian officers

and so he left the Army. He turned his attention to the new science of aviation, in which, at that time, France held the lead. The result came nine years later, with the first flight of this silvery, pencil-shaped vessel, 420 feet long, forty feet wide. She was powered by two 16-hp Daimler motors; her structure was rigid, its strength deriving from the relatively new light metal, aluminium – also a German discovery.

Count Ferdinand von Zeppelin became a hero and a celebrity far beyond the confines of Württemberg. His airship was a prototype; its successors, the *Sachsen*, the *Hansa*, the *Viktoria Luise* and their sisters, were seen all over Germany. By 1914 37,250 Germans had actually flown in Zeppelin airships. On commercial flights Zeppelins had flown 100,000 miles with passengers, without a single accident. The future seemed to be theirs: they could travel far greater distances, they could lift incomparably greater weights, they could climb higher more swiftly than any known aeroplane. If a future in which man would use the air as naturally as he already used the sea suddenly became real in 1900, this was very much the work of Count Zeppelin and his followers in other lands.

The combination of Britain's stored-up and still accumulating wealth, and the vigour of this new Germany which had so swiftly turned herself into the powerhouse of Europe, would alone have been enough to maintain the European economic domination of the world. That domination, after all, did already exist – Europe's only serious rivals were America and Japan, both modelled on the European pattern, both operating in the European style. But what did not exist, in 1900, was the combination; instead there was the rivalry. And whereas rivalry with countries outside Europe was not important, rivalry inside Europe was becoming more dangerous, and that between Germany and Britain was growing day by day.

Once the two countries had been friends, linked by royal ties (it was almost two centuries since the Elector of Hanover had become King of England) and by distant racial affinities dating back to the tribal wanderings at the end of the Roman Empire. In her long wars with France, Britain had generally found German allies, the last famous occasion being the Battle of Waterloo, which, Germans firmly believed, had only been won by the timely arrival of Marshal Blücher's Prussians when the Duke of Wellington's army was at its last gasp. Complicated and romantic engravings showed the two heroes clasping hands on the stricken field. So strong was the pro-German sentiment in Britain that in 1870, when Germany went to war with France, the historian Thomas Carlyle wrote:

That noble, patient, deep, pious and solid Germany should be at length welded into a nation and become queen of the Continent, instead of vapouring, vain-

John Singer Sargent. *The Sitwell Family*, 1900
From the left: Edith, Sir George and Lady Sitwell,
Sacheverell and Osbert

glorious, gesticulating, quarrelsome, restless, and over-sensitive France, seems to me the hopefullest public fact that has occurred in my time.[17]

It was not likely that any Englishman with personal knowledge of Germany would say the same in 1900. British visitors to Germany at the turn of the century found, particularly in the young Germany, the Germany of the middle class and the universities, a hostility which startled them. An aspiring diplomat, studying German, became aware of the phenomenon, and expressed himself forcefully: 'The place was alive with malice; its heart, fuelled with animosities, was continually bursting against Britain, which was to be outnumbered on land, outbuilt at sea, in fact outed everywhere.'[113]

The reason for the prevalence of this hostility in the universities was a certain frame of mind in many of the professors – 'the Pedantocracy', as they were called by unfriendly critics. Among these professors were such diverse figures as Heinrich von Treitschke and Friedrich Wilhelm Nietzsche. Treitschke – born in Dresden, professor of history first at Freiburg, then at Heidelberg, finally at Berlin – was a pure German patriot who believed that the supremacy of Prussia and the Hohenzollern dynasty was the best thing that had happened to his country:

so was it the duty and destiny of united Germany, under these happy auspices, having been taught and seasoned by long centuries of stern and painful apprenticeship, to issue forth in the meridian vigour of her age and seize upon the Mastery of the World.[92]

Naturally, to those who agreed with Treitschke's thinking, the position of England straddled imperially across the globe was an intolerable obstacle and affront. Nietzsche – of Polish ancestry, and cheated of a military career by an unfortunate injury – was quite open in his hatred and contempt. Many of his fellow countrymen, in their delight at his scorn for the British, failed to recognise that they themselves were also part of his target. It was the whole Teutonic race, of which he considered the British to be merely the baser part, that Nietzsche derided: 'Wherever Germany extends her sway, she *ruins* culture.' 'Every great crime against culture for the last four centuries lies on [the German] conscience . . .'[88] Independently of race, Nietzsche believed in an oligarchy of super-men, an aristocracy of intellect, beauty, courage, self-control and power. His message, in fact, was very different from Treitschke's; yet the two could merge into a dangerous confusion. The sound of German speech, the speech of German intellectuals, was becoming unfriendly to British ears, and the unfriendliness was reciprocated.

Not all German speech grated, however; it was Robert Vansittart, travelling from Germany to Austria, who wrote:

So Vienna it was, and the atmosphere changed joyously. Here was kindness remembered with gratitude. 'Public opinion on the Continent', said Cavour, 'is not usually favourably disposed towards England', but here it did not hurt. [113]

Vienna, in 1900, was more than a political capital, it was one of the capitals of the European music world, relishing a great past – the days of Haydn, Mozart, Beethoven, Brahms and Johann Strauss – and a vigorous present.

In 1900, Vienna's State Opera was a magnet drawing the world's most famous singers, its best conductors and composers. To perform at the Vienna Opera, or at the equally renowned Concert Hall, was a great accolade. The principal conductor of the Vienna Philharmonic was Gustav Mahler; in 1900, he was forty years old, and composing his Fourth Symphony. In a very different style, but peculiarly Viennese, was the work of Franz Lehar. He was a Hungarian, trained in Prague, but it was Vienna that supplied the stage he needed for *The Merry Widow* and *The Count of Luxembourg*. The gala nights of the State Opera saw imperial Vienna on display: the gowns, the furs, the jewels, the titles and decorations of Habsburg Vienna in the last days of its glory. The glitter was very dazzling; yet beneath it all there were sounds and signs of disturbance.

In the coffee-houses of Vienna, where ladies who should have known better ate cream cakes and men scanned the newspapers by the hour, there was a continous traffic of ideas. Revolutionaries talked sedition against a regime more apparently despotic than it really was. Artists and writers talked – and talked. The painter Gustav Klimt had just founded the Vienna Sezession movement; this was the plastic expression of a mood of unrest and experiment whose musical equivalent might be found in the works of Arnold Schoenberg, and which was put into words by novelists like Arthur Schnitzler, or the poet Hugo von Hofmannsthal (who would later be the founder of the Salzburg Festival).

There was plenty to talk about in the coffee-houses, much to undermine the settled ideas of a society which at some levels seemed to have settled into petrifaction. The exploration of man's inner nature had begun, and very unsettling that would prove to be. In 1900 Sigmund Freud published his *Interpretation of Dreams*. It was an interesting title to come out of Vienna, where life was already partaking of the quality of a dream, in the waking world of the twentieth century.

2   The Day of Empires

'Blessed are the meek: for they shall inherit the earth.' And so they may, but so far there is not much sign of it. In 1900 it would not have been difficult to imagine that Europeans had inherited the earth, but meekness was not their most obvious characteristic. It was the drive, the endurance, the patience, the skill, the greed, the pride — never the meekness — of Europeans that had brought them collectively nearer to being masters of the world than any group of people had ever been before. They put on the uniforms and shouldered the guns that carried their power to the corners of the globe. They made the machines that made the goods for a vast web of international commerce. They made the ships that carried the goods, and sailed them in all the oceans. They dreamed dreams of power which planted the European image and created European empires in every continent. They were not meek.

Europe herself, as we have seen, was a continent of empires in 1900. She was also a continent of very distinct nationalities, much more sharply separate than they are today. The rivalries of the empires and the nation-states, the aspirations of the nationalities, dominant or suppressed, and the conflicts produced by both, came very near to destroying European society twice in this century. And because national conflict has until recently seemed so normal, because war in Europe has been such a regular occurrence down the decades, one may well question whether there ever has been, or is, or will be, such a thing as a European — as opposed to a Frenchman, a German, a Hungarian, or a Pole, or even an Englishman. Is Europe only a feature of geography? Was the mighty continent only the sum of individual grandeurs? Or are there, in modern times, networks resembling the feudal system which unified a large part of Europe during the Middle Ages?

In 1900 various networks of European internationalism were, in fact, easily visible. There was the obvious network of royalty. Apart from two republics, France and Switzerland, the whole of Europe lived under some form of monarchy; it might be autocratic, or it might be in varying degrees constitutional, but either way the Head of State wore a crown. The royal 'occasions' — coronations, addresses to loyal subjects in or out of parlia-

Queen Victoria in 1890, surrounded by relatives: some of those who filled or were about to fill the thrones of Europe. They include Wilhelm II and Edward VII.

ments, weddings, funerals – were more than mere survivals of traditional pageantry from departed ages; they still spelt, or seemed to spell, political realities. Bad feelings between the Emperor of Russia and his cousin the Emperor of Germany could be bad news for the people of Russia and Germany, and for the allies of both countries. The jealousy and antipathy of the Emperor of Germany towards his uncle the King of England was a political fact, not simply a family feud.

And yet it *was* a family matter, nevertheless – as we recognise when we consider the vast array of Queen Victoria's descendants:

They filled or were about to fill the thrones of Europe: they carried the distinguished tradition of Victoria and Albert to the Empires of Germany and Russia, to the Kingdoms of Greece and Roumania and later to those of Norway and Spain: as well as to countless duchies and dynasties in the heart of Germany. As we turn to those great family gatherings which she loved, and look perhaps on the picture of the Queen and her descendants painted for the Jubilee of 1887 and see the gay uniforms and the long, shrewd Coburg faces we become conscious of an international force which was powerful so long as the central figure lived to keep it together and might – if the conditions of the nineteenth century had lasted longer – have proved an abiding influence in the fortunes of Europe.[39]

Those who mourned Queen Victoria's death in 1901 were mourning also, whether they knew it or not, the passing of a force for unity in a continent which could not afford to part with such a thing.

However, other international networks also existed; beneath the royalty, but close to it, came the aristocracy. The Europe of 1900 preserved class distinctions far more sharply than today, and paid them much greater respect; the landed aristocracy, particularly when fortified by gilt-edged securities, represented (under the throne) the very pinnacle of class distinction in every country of Europe. Even in republican France, where this aristocracy had been so spectacularly overthrown just over a hundred years earlier, the summit of social endeavour was once again an invitation to one of those parties in houses whose owners' blood was bluest of blue. This might be at a magnificent town mansion in the Faubourg St Germain in Paris, or, better still, at a château in the midst of the still immense estates belonging to names which echoed the history of France herself: de la Rochefoucauld, Alençon, Montmorency, La Tour d'Auvergne. And at such a party, according to the season of the year, if sufficiently honoured, one might meet visiting specimens of the aristocracies of all Europe, linked together by class, by marriage, by community of taste, or even – some might say – by the lack of it. And this network, like the monarchies, was absolutely international.

Royals and aristocrats, their prestige was no illusion in 1900. They did

Uncle and nephew. Edward VII and Wilhelm II in 1906, with two of the Kaiser's sisters

44

possess power, but not enough of it by themselves to assert the unities which they represented strongly enough against the discords of the continent. What else was there? Where else could one persuade oneself that resemblances outweighed diversities? Could it be at the top of the great flights of ornamental steps and through the classical porticoes of Europe's Stock Exchanges? Was the language of money, which was readily enough understood in most parts of the continent, the true unifying factor? An institution like, say, the House of Rothschild suggested that it might well be. The name 'Rothschild' was synonymous with enormous wealth, and had been so since the end of the Napoleonic Wars. But all these riches and the power that went with them had begun with a second-hand clothes and coin business in the harshly restrictive confines of the Frankfurt ghetto. There, in a two-roomed house, Mayer Amschel Rothschild brought up his family of five sons, and worked his way up by sheer business sense to the position of banker to the Prince of Hesse-Cassel. His eldest son, Nathan, inherited all his father's business ability and more:

> At his accustomed pillar in the London Stock Exchange, his face was carefully examined for the least expression. A stock that he bought would immediately become popular; and his bear squeeze, even on a government loan, could and did kill.[114]

Nathan Rothschild made London his headquarters. By the time he died, in 1836, he and his four brothers, James in Paris, Solomon in Vienna, Amschel in Frankfurt and Karl in Naples, could regularly make fortunes for one another. By 1900 the Rothschilds had concentrated their interests in London, Paris and Vienna. Between 1901 and 1904, the total sum of the loans with which the London branch alone of the House of Rothschild was concerned was £1,300,000,000. They represented financial activities which were not merely transcontinental, but worldwide. The fact that the family was Jewish emphasised its independence from the countries where the Rothschilds made their millions. Their very existence seemed to suggest that the tendency of international finance, banking, trade and industry was towards continental unity, and at the turn of the century there were many influential people who firmly believed that that was so.

This coin had another side: it was not merely the magnates of finance, the 'captains' of industry who felt affinities with each other across the frontiers, it was also the workers. Among the proletarian masses in the industrialised countries where the great capitalists were making their fortunes, there was perhaps an even profounder spirit of internationalism, based on the ideas of class struggle, the idea that the interests of workers were the same everywhere, and that nationalism was only another mode of

Jean Jaurès, the French socialist leader, speaking at a meeting in 1913

capitalist exploitation. As far back as 1848 Karl Marx had identified the nation state with the bourgeoisie, the enemies of the proletariat:

... the bourgeoisie has at last, since the establishment of Modern Industry and of the world market, conquered for itself, in the modern representative State, exclusive political sway. The executive of the modern State is but a committee for managing the common affairs of the whole bourgeoisie.[75]

Marx and Friedrich Engels had founded the First International Workingmen's Association in 1864, but it had only lasted for twelve years. In 1889 the Second International was formed in Paris, and in 1900 it was this organisation which represented the solidarity of Europe's workers. Among its most prominent leaders were Karl Kautsky, the German Socialist, born in Prague and once a friend of Marx, and the Frenchman Jean Jaurès. In 1904 Jaurès founded the newspaper *L'Humanité*, now the famous organ of the French Communist Party. In 1905 the various Socialist parties in the French Chamber amalgamated under his leadership. Jaurès was a believer in reform by parliamentary methods, but he accepted the ruling of the Second International at its Amsterdam Congress that Socialists should not participate in 'bourgeois coalitions'. Like Kautsky, he was also a firm believer in the idea that international action by the workers would prevent the outbreak of war in Europe. This seemed perfectly possible in the first decade of the twentieth century; working-class internationalism had a look of simple reality; men like Kautsky and Jaurès were regarded as highly dangerous by nationalist extremists, of whom there was no lack.

These, then, were the international networks which possessed power, economic or political, in recognisable forms. There was, of course, another, which did not possess power in any obvious way – or perhaps one should say that the power it possessed was of an altogether different kind. This was the network of the Arts. Painters, musicians, actors, singers, dancers were international in two senses. First, the artists themselves were interchangeable across the national frontiers; nationality was irrelevant, and physically they passed to and fro across the frontiers continuously as they plied their professions. The art centres of Europe – Paris, Vienna, Munich, Dresden, Milan – witnessed truly international gatherings both of artists and their followers, the audiences of music festivals, the connoisseurs of canvases. Wherever the great composers, the renowned orchestras, operatic companies and ballets were to be found, wherever the art galleries were flourishing with novelty, this entourage was certain to be seen. And secondly, of course, there was the patent fact that artistic ideas, artistic 'schools', simply did not acknowledge the frontiers of the political world. Without benefit of radio or television, ideas passed between countries, revealing links of communication which seemed to make non-sense of such things as frontiers. This was power indeed; ultimately the greatest power of Europeanism.

And yet there was no escaping the fact that the frontiers existed. The nation-states existed. The empires existed. Inside Europe herself there were four empires, areas where one set of Europeans ruled over other sets of Europeans, or where Europeans lived under alien rule. None of the four empires was homogeneous. The German Empire in the north contained a piece of what had quite recently been Denmark, a larger piece of what had even more recently been France, and another large piece of what had once been Poland. The Russian Empire in the east had swallowed up numerous once-independent kingdoms, grand-duchies and duchies in the quest for security along its western borders. The Turkish Empire in the south-east was only a miserable remnant of what it had once been, but it still straddled the Balkans from the Aegean to the Adriatic, a provocation to European national instinct in that area. And in the middle of the continent there stood the Empire of Austria-Hungary, a thing apart.

The Austro-Hungarian Empire sprawled across the very heart of Europe; its true capital was Vienna, although in theory it had three – Vienna, Budapest and Prague. This was the direct heir – or, as some would say, the rump – of the Holy Roman Empire of the Middle Ages, when the Emperor in Vienna was just 'the Emperor', the only one in Europe. The Holy Roman Empire itself was the descendant of the Roman Empire, a revival of the concept of European unity first made practical by Rome, so the pedigree of the institution was considerable. The Emperor's titles tell the tale:

We, by God's grace Emperor of Austria; King of Hungary, of Bohemia, Dalmatia, Croatia, Slavonia, Galicia, Lodomeria and Illyria; King of Jerusalem, Archduke of Austria; Grand Duke of Tuscany and Krakow; Duke of Lorraine, of Salzsburg, Styria, Carinthia, Carniola and Bukovina, Grand Duke of Transylvania, Margrave of Moravia; Duke of Upper and Lower Silesia, of Modena, Parma, Piacenza and Guastella, of Ausschwitz and Sator, of Teschen, Friaul, Ragusa and Zara; Royal Count of Habsburg and Tyrol, of Kyburg, Gorz and Gradisca; Duke of Trent and Brixen; Margrave of Upper and Lower Lausitz and in Istria; Count of Hohenembs, Feldkirch, Bregenz, Sonnenberg etc.; Lord of Triest, of Cattaro, and above the county of Windisch; Grand Voivode of the Voivodina Serbia etc....[42]

Each title, each name, no matter how long forgotten, how archaic, how implausibly Anthony Hope-sounding, is in fact a reminder of a stage in the aggrandisement of the House of Habsburg which had held the imperial throne since 1273,* and a reminder, too, if we care to relate the names to a

---

* A rival contestant had been Richard of Cornwall, brother of Henry III of England, until his death in 1272.

Vienna, about 1900. A party of officers in the Sacher garden in the Prater

map, that a very large part of the Habsburg Empire was their personal, family possession.

In 1900 the ruler of the Habsburg Empire, whether operating from the sombre red and gold and mahogany of the apartments in the Hofburg Palace in the heart of Vienna, or from the great sunflower-yellow sweep of the Schönbrunn amid its gardens just outside the city, or from the brooding palace on the hill above Budapest, was the Emperor Franz Josef. He had mounted the throne as a handsome young Archduke in a year of troubles, 1848, and trouble had been his constant companion. The fifty-two years of his reign had already been filled with personal tragedies and political setbacks which, by 1900, had turned him into an aged, careworn figure.

His beautiful and much-loved Empress, Elizabeth, whom he married in 1854 when she was only sixteen, was almost never at his side. Coming from a junior branch of the Wittelsbach family, Elizabeth was really a country girl. Her delights were all out of doors, and as often as possible on horseback; the stifling atmosphere of one of the most ossified courts in Europe, where almost every act was governed by hardened ritual, repelled her. She adopted the simplest device of escapism: she fled. Her absences from the husband who never ceased to cherish her became more normal than her presence, and in 1898 absence became final when she was stabbed to death by an anarchist as she stepped off a lake steamer at Geneva. Meanwhile Franz Josef had been beset by other sorrows. In 1867 his brother Maximilian, after a brief reign as Emperor of Mexico, was captured and shot by victorious Mexican rebels who saw no necessity for a Habsburg emperor, and wished to discourage further adventures in their country. Then, in 1889, the Emperor's son and heir, the Archduke Rudolf, committed suicide with his mistress at Mayerling. Soon all Europe would have cause to mourn another Habsburg death by violence, at Sarajevo.

Besides personal grief, the Emperor had endured political defeats – by the French in 1859, and by the Prussians in 1866 – which diminished both the authority and the extent of his empire, and added to its internal tensions. And these tensions were never in short supply, for the Habsburgs ruled over a remarkable conglomeration of peoples in Central Europe: Czechs, Slovaks, Croats, Slovenes and Ruthenes, all in varying states of resentful subjection; Poles and Italians who enjoyed a certain amount of privilege (the vast estates of the Polish nobility, for example) and power (the Italian element in the Imperial Navy was very strong); and at the top, Austrians and Hungarians, the dominant peoples of the 'Dual Monarchy'. This extraordinary institution had come into existence in 1867; by the terms of the new constitution of that year,

The marriage of Archduke Karl to Princess Zita in 1911.
The emperor Franz Josef is on Karl's right; the Archduke
Franz Ferdinand is towards the left of the photograph,
and his wife Sophie is next to the emperor

The Austro-Hungarian Empire, 'not the feeble
thing it is often made out to be': an
infantry regiment parading in Brünn (Brno),
the capital of Moravia 1900

each half of the Empire was totally independent of the other save for the army, the common Ministry of Foreign Affairs, and certain financial arrangements connected with these. Each half had its own Ministry under a Prime Minister responsible to Franz Josef as King of Hungary and Emperor of Austria.[26]

Attempts to analyse and explain the Habsburg Dual Monarchy have generally had to combat clouds of prejudice which are only slowly dispersing. Even those who reflect upon the thing with basic kindness are often also somewhat satirical; it is difficult not to be:

On paper it called itself the Austro-Hungarian Monarchy; in speaking, however, one referred to it as Austria, that is to say, it was known by a name that it had as a state solemnly renounced by oath while preserving it in matters of sentiment, as a sign that feelings are just as important as constitutional law and that regulations are not the really serious things in life. By its constitutions it was liberal, but its system of government was clerical. The system of government was clerical but the general attitude to life was liberal. Before the law all citizens were equal but of course not everyone was a citizen. There was a parliament which made such vigorous use of its liberty that it was usually kept shut; but there was also an emergency powers act by means of which it was possible to manage without Parliament, and every time when everyone was just beginning to rejoice in absolutism the Crown decreed that there must now be a return to parliamentary government. Many such things happened in this state and among them were those national struggles that justifiably aroused Europe's curiosity and are today completely misrepresented. They were so violent that they several times a year caused the machinery of State to jam and come to a dead stop. But between whiles, in the breathing spaces between government and government everyone got on excellently with everyone else and behaved as though nothing had ever been the matter.[82]

It is partly for these reasons that the Habsburg Empire, despite appearances of extreme reaction at times, was never entirely repressive to its assorted subjects – indeed, was far less repressive than many of the regimes that have replaced it. There is a Viennese word, 'Schlamperei'; it means 'letting things slide', a general tendency towards procrastination and slovenliness, 'muddling through'. According to Viktor Adler, the notable Austrian Socialist, the Empire of Austria-Hungary was ruled by 'despotism modified by Schlamperei'. There could be worse influences.

There are many misunderstandings about the Habsburg Empire. A favourite epithet for it has been 'ramshackle', which is a convenient word to use for propaganda against an enemy, but always liable, of course, to modification according to shifts of foreign policy. If it had not later suited the policy of Europe's major powers to pull the Habsburg Empire to pieces, other attributes of the Empire might have received more attention. Only when it was too late did pundits ruefully reflect that the Empire, in its prime, had been a large free-trade area in the centre of Europe, without customs barriers, a complex of industry and agriculture and markets for both, linked by a common railway system, a great waterway, the River Danube, and possessing an outlet to the Adriatic Sea. This was a form of economic strength which the 1960s decided to call a 'Common Market', and under that name was widely regarded as highly desirable; it certainly helped, by offering a degree of economic stability, to offset the social and political tensions of the Habsburg Empire. Nor can one neglect, in 1900, the power of religion; the Habsburgs enjoyed the almost unswerving support of the Catholic Church. Both Austria and Hungary counted as strongly Catholic countries – another cause of friction with their pre-dominantly Orthodox Slav subjects, but a useful fact wherever Vatican diplomacy might have effect.

So the Empire was not without supports; nor did it lack enemies. Its chief enemies were in the east and south-east: the rival autocratic empires of Russia and Turkey which, fortunately for Austria-Hungary, were also irreconcilable enemies of each other. The quarrel with Turkey had deep roots in a distant past when Islam was in its full flush of vigour, threatening to overrun all Europe. In the sixteenth century Soleiman the Magnificent attacked Malta. This threat to the Western Mediterranean was defeated in 1565 by forces in theory created by the crusading zeal of Christendom, but in fact largely provided by the other branch of the Habsburg family, in its capacity as ruling house of Spain. In 1571 Don John of Austria won his resounding naval victory over the Turks at Lepanto. But in 1683 they were back again, besieging Vienna itself. It was their defeat outside the walls of Vienna that really marked the beginning of the recession of Turkish power, accelerated during the next decades by the victories of Austria's great soldier, Prince Eugene. In Britain and possibly in France he is better known for his part as the Duke of Marlborough's ally in the Battle of Blenheim; in the wider view of European history, especially of the survival of the Romano-Hellenic-Christian cultures of the West, Eugene's battles against the Turks seem vastly more important, and his stature wrongly neglected.

At the time of the French Revolution in 1789 the Turks still occupied almost the whole of the countries which later emerged as Rumania, Bulgaria, Yugoslavia, Albania and modern Greece. By 1900 they had lost a great deal of this territory, but the Sultan's banners were still to be seen on the shores of the Adriatic as well as the Aegean. Sultan Abdul Hamid II ruled over Bulgarians, Greeks, Macedonians and Serbs; his regime was a byword for reaction and oppression throughout Europe. To all the Sultan's Christian subjects Turkish rule certainly was oppressive, though not the continuous reign of terror sometimes represented; it was the more distasteful because it was the rule of an alien culture and religion. By the turn of the century, the hallmark of the Ottoman Empire (as it was still generally known) was inefficiency, a lethargic backwardness stultifying thought and enterprise, rather than actual cruelty, though in moments of crisis or rebellion the Empire could awake to spasms of startling ferocity. It was this combination of torpor and savagery which, down the years, had aroused national ambitions among the Balkan peoples which once had been unknown. Now the Balkans were a danger area for all Europe, watched over by the Great Powers with a mixture of anxiety and greed.

In the political jargon of the time, Turkey had for years been known as 'the sick man of Europe', which was a convenient way of expressing justification for the desire to dismember her empire. That desire had been a factor in European politics for centuries, a natural consequence of Europe's resentment at the impudence of the Turks in capturing Constantinople in 1453 and making it their own capital. Constantinople, after all, had been the Byzantium of the Greeks, the capital of the Roman Empire after Rome herself had fallen, and the centre of the Greek Orthodox Church. The great city stood at the gateway to the Black Sea – or, looking from a different direction, at the gateway to the Mediterranean from the Black Sea – which in later centuries made it a natural object of Russian strategic ambitions. Constantinople was a lure, a prize, a temptation; the very thought of it awoke memories and passions all over Europe. In the nineteenth century the English poet Lord Byron won himself European fame independently of his poetry by joining in the Greek fight for liberation from the Turks. Soon after the opening of the twentieth century another English poet, Rupert Brooke, would be writing: 'I suddenly realize that the ambition of my life . . . has been to go on a military expedition against Constantinople!'[78] Surveying the animosities, the jealousies, the greeds that surrounded the Ottoman Empire at the beginning of the century, no vast perspicacity was needed to perceive that there undoubtedly would be military expeditions against Constantinople.

All the Slavs who lived under Turkish rule, like most of the Slavs who lived under Austrian rule, looked for protection and for the fulfilment of their aspirations towards Russia. The vast empire of the Tsar, stretching away across unimaginable distances, beyond the Ural Mountains, through Siberia to the Sea of Japan, was a champion or an ogre, a promise or a threat, according to your birth or your beliefs. Under the snows of Russia's winter, obliterating its landmarks, the empire extended, as Joseph Conrad

Van Gogh. *Potato planting*

wrote in 1911, 'like a monstrous blank page awaiting the record of an inconceivable history'.[24] That history would soon be written, and it would, indeed, be inconceivable.

The capital of the Tsar's empire was St Petersburg, in the north on the Gulf of Finland. This was the city built by Peter the Great, on a scale which matched that of the empire itself. In 1800 St Petersburg proclaimed the magnitude of Russia and the might of the Tsar to all who came there, and yet, of all Russian cities, this St Petersburg with its elegant façades, its delicate spires, its sense of floating lightly on the broad waters of the Neva, was the most truly European. It was a deliberate insertion of Europeanism into Russia, a denial of the primitive aspects of Russia which repelled so many Europeans – and also repelled a good many Russians.

In the Balkans the Tsar, Nicholas II, was thought of as the Protector of the Slavs. But in the minds of many Europeans he was more than an autocrat: he represented the very principle of autocracy, the thing in its purest form, and was hated and feared accordingly. The first of the Fundamental Laws of the Empire stated the proposition unequivocally: 'To the Emperor of All the Russias belongs the supreme autocratic and unlimited power. Not only fear, but conscience commanded by God himself, is the basis of obedience to this power.'[54] This was a harsh doctrine, not least from the point of view of the Tsar himself; Nicholas II wrote:

In the sight of my Maker I have to carry the burden of a terrible responsibility and at all times, therefore, be ready to render an account to Him of my actions. I must always keep firmly to my convictions and follow the dictates of my conscience.[54]

This responsibility was a penalty of supreme autocracy; there were others. There was the penalty of isolation: isolation from movements of fresh thought if these tended towards social change and democracy; isolation in deceptive imperial splendour from the hard lives of Russia's tens of millions of peasants living near the borderline of utter poverty; isolation from the ideas of the intellectuals who despised the entire institution of Tsarism; isolation from the desires of the still few, but multiplying, industrial workers in the towns whom the prophets of Socialism called 'the class of the future'. All this isolation was a penalty, but more than a penalty, a grave peril of the Tsarist regime.

And if Nicholas II was detached, on this pinnacle of absolute rule, from so many of his Russian subjects, he was detached even more from those who were not Russian. Like the Emperor of Austria and the Sultan of Turkey, he had to reckon with the ambitions of subject and persecuted races. Jews were constantly persecuted in Russia, a tradition which dies

'The power of the Tsar . . . embodied in the great Russian army'. Military review, Moscow riding-school, built on a scale to match the Empire itself

Wilhelm II head and shoulders above a group of officers while on manoeuvres. 'The most professional military leadership in the world: the Great General Staff'

hard. But it was not only on the Jews that Russian rule pressed heavily. All of Finland, in 1900, was a Russian Grand Duchy. The Baltic states, Estonia, Latvia and Lithuania, which had once enjoyed independence and power, were provinces of the Empire. A huge section of what had been Poland, including the cities of Lodz and Warsaw, belonged to Russia. Bessarabia belonged to Russia. The Ukraine and the Caucasus belonged to Russia, despite nationalist movements and revolts that kept a spirit of independence alive among their peoples.

All autocracy depends upon power, autocracy on this scale particularly so, and the power of the Tsar in 1900 was embodied, in the eyes of the world, in the great Russian army. Its peacetime strength was about $1\frac{1}{2}$ million men; its immediate wartime strength was at least twice as many, and behind them stood limitless reserves of manpower, if they could only be mobilised and armed. It was the army that had pushed the Tsar's power eastwards to the borders of China and Japan, south towards India (to the great consternation of Britain). It was the army that guarded Russia's European frontiers against the threats of other empires, and the Caucasus against the Turks. It was the army that was counted on to suppress revolts inside Russia, and maintain the autocracy intact. In the link between the Tsar and his army lay the whole sanction of the Russian Empire, and in 1900 there was no apparent reason to doubt the strength of that link.

Turkey and Russia were what, for a large part of this century, would be described as 'natural enemies' of Austria-Hungary. When the Emperor Franz Josef looked for friends, he looked north, to the young German Empire, ruled over in 1900 by the Emperor Wilhelm II (generally known as 'the Kaiser', although Franz Josef was also, of course, a Kaiser). The logic of the Austro-German alliance may seem obvious now; after all, the two groups shared a language and a culture; most of Germany had for centuries paid some degree of obeisance to the Habsburgs; and links between Austria and South Germany had remained close. It requires an effort to recall that, in 1900, the Austro-German axis was a relatively new and still untested arrangement, viewed with some distrust by members of both parties.

For Franz Josef and the House of Habsburg the very existence of the German Empire was a reminder of defeat – the wholly unexpected and humiliating defeat of Austria and the South Germans by Prussia in the seven-week war of 1866. On that occasion one day's fighting, at the Battle of Königgratz (Sadowa) sufficed to deprive the Habsburgs of their centuries-old supremacy in Germany. In the words of the *Spectator*, 'the political face of the world has changed as it used to change after a generation of war – Prussia has leaped in a moment into the position of the first

Power in Europe'.[12] The point was rubbed home four years later when Prussia led the German states to victory over France in another lightning campaign. On 18 January 1871 the King of Prussia was proclaimed Emperor Wilhelm I of Germany in the Palace of Versailles and the Second German Reich was born.

The man responsible for all these remarkable events, the visionary who had taught Prussia her destiny and so created the new Germany which he would now proceed to fashion in Prussia's image and his own, was Count Otto von Bismarck. Bismarck has been called 'the Iron Chancellor', but under the iron he was a subtle statesman with more wisdom than the seekers of imperial destiny usually display. After Königgrätz he had taken care not to add to Austria's humiliation. The defeated Austrian army was not pursued; there was no triumphant march into Vienna; the peace treaty offered terms which Austria could accept without everlasting bitterness. The defeat of France was a somewhat different matter; this time Bismarck intended a definite diminution of the defeated enemy's status. But he knew that victory can bring its own penalties: two great powers had been beaten by superior military force, two potentially hostile neighbours who might one day perhaps combine with Russia to reverse the verdict of this recent history. Germany had to be ensured against that possibility; she needed an ally, and in 1879 the treaty with Austria was signed. Three years later, against all seeming probability, Bismarck was able to bring in Italy alongside Austria, and the Triple Alliance came into being; by 1900 it was an established fact of European power politics.

Much of all this had been intensely distasteful to Franz Josef of Austria; it had scarcely been less so to many of the German princes who now had to accept Prussian suzerainty. Indeed, some of them were not at all sure how to interpret that suzerainty, and their subjects were liable to share their uncertainites, '''The Emperor is not my Monarch,'' said a Württemberg politician. ''He is only the Commanding officer of my Federation. My Monarch is in Stuttgart.'' '[5]

Some of the royal and princely dynasties of Germany — the Wittelsbachs of Bavaria are a good example — were much older and more illustrious than the relatively upstart Hohenzollerns of Prussia to whom they now all paid allegiance. By 1900 the German princes had lost most of the independence which they had enjoyed for centuries, and some resented this deeply. Nevertheless, the Hohenzollern Empire represented German unity, a cause near to the hearts of Germans everywhere, and which none of the princes was disposed to dispute.

One thing is certain: the creation of the Empire coincided with an astonishing burst of national energy in Germany. There was a population explosion: 41 millions in 1871, 56·3 millions in 1900. There was an 'economic explosion'. There was a great upsurge of German influence, right through Europe and beyond. Under Prussian leadership, this influence always bore a strong military flavour. Prussia, the spear of Germany pointing at the East, hardened by centuries of frontier warfare, was a military state, and the German Empire, under a Prussian dynasty, took on the Prussian image.

If not in numbers, certainly in efficiency, the German Army was the most powerful in the world. It was well equipped, admirably organised, and commanded by a dedicated and privileged military caste which provided its officer corps – a combination not without its dangers:

The German military system had raised the corps of officers to the position of an autocracy, but had failed to provide them with the means of maintaining the exalted role they were asked to play in the national life. The great majority were very poor, and they saw around them the commercial and manufacturing classes steadily growing in wealth and setting a standard of living with which they could not compete. Promotion was slow, the work hard and monotonous, and discontent with their straitened circumstances was rife. A very large number of German officers made no attempt to conceal their longing for a war, which they were certain would be a German triumph, and in moments of expansion spoke of the loot to be had in rich France.[77]

At the pinnacle of the German Army stood a small élite which provided the most professional military leadership in the world: the great General Staff. In 1888 there were 239 General Staff officers, of whome 197 were Prussians; by 1914 the total had risen to 625, a very small number for an army whose active strength and trained reserves amounted to over three million men. Nevertheless, 'the Staff Officer remained, as he had done for at least a century, the driving-wheel of the whole organisation, and possessed an authority probably unknown in other armies.'[111]

The German nation and the German Army were closely identified; the symbol of Germanism was the soldier. And because the world also respected the German soldier, Germany now had a 'place in the sun'. Besides being an empire in Europe, Germany, in 1900, possessed an empire overseas. This was the result of a remarkable volte-face by Bismarck:

In 1871 he refused a suggestion that France surrender Cochin-China instead of Lorraine; in 1876 he rejected a proposal to set up a colony in South Africa; in 1880 he ignored a plan for the colonisation of New Guinea; in 1881 he asserted that, as long as he was Chancellor, Germany would carry on no colonial activities; in 1882 he announced that the political situation prevented the government from taking any part in the work of the Colonial Society; in 1884 he proclaimed German sovereignty over five colonial areas in rapid succession.[5]

Naval review, Spithead, 1911. 'The British Empire was founded absolutely on sea power'

Whatever may have prompted this change of mind (and Bismarck's motives were seldom straightforward), its effect was to plant the German flag in South-west Africa, East Africa (later Tanganyika), Togoland, the Cameroons, in part of New Guinea, in Samoa, and on the Chinese mainland at Tsing-tao, which became a German naval base: two million square miles of territory acquired 'without a fleet and without moving a soldier'.

Wilhelm II took great pride in Germany's overseas possessions, and many of his subjects shared his enthusiasm. There were some, however, who questioned whether Germany's empire did anything for her except squander her assets and aggravate the fears and envy of other nations. When, in addition to an empire, Germany set out to acquire a large fleet, their fears increased. But the fleet itself aroused great enthusiasm; it even created a new national cause. A later Chancellor of the Empire wrote: 'The fleet was the favourite child of Germany, for in it the onward-pressing energies of the nation seemed to be most vividly illustrated.'[51] Oddly enough, by comparison with the Army, which had always been dominated by the nobility, the new Navy was a democratic institution in imperial Germany.

No chief of the General Staff nor any Minister of War before 1914 was of bourgeois origin. The contrast with the Navy is striking. Of the fifty-seven admirals and senior officers who served as heads of departments in the Admiralty Staff between 1899 and 1918, only seven belonged to the nobility and only three . . . to the higher, titled nobility. At the Imperial Naval Office, the general pattern was much the same. Only six of the thirty-three naval officers on duty at the beginning of 1898, only two of the twelve department heads and none of the three admirals belonged to the nobility.[102]

This new fleet was a curious phenomenon; what was it really for? The answer, had it been known, was succinctly provided in 1897. In June of that year a significant figure made his appearance on the European – as opposed to merely German – stage: Admiral von Tirpitz became State Secretary of the Imperial Naval Office. In a secret Memorandum of that very month, von Tirpitz declared the purposes of a large, expanding German Navy:

For Germany the most dangerous naval enemy at the present time is England. It is also the enemy against which we most urgently require a certain measure of naval force as a political power factor . . . Our fleet must be so constructed that it can unfold its greatest military potential between Heligoland and the Thames . . .[102]

The sole purpose, in other words, of the German fleet was its obvious one – to threaten Britain. At first the complacent British took no notice, but the promulgation of the Second Navy Law in 1900 opened their eyes. This laid down a *minimum* building programme for the next twenty years, giving definite assurances to the steel industry and the shipyards, with financial guarantees by the government. There was no mistaking the meaning of this, except by wilful blindness, and so the antagonism which we have already noticed between Germany and Britain was intensified. Tragic irony could scarcely go further, because, as A. J. P. Taylor says,

Nothing could better express the roaring spluttering energy of Germany, like a ship's propeller out of water, than this vast naval force, absorbing great quantities of economic power, engendering disastrous international friction, destined never to be used to any decisive purpose in war, but to perform a role in history only as the match which began the explosion and collapse of the Hohenzollern Reich.[104]

The British could not fail to react to the building of the German fleet; in 1900 they possessed by far the largest of Europe's empires, and it was an empire founded absolutely on sea-power. Any threat to British sea-power was a threat to the British Empire. The life-lines of that empire were the oceans of the world, which linked the ports of Britain to the four great ports which the British had created in the Far East: Bombay, Calcutta, Singapore, Hong Kong; linked the British Crown to its 'brightest jewel', India; linked the people of Britain to the British lands which they had brought into existence overseas, in Canada, in Southern Africa, Australia and New Zealand.

The British Empire was, above all, the product of a population explosion.

Ten generations ago, in the age of Shakespeare and Raleigh, these small islands were inhabited by six or seven millions of people whom we may loosely call the British race. For the most part they were rustic, though they were showing signs of a change from a life of agriculture to a life of commerce. In the course of this change which transformed them, for a time, into the richest and strongest community (or rather group of communities) in history, two phenomena may be observed, each of them unique, so far as our meagre records show. In the first place the British, with whom for brevity of reference I include the Irish, increased in numbers from something less than 7,000,000 to something more than 140,000,000, a rate of multiplication unequalled by any other nation in Europe or Asia. In the second place the majority of the British race have abandoned the British Isles and made their homes elsewhere, a diaspora which in its effect upon the progress of mankind can be compared only with the Dispersion of the Jews.[18]

The British communities which had grown up in distant parts of the world shared Britain's language and culture, and also her political institutions. In 1900 Queen Victoria was the monarch of them all; their Parliaments were modelled upon Westminster; their Law was British Law. Political democracy and self-determination were concepts absolutely inherent in these communities: the North American colonists had won their total independence by war against Britain as far back as 1783; Canada became self-governing in 1867, New Zealand in 1852; in 1901 the Commonwealth of Australia, federating the previously separate states of that continent, came into being. All these were free peoples, linked to each other and to Britain under the Crown.

The strength of the link was being tested in 1900. For the first time in history it was possible to say that the British Empire – not just Great Britain – was at war. Canadians, New Zealanders, Australians, South Africans and others were actively aiding Britain in her war against the Boer republics in South Africa, the Transvaal and the Orange Free State. Public opinion in Europe was bitterly anti-British over this war; every available drop of envy and malice fermented briskly. The Boers – the word means simply 'farmers' – were, after all, people of European descent: the original Dutch settlers whose first colony at the Cape of Good Hope was founded in 1652, French Huguenot refugees after the revocation of the Edict of Nantes in 1685, and an admixture of German Protestants. None of these people had any share in British political or constitutional ideas. Their society evolved out of a grim struggle for survival in a continent which was rarely hospitable. Its only reliable asset that they could develop was space, and the Afrikaner's endless quest for space produced the personality of the Voortrekker, the everlasting emigrant:

> His neighbours' smoke shall vex his eyes, their voices break his rest.
> He shall go forth till south is north, sullen and dispossessed.
> He shall desire loneliness and his desire shall bring,
> Hard on his heels, a thousand wheels, a People and a King.[61]

It was the Voortrekkers who had created the Transvaal Republic and the Orange Free State. But now, in 1900, came the thousand wheels of the British Army, the weight of the combined British race and its monarch pressing down upon the Boer states. Most Europeans regarded the British as greedy oppressors of these simple people, and greatly rejoiced at every British setback. There was no lack of these; the British Army had not fought a white enemy since the Crimean War in 1855, and was at a low ebb of efficiency. Also, to be fair, it was making a first acquaintance with a new and disturbing phenomenon of war: the empty battlefield. This was the product of magazine rifles and smokeless powder; it did not need the additional factor of Boer marksmanship. The empty battlefield made nonsense of traditional tactics, as the British now discovered and other European nations would learn later. While Europe mocked the British plodded on, and the Boers constantly eluded them; it took the might of the British

Empire three years to defeat these tough, bigoted, obstinate men. Even then, the defeat was more apparent than real; the war ended in 1902, but in 1910 South Africa became a self-governing dominion led by the very men who had fought the British, and in 1961 the link with Britain was broken by their descendants.

Empires clash. In September 1898 – the year before the South African War broke out – Lord Kitchener won his famous victory over the Mahdists of the Sudan at Omdurman. No sooner was the battle won than Kitchener learned to his annoyance that other Europeans had established themselves in the Sudan, at Fashoda on the White Nile. This was a French expedition from the Congo; led by the powerfully anglophobe Major Marchand, the expedition had overcome incredible difficulties in its long march from Brazzaville, and from that point of view its story is one of the many epics of France in Africa. From Lord Kitchener's point of view, however, Marchand's expedition was an excrescence; Fashoda, Kitchener considered, was part of the Sudan, part of the legitimate spoils of his victory at Omdurman.

Kitchener decided, wisely, on a massive show of strength. He set off at once up the White Nile with five armed steamers, a company of Highlanders, two battalions of Sudanese infantry and a battery of artillery – the most powerful European army to penetrate that distant region. Marchand had only nine French officers and 150 Senegalese soldiers; proud, embittered and hot-tempered as he was, he could not pit this tiny company against the weight of Kitchener's force. In any case, he would not have been supported by his government if he had come to blows with the British. The French Foreign Minister at the time, M. Delcassé, carefully steered his country away from the possibility of war with England. The French evacuated Fashoda, a decision as painful to French self-esteem as it was to the disappointed Marchand himself. There was a great deal of bitterness in France, well reflected in the French Press by satirical cartoonists when the British ran into their difficulties in South Africa the following year; but there was no war. It was the shadow of Germany that Delcassé had seen over his shoulder.

Indeed, the French Empire in 1900 owed its existence in some part to the shadow of Germany. France's imperial role was as old as any in Europe; in the Americas, the Caribbean, Africa, India and Indo-China the banners of France – royal, republican, imperial – had been displayed. In the 1830s French martial energy, which had so recently kept all Europe in a state of alarm, was channelled into the conquest of Algeria. A famous military unit was born out of this – the French Foreign Legion. 'Algeria was the cradle of the Legion, it made the Legion, and it is true to say that the Legion in turn did much to make Algeria. The conquest of that country is largely the history of the Legion: the two are almost inseparable.'[89] The Legion, of course, soon found employment elsewhere: Cambodia and Saigon in the 1860s: Annam, Hanoi, Laos in the 1880s and 1890s. This was the peak period of French imperial expansion in Asia and Africa. French military prestige had taken a hard knock in the defeat of 1871; there were many Frenchmen who dreamed of nothing but ultimate revenge upon Germany. But there were also some, like Jules Ferry (Prime Minister, 1880–1, 1883–5), who saw war with Germany as a disastrous prospect. Ferry preferred to direct French energy into the conquest of North Africa: 'the capture of some green flags would calm the impatience of those who dreamed of taking other trophies.'[64]

So the great powers of Europe carried their ambitions and their rivalries to the corners of the globe. Britain possessed an empire 'on which the sun never set' – children were proudly informed that at any hour of the day or night the sun would be shining on some part of the British Empire. Germany had her 'place in the sun', the fulfilment of her 'right and destiny' which her Emperor promised to defend 'with mailed fist'. France pursued a substitute for 'La Gloire' with moderate contentment, despite the fact that, as a sardonic English minister remarked, some of her acquisitions consisted chiefly 'of very light soil'. But Europe's empires were not confined to the great powers.

As early as 1415 the Portuguese had found a foothold in Africa. Portugal's bold sailors planted her imprint in every continent but one, and the empire founded on their explorations was destined to outlive those of some bigger nations. Portugal's neighbour, Spain, had once possessed an empire which included almost the whole of South America. In 1900 the Spanish Empire was reduced to a fragment in Africa. A disastrous war with America in 1898 had cost her Cuba, Puerto Rico and the seven thousand islands of the Philippine Archipelago. As an ironic consequence, the United States (herself a product of European imperialism, but always very vocal in condemning it) became an imperial power, laboriously conquering the very Filippinos whom she had 'freed' from Spain.

The Dutch, who had once owned New York and the Cape of Good Hope, remained an imperial nation. They held Surinam in South America, and jealously clutched the treasure-house of the East Indies. Here Dutch rule extended through Java, Sumatra, most of Borneo, half New Guinea and some three thousand other islands, covering 576,000 square miles of land. The thirty-five million people ruled by Holland included three hundred ethnic groups, speaking two hundred and fifty languages or dialects.

Belgium had only existed as an independent state since 1830, yet in 1900 she too possessed a large empire – which was also an international scandal.

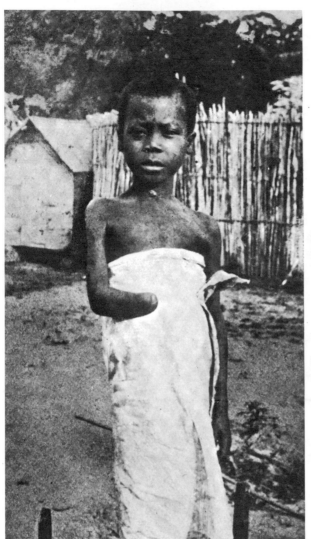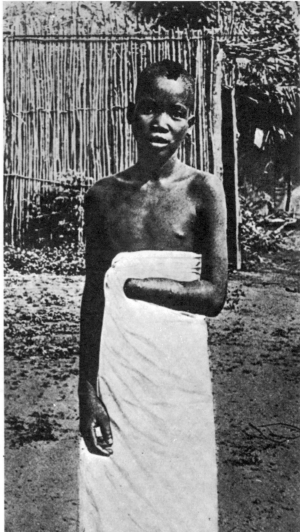

The Belgian Congo. 'In exploiting the Congo the Belgians established a regime so harsh as to be almost indistinguishable from slavery'

With the aid of the American explorer H. M. Stanley, King Leopold II set up an international body to federate the tribes of the Congo basin, ostensibly for philanthropic purposes: the abolition of tribal warfare, with all the benefits that that could bring. But Stanley departed, and soon afterwards King Leopold's agents replaced the other international officers. The ivory and rubber of the Congo became strict state monopolies, and the methods which the Belgians used to make the Africans bring in their quotas of these products were so harsh and oppressive as to be almost indistinguishable from slavery.

The King himself bore heavy responsibility for this state of affairs. His private estate in the Congo, 'la domaine de la couronne', covered 100,000 square miles (practically nine times the size of Belgium herself), and from it he drew at least £4,000,000 for his privy purse. But it was difficult to say where blame for the Congo scandal began and ended in Belgium. Money wrung by cruelty out of the Congo people enriched Belgian cities with parks, art galleries and theatres; it also enriched the pockets of many private individuals. This was sheer colonial exploitation. Anti-imperialists would say that every imperial power was guilty of the same thing; certainly no empire was entirely free from the stigma of oppression. But there was a difference of degree and blatancy about the Belgian performance which made it a difference of kind. All Europe was affronted, and there was loud protest. But as long as King Leopold lived all pressures were resisted; the exploitation continued, and the seeds of hatred thus planted germinated briskly.

Finally there was Italy. She too, in the modern sense, was a young country; she had only effectively existed since 1870. Yet she too felt the need for an empire, and her efforts to obtain one provided some salutary warnings. Italy had wanted Tunisia, and it was her indignation at being forestalled by the French that had caused her to forget for a time her old enmity with Austria and join the Triple Alliance. She had also compensated herself by the acquisition of territories which became known as Eritrea and Italian Somaliland in the area known as the Horn of Africa. But horn is a hard substance, and these colonies brought Italy little except expense and temptation. In 1896 she tried to impose a protectorate over the neighbouring Empire of Abyssinia. This led her to outright military defeat in the Battle of Adowa: an Italian army of 15,000 was almost wiped out – 6000 killed, 4000 wounded and 2000 captured by the Abyssinians. 'Civilised' Europeans did not always hold all the trumps in their fights with 'savage' peoples in those days. But Italy was not put off; she was still looking for more colonies in 1900.

Europeans, by and large, were unselfconscious about empires at the beginning of the century. Habsburgs in Vienna, Hohenzollerns in Berlin, Romanovs in St Petersburg, Queen Victoria and the President of France, all considered it natural that they should rule different peoples and occupy their lands. The British statesman, Joseph Chamberlain, pronounced in a speech at Birmingham, on 13 May 1904: 'The day of the small nations has passed away; the day of Empires has come.' Inside and outside Europe, this seemed to be the obvious truth. Revolutionaries like Vladimir Ilich Ulyanov (generally known as Lenin) might proclaim that 'Imperialism is capitalism in the throes of death', but it did not look like that in 1900. The pomp of empire spelt prestige, a much sought-after commodity. The danger, of course, was that the pursuit of empire also spelt conflict, a sharp note of fresh competition added to the antagonisms of race, political ambition, language and religion which made up European history. There was France's feud with Germany; Russia's feud with Germany and Austria; Austria's feud with Italy; the Slav feud with the Turks; the Greek feud with the Turks and Italians; almost everybody's feud with England. All these were plants with deep roots. The feuds flared up and died away and flared up again; they were hardly ever absent from men's minds and calculations.

But in 1900 an extraordinary thing happened. For one brief, unique span of time the powers of Europe found a joint purpose and identity. The Boxer Rising in China was an upsurge of Chinese national pride directed against the foreigners, Europeans, Americans and Japanese, who had fastened on China like leeches during the last half of the nineteenth century. The Boxers began as a nationalist secret society, 'the righteous-harmony-boxers'. They carried out savage assaults on missionaries, traders and foreign officials which in due course led to attacks on the foreign legations in Peking and the murder of the German Minister. This was more than Europe could stand. Her pride and her pocket were injured, and for a moment her feuds were set aside. For the only time in her modern history the mighty continent responded continentally to what was considered a common outrage. An International Force was assembled in China: Russians, Germans, French, British, Austrians, Italians (to say nothing of Japanese and Americans). Side by side, in the uniforms which had always symbolised their hostility to each other and would do so again, the contingents of the European empires marched to Peking.

And that was the end of the Boxers. It was also very nearly the end of European cooperation. Only a short time was left for Europe to enjoy her might and riches, before the feuds devoured them.

Boxer rising, 1900. A joint guard of nine nations – from the left,
British, American, Russian, Indian, German, French, Austrian, Italian and Japanese

3   A World to Win

Royal and imperial, aristocratic and bourgeois, proud and opulent, the European 'establishment' in 1900 could survey itself with confidence and satisfaction. Europe leaned upon the traditions of a lusty past, savouring the pomps and parades, the circuses of ceremonial, the music and the glitter with which they filled her years, and some of which survive today. She also took pride in a crop of new inventions and ideas which seemed to give her as sure a grip on the future as on the past. The order of things had an air of being settled. Society was a firmly-based pyramid; royalty was its unshakable peak.

Religion gave its blessing to this sense of established permanence. 'Render therefore unto Caesar the things which are Caesar's; and unto God the things that are God's.' In 1900 God and Caesar divided men's loyalties between them as though by contractual agreement. Republican France might rail against Clericalism; royal Italy might wish to contest the Vatican's political power – but the Catholic Church was a pillar of the Austro-Hungarian Empire; the Anglican Church was the Established Church of the British state, with the monarch equally Head of Church and State; the Protestant Churches of Germany backed the Empire; the Orthodox Church was at times scarcely distinguishable from the Russian Empire. All were tranquillisers. All preached – more or less – acceptance of the existing order. The twin foundations of Church and State seemed to be immutable factors of life.

But Europe was changing, outwardly and inwardly. Her very landscape was changing, into a scenery now universally all too familiar, and owing its birth to the same universal phenomenon. Europe's own energy in the nineteenth century, the swift industrial expansion which had occurred in certain regions, had brought into existence a new population in a new environment. Industry required workers – a proletariat – to be housed close to it; people were accordingly lured or forced out of villages into towns, new towns arising round the industries, or old towns expanding hastily to accommodate them.

Towns were taking over. In 1871, when the German Empire was born, 36·1 % of its population lived in towns; in Britain the figure was 54·5 %.

Three generations of a German peasant family. By 1901 less than half Germany's population lived on the land. (August Sander)

Thirty years later, 54·3% of Germans lived in towns, and 71·3% of the British. London's inhabitants had increased by two million in thirty years; Paris added a million in the same time; Berlin quadrupled her population in forty years. As the first decade of the new century passed, Barcelona and Milan, Marseilles and Budapest all topped the half-million mark. And so a new phenomenon came into being, and into men's vocabularies: megalopolis, or, hardly more mellifluous, conurbation. Mining villages, in South Wales or Belgium, ran into each other to form built-up agglomerations which were certainly not country but did not truly deserve the name of town which they were given; the district round Lille in northern France, under many place-names, was a continuous area of industry; the Five Towns of the English potteries were really one; the coal and iron-ore mines of the Donets and the oil-wells of the Caucasus repeated the process in Russia; the shipbuilding section of the Clyde did the same for Scotland, the mines and factories of the Ruhr for Germany.

The new, rapidly increasing, uprooted populations of these urban warrens did not always share the bourgeois reverence for Church and State. On the contrary, these people, this proletariat, increasingly regarded themselves as the enemies of the bourgeoisie:

Of all the classes that stand face to face with the bourgeoisie today, the proletariat alone is a really revolutionary class. The other classes decay and finally disappear in the face of modern industry; the proletariat is its special and essential product . . . The proletarian is without property; his relation to his wife and children has no longer anything in common with the bourgeois family relations; modern industrial labour, modern subjection to capital, the same in England as in France, in America as in Germany, has stripped him of every trace of national character. Law, morality, religion, are to him so many bourgeois prejudices, behind which lurk in ambush just as many bourgeois interests.

So wrote Marx and Engels in their Manifesto of 1848; it is easy enough to observe how, proposition by proposition, the future made nonsense of their analysis. As far back as 1900 the fulfilment of the analysis was already beginning to recede, and yet some of the conditions that prompted it were very real. The proletariat may not have been the revolutionary class that Marx and Engels believed it to be, but its antagonism towards the bourgeoisie was founded on some grim realities. The chief of these was the grinding poverty and the appalling living conditions that went with it in the new 'conurbations'.

Poverty, filth, malnutrition, disease, exploitation of women and child labour . . . small wonder if bitterness fermented and rebellion was talked of among the urban proletariat. Small wonder if nearly nine million Europeans registered their discontent with their mighty continent by emigrat-

Krupp's Essen works in about 1912. 'This new
Germany which had so swiftly turned herself
into the power-house of Europe'

A group of ironworkers: 'This
proletariate increasingly regarded themselves as
the enemies of the bourgeoisie'

ing to America in the century's first decade. For those who remained, the remedy of their ills was to combine, organise, and fight for better conditions. This, of course, was the origin of Trade Unions, which in most countries had won the battle for recognition (though not necessarily for acceptance) by 1900: in Britain they were legalised in 1871, in France in 1884; in Germany legislation improved their status in the 1890s, but in Russia they were still forbidden. At the turn of the century only about 25% of Europe's industrial workers belonged to Trade Unions; the next battles would be to enlarge their numbers and make them truly effective.

Trade Unions existed to reform society, to improve the worker's share of its wealth, not to change it fundamentally. The idea of change itself, the possibility of change so drastic as to imply the overthrow of the whole of society in its existing form, had been planted in Europe by the example of the French Revolution. Throughout the nineteenth century this remained a living inspiration; the idea developed, adopting new doctrines, hardening into a recognisable political force. 1848 had been a year of revolution all over Europe, a frightening event for the emperors and kings; they survived, but some were very conscious of 'a close-run thing'. And then came 1871. This not only was the year of the birth of the German Empire; it was also the year in which the working class in a major European capital appeared to take power – briefly, certainly, but what a portent!

The Paris Commune of 1871 rapidly assumed the quality of a legend; it was still a recent memory as the twentieth century began. Many of those who had taken part in it were still active figures in politics: Georges Clemenceau, once mayor of revolutionary Montmartre and near to being executed, was about to become a Senator; General Gallifet, the ruthless suppressor of the Commune, was now Minister of War. Every year the delegations of the Left came to Père Lachaise Cemetery and wound their way along its cobbled paths, to lay wreaths along the 'Mur des Fédérés' where captured Communards had been mown down in May 1871; this is still sacred soil of the revolutionary faith.

The Commune served as an inspiration and as a warning. 'What is happening', wrote Edmond and Jules de Goncourt in their Journal, 'is nothing less than the conquest of France by the worker . . .'[56]* This was untrue, but sufficiently widely believed to provoke a reaction full of the violence of fear. According to the French historian and statesman Gabriel Hanotaux, from beginning to end of the Commune 'Paris lost altogether 80,000 citizens'. In the 'Semaine Sanglante' (the 'Bloody Week', 21–28 May 1871), which marked the fall of the Commune, a modern French

*Alistair Horne points out that only twenty-one members of the commune out of sixty-four 'could be rated genuine workers' (*The Fall of Paris*, pp. 292–3).

historian estimates the number of Parisians killed as 'more than 17,000, perhaps 20,000'.[21] The proletarian political movement was now supplied with its martyrs, not by scores and hundreds, but by thousands: 'condamné à mort' (condemned to death), 'condamné à mort et fusillé' (condemned to death and shot), 'condamné à déportation' (condemned to deportation) – the register goes on and on.

The Right and the Moderates also had their memories: the Archbishop of Paris, many priests and many other hostages shot by the Communards, 480 of them during the course of the 'Bloody Week' alone.[21] And there was the physical destruction of much of Paris herself: the Tuileries Palace burnt down and the treasures of the Louvre very nearly lost; famous streets, like the Rue de Rivoli, turned into battlefields. The Arc de Triomphe was sandbagged and used as a gun position; Government forces fought their way down the Champs Elysées; barricades blocked the entry to the Place Vendôme. Wherever these barricades (which sprouted all over Paris) were firmly defended, there was usually a slaughter when the Army finally took them. And all the time what was particularly sickening, and made the bitterness more intense, was the thought of the victorious Germans just outside Paris, watching Frenchmen tear each other to pieces.

Outside France, the Commune was also taken as a warning, a lesson which was noted all over Europe; the memory and fear of it helped to accelerate the pace of social reform. In Germany, under Bismarck, the outlines of a kind of Welfare State were drawn, but it was a Welfare State with a difference.

Social security did not achieve its immediate aim; it did not arrest the growth of the Social Democratic Party. In a more profound sense it was successful; it made the German workers value security more than liberty and look to the state rather than to their own resources for any improvement in their condition. . . . If social security had been won by political struggle, it would have strengthened the confidence of the working-class movement to make political claims; as it was, the workers seemed to have received social security as the price of political subservience, and they drew the moral that greater subservience would earn a yet greater reward.[104]

However, the rewards obtained by the German workers through a process of legislation between 1883 and 1889 included compulsory insurance (contributed by employers and workers and organised by the State) against sickness, accident, incapacity and old age.

Reform was a pressing topic during the last decades of the nineteenth century as the evils of unrestricted capitalism became more apparent. In Britain and France, liberals warmly pressed reforms as an antidote to revolution. In both countries the political system permitted more democratic methods of reform than Bismarck's authoritarianism, but such are the confusions and delays of democracy that the lot of the German workers often seemed infinitely preferable to that of their brothers in 'freer' lands. Even the Papacy now concerned itself with workers' material conditions, and gave its blessing to the mission of improving them. In 1901 a papal encyclical, 'Graves de Communi', commended, for the Church's efforts to improve wages, working hours and working conditions, the name 'Christian Democracy'.

Yet, despite all reform and talk of reform, the idea of revolution persisted; the idea itself was altogether international, its inspiration drawn from all over Europe. It was a Frenchman, Auguste Blanqui (1805–81), who first proclaimed 'the dictatorship of the proletariat'. At his first trial, in 1832, he anticipated Marx by stating: 'There is a war between the rich and the poor. The rich have made it so, for they are the aggressors. . . .'[38] Blanqui called himself a professional proletarian, and spent almost a lifetime in prison to prove his point. He believed in revolution by conspiracy, in carefully organised secret societies which would gnaw continuously at the fabric of the state. Victor Hugo called him 'a sort of baleful apparition in whom seemed to be incarnated all the hatred born of every misery'. The Commune should have been the triumphant moment of Blanqui's life; instead, it found him once again in prison, but his followers dominated all its transactions. Blanqui supplies a necessary link between the French Revolution in the eighteenth century, the evolution of Marxist theory in the nineteenth, and the Bolshevik Revolution in the twentieth.

The introduction of a scientific, philosophical content into the idea of revolution came from two Germans, Karl Marx and Friedrich Engels, living in exile in London. Together they evolved a materialist concept of history, known as Dialectical Materialism, which they proclaimed as a guide to revolutionary activity. The goal was Communism, and the approach would be through the political education and organisation of the workers, especially a selected leadership of the workers. These would provide the true, scientific revolutionaries who alone could bring about the dictatorship of the proletariat which, in turn, would give way to Communism itself. Marx and Engels drew up their Manifesto in 1848, the year of revolutions; it began with these words: 'A spectre is haunting Europe – the spectre of Communism.' And it ended: 'Let the ruling classes tremble at a Communist revolution. The proletarians have nothing to lose but their chains. They have a world to win. Working men of all countries, unite!' They did not foresee that the world would have to wait until the twentieth century for the implementation of their ideas, nor could they have foreseen the amazing result.

The Potsdam Bridge, Berlin,
at the turn of the century

Inspired by Marx and Engels, Socialism grew as a political force in Europe. The First International Working Men's Association was formed in London in 1864, and held its first meeting in Geneva in 1866. In the following year Marx wrote to Engels: 'Things are moving, and in the next revolution, which is perhaps nearer than it appears, we (i.e. you and I) will have this powerful engine *in our hands*.'[46] When the Paris Commune came into being only four years later, it looked as though the hopes of Marx and Engels were being fulfilled. But the Commune was suppressed, and in the very next year, 1872, the Working Men's International split and lost its dynamic.

It was a Russian, Michael Bakunin, who brought this about. Bakunin (1814–76) was an anarchist; he rejected the state and everything to do with it; he rejected political action within the state; he believed only in direct action against the state. 'We must overthrow from top to bottom', he said, 'this effete social world which has become impotent and sterile.'[57] In 1869 Bakunin became associated with a twenty-two-year-old Russian, Sergei Gennadevich Nechaev, a fanatical terrorist; together they evolved much of the doctrine which was to become holy writ for innumerable anarchists in the years to come:

The revolutionary despises and hates present-day morality in all its forms . . . he regards everything as moral which helps the triumph of the revolution. . . . All soft and enervating feelings of friendship, relationship, love, gratitude, even honour, must be stifled in him by a cold passion for the revolutionary cause. . . . Day and night he must have one thought, one aim – merciless destruction. We recognise no other activity but the work of extermination, but we admit that the forms in which this activity will show itself will be extremely varied – poison, the knife, the rope, etc. In this struggle, revolution sanctifies everything alike.[57]

The language of violence found ready listeners in many places: Italy, Spain, Belgium and America, for various reasons, offered good growing soil for Bakunin's ideas. The Anarchist movement grew and shocked the establishments of the world by demonstrations that it was not interested only in ideas and talk. In 1892 three bombs exploded in Paris; in December 1893 a bomb was thrown in the Chamber of Deputies and wounded a number of them; in February 1894 a particularly mindless explosion in the Café Terminus at the Gare St Lazare killed one person and wounded twenty out of a predominantly working-class clientèle; in April yet another bomb, thrown in a restaurant, succeeded in gravely wounding the poet Laurent Tailhade; and then, in June, came the summit of the whole campaign, the assassination in Lyon of the President of the Republic, Sadi Carnot, by a twenty-one-year-old Italian, Santo Hieronimus Caserio, who hated all Heads of State on principle. So much for France; not long afterwards it was Switzerland's turn: in September 1898 the sad, lonely Empress Elizabeth of Austria was assassinated by another Italian at Geneva. Her endless journeyings were over at last. In 1900 the King of Italy fell to another assassin, and in 1901 President McKinley of the United States was the victim of yet one more glorious blow for anarchy.

It was Alejandro Lerroux, in 1905, who issued to his followers in the fermenting slums of Barcelona a manifesto which may stand for the passions of the anarchists everywhere:

Young barbarians of today! Enter and sack the decadent civilisation of this unhappy country! Destroy its temples, finish off its gods, tear the veil from its novices and raise them up to be mothers! Fight, kill, and die![110]

This was a language which would be heard again and again, the language of an underground sapping the very foundations of society. Its political manifestations were, on the one hand, a steadily increasing Socialist vote at elections, and on the other, catering for the more impatient, the violent deeds of the Anarchists. But so much anger, so much excitement, justifiable or otherwise, was not to be contained only by politics; it spilled over into the arts. In that field the word 'modern' had already taken on a fresh significance. One writer says: 'The twentieth century could not wait fifteen years for a round number; it was born, yelling, in 1885.'[99] 1885 was the year of Victor Hugo's funeral. He was the Grand Old Man of French literature – poet, playright, political martyr, patriot. When he died his body lay in state at the Arc de Triomphe for twenty-four hours, while Paris gave herself up to an orgy – literally an orgy – of emotion. That night, 'how many women', asked Maurice Barrès, 'gave themselves to lovers, to strangers, with a burning fury to become mothers of immortals!' The next day Hugo's body was escorted to the Panthéon by a vast crowd, with several brass bands. There were speeches from numerous exalted political and literary figures, and several people died in the press of the crowd.

By this orgiastic ceremony France unburdened herself of a man, a literary movement, and a century. . . . Exactly in the years following Hugo's funeral, all the arts changed direction as if they had been awaiting a signal . . . 1885 is the point from which we must reckon the meaning of the word 'modern'.[99]

Paris now became the epicentre of a series of artistic earthquakes which closely matched, in their social disturbance, the political agitation of the bomb-throwers. In the cafés and boîtes of the Left Bank, the Latin Quarter, ideas seethed, flourished, faded and yielded every day to the temptations of tomorrow. A phenomenon occurred which has been part of the twentieth century ever since:

. . . the fluid state known as Bohemia, a cultural underground smacking of failure and fraud, crystallised for a few decades into a self-conscious avant-garde that carried the Arts into a period of astonishingly varied renewal and accomplishment.[99]

These decades were marked by a curious penchant for collective endeavour; the Art movements followed each other like regiments behind their banners, except that, being artists and therefore fundamentally individualists, the personnel of the 'regiments' was remarkably interchangeable. The names of men of such varied genius as Cézanne, Matisse or Picasso could never be confined to one catalogue. The 1870s sustained the superb impact of the Impressionists; in the 1880s came the Neo-Impressionists; the 1890s were rocked by Art Nouveau; and then in the 1900s came Post-Impressionism. All these movements and groups, no matter how fiercely they might from time to time dispute among themselves, were in direct, constant conflict with the art of the Establishment, the Academicians. Establishment art was annually displayed in the Salon des Artistes français (which Cézanne called 'Bouguereau's Salon', after one of the outstanding practitioners) and the Salon National, presided over by Puvis de Chavannes. Here the graceful nude goddesses and mortal ladies annually displayed on canvas their soft, inviting slopes; menageries of animals as sleek as the nymphs stalked imaginary jungles and deserts; classical allegories and romantic myths were suitably interpreted; pompous portraits frowned and leered; often it was enough to make you sick.

In reaction to all that, the artists and writers of the avant-garde cultivated, in the cafés of the Latin Quarter or Montmartre, their own simmering way of life, erupting periodically in uproars and scandals which some people believed were their sole purpose. Montmartre in 1900 was just reaching the height of its fame as an artistic colony. It was still a place of windmills, with cows and goats and chickens in its steeply sloping streets where now the cars thread their way with difficulty through the tourist herds. At that time the great basilica of Sacré Coeur was still unfinished. The Chat Noir cabaret, for a long time the headquarters of the avant-garde, was reaching the end of its primacy. At the Chat Noir it was correct form for the proprietor to insult every customer as he came in; the surly waiters wore the robes of the Académie française; the cabaret had its own weekly newspaper and conducted its own literary soirées. At the turn of the century its popularity gave way to that of the Lapin Agile, which still crouches modestly among the tall straight-faced houses of modern Montmartre. There there was a donkey called Lolo which painted a picture by twitching its tail. Lolo's picture was called 'And the Sun Went Down over the Adriatic'; it was hung in the Salon des Indépendants, and several critics praised it. Guillaume Apollinaire the poet, looking back on this period, said: 'We learned to laugh'.

90

In 1905 the avant-garde produced one of its greatest sensations. The Salon d'Automne presented in one room paintings by Matisse, Derain, Rouault, Vlaminck, Friesz, with the Douanier Rousseau's 'Le lion ayant faim' in amongst them. The total effect was a blaze of raw colour, so violently assaulting eyes more familiar with the softer tones of the impressionists or the treacly confections of the academicians, that one critic called this room 'une cage aux fauves' – a cage of wild beasts. The artists accepted the description with pleasure, and it became their title: they were the Fauvists, one more avant-garde group in a never-ending succession.

By the standards of what was to come, the artistic 'wild beasts' of 1905 looked even tame, just as the crudities of the anarchist outrages would soon be overshadowed by a much vaster violence; but in their own day, set against Establishment art and Establishment morals, avant-garde and anarchists were shock troops. Painters gave plastic form to the sense of imminent explosion; writers supplied words to match this fever of ideas; the anarchists merely added some high explosive. The famous French Socialist, Léon Blum, then in his thirties, summed it all up: 'The whole literary generation of which I was a part was impregnated with anarchist thought.'[57] Somewhere, soon, there was bound to be an eruption.

Unexpectedly, the place was Russia, and the event occurred in that very year, 1905, a year of peculiar tragedy. Europe's most backward economy had at last been making some remarkable progress: in ten years railway mileage had increased by 46%; coal production had doubled; pig iron production trebled; oil production quadrupled. A new population of industrial workers had come into existence to man this new industry. By most western European standards, this Russian proletariat was small and grotesquely underprivileged, but to the Marxist Socialists this was the class of the future, the soil in which their ideas of revolution would take root. But it needed to be larger; without allies, the ranks of the proletariat were all too thin.

In 1905, however, it found allies. The twentieth century had come painfully to Russia. Modernisation and autocracy confronted each other without sympathy. Russia remained, despite her economic advances, predominantly a nation of peasants. Only forty years before the turn of the century they had been serfs living in medieval bondage, and many of the attributes of serfdom still clung to them. Even when they moved to the towns to join the new working-class, they either had to give up all their land rights, or they were compelled to return each year to their villages for the harvest. So they became neither real peasants nor real proletarians, just unskilled casual labourers. Their poverty was chronic; wages were pitifully low, working hours were long; health and safety regulations were practically non-existent; there were no Trade Unions, no right to strike. In the countryside, the peasants were increasingly irked by the restrictions which governed their lives and coveted the ownership of land. In country and town alike there was mounting discontent, to which the autocracy knew only one answer: repression.

Under the autocracy political parties were not permitted – though that did not prevent them from existing. But there was no parliament or national assembly which they could try to control by general elections, or, as an Opposition, where they could voice the people's demands; so the parties were forced into a revolutionary position. And this was also the almost universal frame of mind of the younger generation, whose un-challenged mentor was Count Leo Tolstoy, and the middle-class intellec-tuals. 'The feeling among educated society was that it was everyone's moral duty to aid the cause of revolution, a sacred obligation to the ex-ploited people of Russia.'[101]

Because the parties had no other outlet than revolutionary activity, their leaders were generally to be found either in prison, or in Siberia, or in exile abroad: Geneva, Brussels and London were favourite places of refuge. It was in London, in 1903, that the Russian Social Democrats (SDs) held their vital congress at which the faction led by V. I. Lenin defeated G. Plekhanov and so divided the party into Bolsheviks (= majority group) and Mensheviks (= minority group). Lenin and the Bolsheviks stood for a tightly-organised party limited to active and disciplined revolutionaries, as opposed to a mass party modelled on those of democratic states. The characteristic of 'double-speak' was implanted early: very soon the Bolshevik 'majority' was seen to be a minority, and the Mensheviks gained control of the party. But Lenin never departed from his ideas, and never ceased to work for their fulfilment.

It was the Socialist Revolutionaries (SRs), however, not the SDs who formed Russia's largest and most important party at the beginning of the century. This was for a very good reason: whereas the SDs sought their support among the growing but still small industrial working-class, the SRs were quite frankly the party of the peasants. Much less concerned with 'scientific' theories of historical materialism and precise definitions of socialism, their organisation was adapted to the crudest assault upon the autocracy: SR politics were the politics of pure violence. They organised strikes and student riots (which were brutally repressed), peasant upris-ings (which were equally brutally repressed), and a steady attrition by assassination: in 1901 the Minister of Propaganda (Bogolyepov), in 1902 the Minister of the Interior (Sipyagin); in 1904 another Minister of the Interior, Plehve (the holder of this post was always a favourite target), and

Father Gapon with the Prefect of St Petersburg, General Ivan Fullon, a picture which displays the envious ambiguities of the Russian autocracy.

Bobrikov, the Governor-General of Finland; in 1905 the Grand Duke Sergey, Governor of Moscow.

To all these deeds the autocracy – that peculiar apparatus of government for government's sake which nailed Russia into the coffin of her past – could only find one dismal answer: violence of its own, turned in a different direction. By 1904 it appeared that the last expedient left to the Russian autocracy was 'a small victorious war'. The enemy was not difficult to discover: the rising Empire of Japan with which Russian interests constantly conflicted in Manchuria. War broke out (without any declaration) in February 1904, and from the very first it went badly for Russia, with defeat following defeat on sea and land. This was not what the autocracy needed at all; this disastrously unvictorious war merely accentuated the problems at home that it was meant – somehow – to solve. The strain on transportation caused a breakdown of supplies to the cities. Bread prices soared. Once more there were strikes and riots.

In St Petersburg on 22 January 1905 a priest, Father Gapon (who may or may not have been an agent-provocateur) led a large procession carrying portraits of the Tsar and singing hymns and patriotic songs towards the Winter Palace to present a petition to their 'Little Father':

Lord! We workers, our children, our wives and our old, helpless parents have come, Lord, to seek truth and protection from you. We are impoverished and oppressed, unbearable work is imposed on us, we are despised and not recognised as human beings. We are treated as slaves, who must bear their fate and be silent . . . Despotism and arbitrariness throttle us and we choke. . . . For us that terrible moment has come when death is better than the continuance of the most unbearable torments . . .[94]

Death was what many found that day. As Father Gapon's procession reached the Narva Triumphal Arch (still some miles from their destination, the Winter Palace) it found police and soldiers drawn up across its route. Father Gapon has left his own description of what followed:

At last we reached within two hundred paces of where the troops stood. Files of infantry barred the road, and in front of them a company of cavalry was drawn up, with their swords shining in the sun. Would they dare to touch us? For a moment we trembled, and then started forward again.

Suddenly the company of Cossacks galloped rapidly towards us with drawn swords. . . . I saw the swords lifted and falling, the men, women and children dropping to the earth like logs of wood, while moans, curses and shouts filled the air . . .

Again we started forward, with solemn resolution and rising rage in our hearts . . .

We were not more than thirty yards from the soldiers . . . when suddenly with-

Bloody Sunday, St Petersburg, 22 January 1905.
Troops and demonstrators in front of the Winter Palace

out any warning and without a moment's delay, was heard the dry crack of many rifle shots . . .

I turned rapidly to the crowd and shouted to them to lie down, and I also stretched myself out on the ground. As we lay thus another volley was fired, and another, and yet another, till it seemed as though the shooting was continuous . . .

At last the firing ceased. I stood up with a few others who remained uninjured and looked down at the bodies that lay prostrate around me. I cried to them, 'Stand up!' But they lay still. I could not at first understand. Why did they lie there? I looked again, and saw that their arms were stretched out lifelessly, and I saw the scarlet stain of blood upon the snow. Then I understood . . .

Horror crept into my heart. The thought flashed through my mind, 'And this is the work of our Little Father, the Tsar'. . .[94]

Similar scenes were repeated in other parts of St Petersburg, culminating in the afternoon in the wide square outside the Winter Palace itself, where the Preobrazhensky Guards fired into an unorganised crowd which had gathered there, on an order from Prince Vasilchikov, the military governor of the capital.

The scene resulting from the execution of that order was to become etched into the minds of the Russian people as the one, above all others of this tragic Sunday, that represented the brutal injustice under which they lived. It was to be described over and over with many embellishments and much bitter vindictiveness.[54]

This was 'Bloody Sunday', the opening act of Russia's 1905 Revolution.

The Revolution was a failure, in the immediate sense, but it was a turning-point. It did not overthrow the autocracy, but the autocracy was never the same again. Deserted by many of his own supporters, the Tsar was forced to concede a measure of parliamentary government for the first time, a Duma elected (for a while only) by universal suffrage. This temporarily satisfied the Liberal opponents of the régime, though the working-class and the peasants remained largely discontented. For them, once more, the prescription was repression, with a new element added: an unofficial reign of terror over and above the acts of the army and police, by reactionary gangs and mobs called the 'Black Hundreds', anti-semitic, anti-minority, anti-revolutionary, people who frequently made patriotism a convenient excuse for hooligan cruelties. And so the 1905 Revolution sputtered out in continuing bloodshed and broken promises, but it had made some instructive points: above all, the working-class had been shown the contents of its armoury — political strikes and workers' councils, called Soviets.

The Revolution had provided a shock and a lesson for all Europe. The Russian revolutionaries condemned to Siberia (among them a young

Jewish socialist Lev Davidovich Bronstein, generally known as Leon Trotsky), or in exile elsewhere, pondered how the thing might be done better another time. European Liberals and Socialists pondered whether it should be done at all by revolutionary means, and if not, what the alternatives were. Of all Europe's Socialist parties the richest and apparently most powerful was Germany's. As early as 1900 the Social Democrats had 56 seats in the Reichstag, backed by two million votes. By 1912 they had become the largest single party in the Reichstag, and yet, as A. J. P. Taylor says, they 'were incapable of imposing on the Reich a single under-secretary'.

The contradictions within the German Social Democratic Party were dangerous not merely to itself but to all Europe. Because the authoritarian character of the German Empire blocked the avenues to high office for Social Democrats, the Party clung to Marxist revolutionary theories. But in reality Bismarck's social security programme had revealed an easier path to greater prosperity which fully satisfied many of the Party's members.

In fact the Social Democrats made the worst of both worlds. Their revolutionary theory prevented any united movement of the Left for liberal reform; their unrevolutionary practice made them incapable of action in a revolutionary crisis.[104]

For Europe the danger of this confusion was this:

The German Social Democrats were the largest and best-organized party of the Socialist International, the unquestioned repositories of Marxist theory. They preached the doctrine of the general strike against war and imposed it on the Socialist parties of every other country. Thus they created the impression that the Reich government, however malignant its intentions, would not be permitted to start on a war of aggression; and so greatly strengthened the opposition to both military and diplomatic precautions against Germany in England and France . . . Germany, with its great Socialist party and its industrial concentrations, was, they argued, practically a Socialist country already; and a German victory would bring a socialist victory all the nearer. Therefore, while it was the duty of French and Russian workers to strive for the defeat and overthrow of their governments, it was equally the duty of German workers to strive for a German victory – a comforting conclusion not, however, appreciated by the Socialist comrades in the International who continued, to the last, to rely with confidence on the German general strike.[104]

Ambiguity could scarcely be more ruinous.

And ambiguities were plentiful: a Marxist Socialist party in Germany turning its back on revolution – and a decidedly non-Marxist Liberal party in Britain striding towards civil war. By tradition the British Liberal Party was the party of reform, still glowing with the recent lustre of its famous leader, William Ewart Gladstone. In 1906 the Liberals won their last great triumph: a landslide victory in the general election under the leadership of Sir Henry Campbell-Bannerman. Campbell-Bannerman and his successor, H. H. Asquith, then launched a sweeping programme of reforms in the name of social justice and national efficiency.

The Liberal programme amounted to a direct attack on the rich, which naturally provoked bitter opposition. When David Lloyd George became Chancellor of the Exchequer in 1908, the Liberals laid down, stage by stage, the foundations of a Welfare State in Britain, not decreed from aloft like Bismarck's essay in Germany, but fought for every inch of the way. In battle after battle the Liberals and their supporters gained old-age pensions, free school meals and medical services, Labour Exchanges, regulations of working conditions, town planning and, above all, a National Insurance Scheme. In 1909 Lloyd George brought in his 'People's Budget', regarded by the Opposition as a direct attack on property, landed property above all. Not surprisingly, this aroused the fierce resentment of the Conservative majority in the House of Lords. This in itself was something of a feat; a new bishop was heard to remark at about this time: 'Divisions in the House of Lords are now so thinly scattered that, when one occurs, the peers cackle as if they had laid an egg.'[29] The Lords now rallied all their forces and threw out the Budget, thus defying the Liberal majority in the House of Commons and beginning a constitutional crisis which led to two general elections in 1910. Twice the Liberals were returned to power (though only with the backing of Labour and Irish members). The first time they forced through the Budget. Then they turned their attention to the House of Lords itself, and a Parliament Bill was introduced to curb the powers of the Upper House. The second election gave the Government a mandate to force this Bill through also, which it duly did in 1911, the House of Lords acquiescing in its own downfall when faced with the threat that the King would be compelled to create four hundred Liberal peers.

All these stormy events unfolded in a Parliament unusually rich in strong and passionate personalities. Asquith, the Prime Minister, and A. J. Balfour, the Leader of the Opposition, were cool, aloof and suave; many of their followers were the exact opposite. On the Government side, Lloyd George, one of the most unforgettable oratorical talents in British political history, was now at his zenith. Winston Churchill had so cultivated the art of inflaming his opponents that on one occasion a heavy book was thrown at his head in the Commons chamber – an episode which King George V called 'serious and deplorable'. Ramsay MacDonald, for Labour, could work upon an audience's emotions without the intellectual blur which later overtook him. For the Conservatives, F. E. Smith habitually deployed a devastatingly brilliant mind and a cruel wit.

It was a time of political emotions with no comparison in modern history. The ill-temper of the Opposition who believed in their inherent right to rule was equalled only by the invective used and the storms that regularly took place in the House of Commons. To this day when politicians wish to find a parallel for bitter, passionate or reckless controversy they go back to the Parliament of 1910.[36]

Parliament merely reflected the mood of the nation. In 1906 a new portent had been seen, a new phenomenon in British politics. Among the supporters of the incoming Liberal Government were twenty-nine members of Parliament who grouped to form a 'Labour Party'. The outgoing Conservative Prime Minister, Mr Balfour, exclaimed: 'We are face to face (no doubt in a milder form) with the Socialist difficulties which loom so large on the Continent. Unless I am greatly mistaken the election of 1906 inaugurates a new era.'[85] He was not mistaken. The working class was on the march. In 1910 there was a strike of South Wales miners which lasted ten months; in 1911 the dockers and railwaymen struck; in 1912 the miners, dockers and transport workers.

It was this period that Ben Tillett, the dockers' leader described as '. . . a great upsurge of elemental forces. It seemed as if the dispossessed and disinherited class in various parts of the country were all simultaneously moved to assert their claims upon society.'[14] The dispossessed and disinherited were not just a class: in 1903 Mrs Emmeline Pankhurst founded the Women's Social and Political Union to fight for women's rights, above all the right to vote. The Suffragette Movement, as it came to be called, grew in strength and determination during the next ten years. By 1913 Suffragette violence had become as regular a part of the British scene as anarchist outrages in France during the previous decade.

This was a bad time for His Majesty's government, with both workers and women in a state of simmering revolt. But there was worse to come, and ironically the most serious upsurge of all came from the very heart of traditional England, from the shires and the stately homes which were the strongholds of the Tory Right. What triggered off this revolt of the least revolutionary of people was the everlasting Irish Question. The Liberal Government (a substantial part of whose support came from the Irish Members at Westminster) wanted to give Home Rule to the whole of Ireland. The Protestants of Ulster bitterly resisted inclusion in the Catholic South. Conservatives all over Britain backed the Protestant demand to continue their union with the rest of the United Kingdom – British Conservatives, in fact, were now called Unionists, and their passions were deeply roused. In March 1914 the officers of a cavalry brigade stationed at the Curragh Camp outside Dublin announced that they would resign their commissions rather than march against Ulster. For a time it looked as though all authority was about to collapse, and the country would be plunged into civil war. In Ireland, volunteers were drilling on both sides of the Ulster border. The problem seemed intransigent; it was quenched by the coming of a much deeper crisis, but only for a time. It would return, evil as ever, in the 1970s.

Those were frightening times – times when gunsmiths' shops in London sold out their entire stock of revolvers. The Liberal Government remained in power with diminished majorities, more and more dependent on its Labour and Irish allies, more and more vulnerable to the triple attack of workers, women and Tories. Parliament itself, the very foundation of British democracy, seemed in danger of collapse. And the violence of the British scene was well matched by violence in Europe. A fresh wave of anarchy in politics and the arts threatened to submerge all bourgeois democracy and parliamentary government.

In France agitation took two forms. Under the leadership of Jean Jaurès, the various factions of the political Socialist movement had unified and were working for the advance of Socialism by parliamentary means. The Trade Unions, on the other hand, were much influenced by former Blanquists, anarchists and syndicalists, who believed only in the weapon of the general strike. Between 1906 and 1910 France, like Britain, was torn by a series of strikes – postal workers, teachers, wine-growers, railway-men – often marked by scenes of very ugly violence on both sides, and edging towards revolution. In 1910 Aristide Briand's government smashed the railwaymen's strike by mobilising the strikers into the army. By such means the State was preserved, and French parliamentary democracy survived, if badly battered; but national unity in France, in the aftermath of these passions in the years just before 1914, seemed to be just a joke.

Spain had no parliamentary system as it was understood in France and Britain; perhaps for that very reason Spain was a stronghold of anarchy – the only expedient available to those who wished to put pressure on the régime. Political strikes there were a weapon of open class-war; in Barcelona in 1902 and in Bilbao in 1903 there were indications of what that might mean. And then, in 1909, the Left added a new name to its list of 'battle honours': the 'Semaine Sanglante', the 'Bloody Week' of the Paris Commune, and 'Bloody Sunday' in St Petersburg were followed by the 'Semana Tragica', the 'Tragic Week' of Barcelona. For one week in July it looked as though revolution had triumphed in the Catalan capital. Anselmo Lorenzo, a leading anarchist, wrote to a friend:

It is amazing! The social revolution has started in Barcelona, and it has been started by something so ill-defined, misunderstood and wrongly identified as that which is sometimes called the vile rabble and sometimes His Majesty the

Sickert. The New Bedford; 'The outward image of a glittering Edwardian decade . . .'

100

101

102   Henri Rousseau. *War*

People. No one started it! No one led it! Neither liberals nor Catalan separatists, nor republicans nor socialists nor anarchists. . . . A week of intoxication, of holy rage, seeing that the fury of the masses was justified by a hundred centuries of misery, oppression and endurance.[57]

But the revolutionaries of Barcelona were shot down by the army, martial law was proclaimed, and the inevitable reprisals followed. Yet the 'Tragic Week' produced one important gain for the anarchists: the foundation in 1911 of the first national anarchist federation, the Confederación Nacional de Trabajo. Anarchism in Spain remained the most powerful instrument of dissent.

Meanwhile the avant-garde writers and artists were stepping up their own attacks on society and its conventions. These took endlessly new and frequently bizarre forms. Thus the French poet Guillaume Apollinaire devised a 'plastic poetry', called the 'calligram', with deliberately fractured typography. Pablo Picasso and Georges Braque invented Cubism as a means of liberation from the 'tyranny' of the subject. This in turn opened the way for 'Orphism' and 'Simultanism'. The names were legion, the purpose was always the same: an assault on accepted values and conventions, with the ultimate result of an undermining of society itself. In Dresden, in 1905, Ernst Kirchner raised the banner of the 'Brücke' School, proclaiming:

With the belief in a new development, in a new generation of creators as well as of spectators, we call on youth to rally, to fight for elbow room and for the right to live our own lives. . . . All those belong to us who reproduce, direct and unadulterated, that which urges them to create.[95]

This was 'Expressionism'. Later it received a new impetus in Munich from the 'Blaue Reiter' (Blue Rider) School — Franz Marc, Vasili Kandinsky, Alexei von Jawlensky, August Macke, Gabriele Münter and others. And always the fight was against the Academies and the world they represented.

At the extreme tip of the avant-garde spear stood the Futurists, the movement launched by the Italian poet Filippo Marinetti. His manifesto appeared in 1909; the words explode like bombs:

We shall extol aggressive movement, feverish insomnia, the double quick step, the somersault, the box on the ear, the fisticuff . . . a roaring motor-car, which looks as though running on shrapnel, is more beautiful than the 'Victory of Samothrace' . . . There is no more beauty except in strife. No masterpiece without aggressiveness . . .

We wish to glorify war — the only health-giver of the world — militarism, patriotism, the destructive arm of the Anarchist, the beautiful Ideas that kill . . .

We wish to destroy the museums, the libraries . . .

Come, then, the good incendiaries, with their charred fingers! Here they come!

Here they come! Set fire to the shelves of the libraries! Flood the cellars of the museums! Oh! May the glorious canvases drift helplessly! Seize pickaxes and hammers! Sap the foundations of the venerable cities!

We will have none of it, we, the young, the strong, the living Futurists![73]

So the new Schools, all over Europe, fuelled the sense of imminent eruption, the overlapping explosions, overlapping discontents beneath the surface of the 'Golden Age' which might merge into some great explosion which would transform the world. Avant-garde artists and political anarchists alike gave expression to Nietzsche's incendiary text: 'Who wishes to be creative . . . must first blast and destroy accepted values.'[95]

'The fleet was the favourite child of Germany'.
Wilhelm II and the crew of the cruiser *Deutschland*

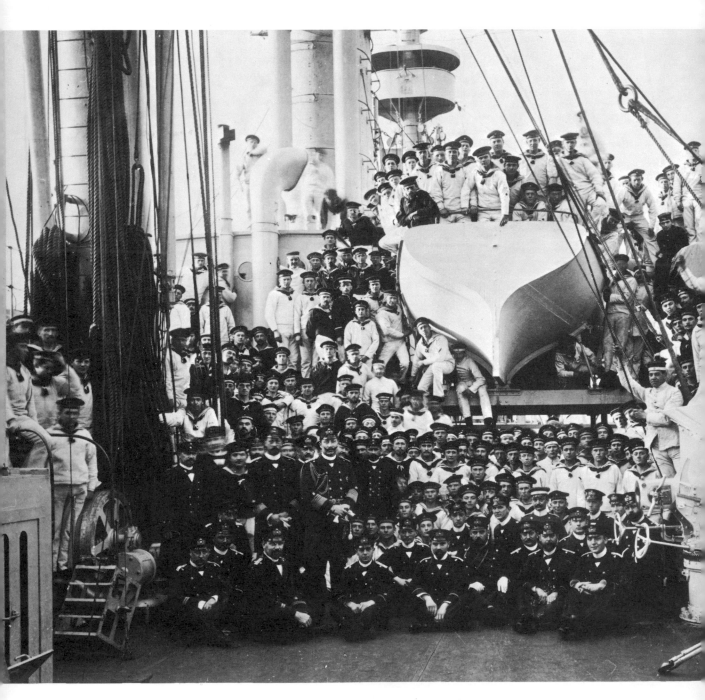

4   When the drums begin to roll

The produce of the world flowed into Europe – not only foodstuffs like cocoa and sugar, raw materials like rubber, from imperial possessions in Africa, the East and West Indies and South-east Asia, but also from independent countries such commodities as American wheat, Chilean nitrates or Argentine beef. The demand was always increasing and the variety of products desired was always extending with each advance of European technology, population and prosperity. Less and less were the nations of Europe able to support themselves (Britain was an outstanding example of this), but in 1900 this hardly mattered because that was the time when 'offices in London or Hamburg or Rotterdam controlled developments in Singapore or Shanghai or Santiago'. If there was trouble in faraway places, Europe possessed the fleets and armies to settle it; gunboats were still good value for money. Money invested overseas seemed to be well placed; Europe's annual overseas investment ran at about £350 million. The shareholders, by and large, were well satisfied, and there did not seem to be any overwhelming reason why this state of affairs should not continue.

And then, suddenly, in 1904 the trajectory of European history entered a steep curve. A tide was reversed. It could even be said that the fall of the mighty continent now began. 1904 was the year in which the vast Russian Empire, in order to avoid the penalties of mounting crises at home, rashly opted for war with the Empire of Japan. On one side in this war stood the largest, most unassailable, and apparently most powerful of the European empires. On the other side stood the only Asian country to have succeeded in imitating European methods, the only Asian country with a modern army and navy, based on modern industry. The focus of the war was Port Arthur in Manchuria. The Japanese had demanded Port Arthur and the Liao-tung peninsula behind it as legitimate spoils of their victory over China in 1895, but three European powers, Russia, France and Germany, had compelled them to settle for a money payment instead. This was a display of European *force majeure* which Japan would not forget or forgive; and the insult was compounded in 1897 when Russia herself leased Port Arthur from China as a naval base. Now, in 1904, the port was heavily protected by modern forts and artillery and defended by a large army;

but Port Arthur was 5500 miles from Moscow, connected to European Russia only by the single track of the Trans-Siberian Railway with its 100-mile gap at Lake Baikal. This stark logistical fact constituted Russia's insuperable strategic problem.

Without declaring war, the Japanese attacked the Russian naval squadron at Port Arthur on 8 February. *The Times* commented:

The Japanese navy, thanks to the masculine decision of the Mikado and his advisers, has taken the initiative, and has opened the war by an act of daring . . . Owing to its position in the outer roadstead, the Russian squadron was open to, and invited, attack. The invitation has been accepted with a promptness and a punctuality that do high honour to the navy of our gallant allies.[65]

In 1904, of course, Japan *was* Britain's ally; thirty-seven years later *The Times* found very different words to describe a similar performance at Pearl Harbour.

The war between Japan and Russia turned out to be full of surprises; it quickly took on a David and Goliath quality. Led by officers who in many cases had begun their military careers wearing chain-armour and wielding battle-axes, the Japanese won victory after victory. They forced the Russians back into Port Arthur, and captured the base after a five-month siege in the first week of 1905 – at a cost of 60,000 casualties. In February they defeated the Russian field army at Mukden, the greatest battle of the war. With over 600,000 men engaged on a front of forty miles, this was also the greatest battle in history to that date.

The last act came in May 1905. The Russian Baltic Fleet, having traversed the North Sea (almost causing war with Britain by idiotically firing on the Hull trawlers off the Dogger Bank), the North and South Atlantic, the Indian Ocean and the Western Pacific, arrived at the Tsushima Straits – and was destroyed in three quarters of an hour. Europe now had to take in the unbelievable facts, not only of large European armies being soundly defeated, but also of a modern European navy being annihilated by an even more modern Asiatic fleet. Such events flouted all historical precepts, contradicted every textbook. As far as Russia was concerned, the Battle of the Tsushima Straits was the final straw; three months later peace was signed. Japan had won, hands down.

The consequences of this now almost forgotten war were prodigious. The defeat of Russia shook all the European empires as they had never been shaken before. A Turkish consul with long experience in Western Asia, told an English visitor:

. . . that in the interior you could see everywhere the most ignorant peasants 'tingling' with the news. Asia was moved from one end to the other, and the sleep of centuries was finally broken. . . . A new chapter was being written in the book of the world's history. . . . The old-time glory and greatness of Asia seemed destined to return.[40]

Another Englishman, Edward Dicey, who had lived in Africa for forty years, wrote:

Suddenly and unexpectedly, the conviction that native forces, however brave, were bound to be worsted by Europeans, was shaken to its base by the discovery that Russia, which was regarded in the East as the greatest military power in Europe, had been driven from pillar to post by the victorious Japanese, that her armies had been put to flight, her navy destroyed, her fortresses captured by a comparatively diminutive and feeble Power, whose people, whatever else they might be, were certainly not Caucasians or Christians. It may be said with truth that the native Africans . . . knew nothing . . . about Japan. But yet I should doubt whether there was a town or village in the whole of Africa where the inhabitants did not learn directly or indirectly that the Russian invaders of the Far East had been scattered like sheep by an unknown non-European race.[40]

Above all the sub-continent of India, the most prized possession of the British Raj, became aware of the new portent. In the northern provinces, even the remote villages talked over the victories of Japan as they sat in their circles and passed round the *huqqa* at night. . . .'[40] An Indian scholar, R. G. Pradhan, says: 'It is impossible to exaggerate the effects of the Japanese victory on the Indian mind.'[40] Indian students began to travel to Japan to study her history and discover the secret of her success. Nationalist politicians took courage from the Japanese example. In the event, it would take another remarkable demonstration from the Japanese in 1941 to complete the lesson, but it was in 1904 that the first step in the long march of Asian nationalism towards independence of Europe was taken.

If the repercussions of Japanese victory were felt all over Asia, the repercussions of Russian defeat made a direct impact on Europe. For a time a power vacuum was created – one of the most dangerous conditions in politics, and on this occasion the danger was intensified by the actions of a restless, disturbing personality. The Kaiser Wilhelm II had ascended his throne in 1888 and soon afterwards he announced to the German people: 'We are destined to great things and I am leading you to marvellous times.'[5] The pursuit of the Kaiser's 'great things' and 'marvellous times' contributed no small amount to the unease of Europe as the twentieth century advanced. One of his Chancellors, Prince von Bülow, said of him: 'Wilhelm II wants to shine and to do and decide everything for himself. But what he wants to do unfortunately often goes wrong.'[5]

Later in his life Wilhelm II came to be regarded by many as an arch-villain; but, as one historian shrewdly remarks, 'later generations have

'The number of popular newspapers was increasing . . .'
The offices of the *Daily Mail*, 1913

seen real villainy and can pronounce him only a nuisance.'[119] The Kaiser's trouble would seem to have been talent without discipline. And he certainly had talents. One of them was for naval design; Wilhelm II was in love with the idea of a strong German Navy, and it was his pastime to design warships on any piece of paper that came to hand, a telegram form or perhaps the back of a banquet menu. The designs were very practical – at least as practical as the architectural plans which later helped to express the personality of Adolf Hitler. The German Navy was also very practical – in its way – and very disturbing to European peace.

Wilhelm II liked to see himself as a war-lord (although 'when real trouble was brewing, he was always for peace and compromise'[119]). He once spoke of himself as 'standing in shining armour'; his words and his gestures all too often exactly fitted the phrase 'sabre-rattling'. His first public utterance as Kaiser was addressed to the Army: and he said: 'We belong to each other – I and the Army – we were born for each other and will cleave indissolubly to each other, whether it be the will of God to send us calm or storm.'[5] Such language, too often and too loudly repeated, can be very dangerous.

At the opening of the century the Chief of Staff of the German Army was Field-Marshal von Schlieffen. This officer was haunted by one fear: that the alliance between France and Russia would compel Germany to fight a war simultaneously on two fronts. His conclusion was that in the event of war Germany must smash France in a lightning campaign before the slow-moving Russians could mobilise. The method by which this was to be done has gone down in history as the notorious Schlieffen Plan. In 1905, however, von Schlieffen's problem was greatly simplified by Russia's defeat and the revolution which accompanied it. For the time being Russia was out of the game (this was the power vacuum) and it seemed that German policy towards France could be shaped accordingly. But could it?

France had found a new friend. Against all expectation, after the humiliation and bitterness of Fashoda, France and Britain reached an understanding. In 1903 Edward VII visited Paris; he was hissed when he arrived as the embodiment of grasping British imperial power, 'perfidious Albion', the perpetual obstacle to French expansion. But when he left he was cheered, and in the atmosphere which the King had created by his good temper and goodwill the French and British were able to settle their differences and arrive at a mutually supporting agreement, the Entente Cordiale.

In 1905 Germany put the new Entente to its first test. The scene was Tangier in Morocco. Ostensibly, Morocco was an independent kingdom, but the terms of the Entente Cordiale promised France a 'free hand' in Moroccan affairs, in return for Britain's 'free hand' in Egypt and the Sudan.

(France also promised Spain an eventual share in the control of Morocco, a mixed blessing if ever there was one.) And then came the German challenge to these bland agreements: in March 1905 the Kaiser appeared in person in Tangier, on the face of it to assert Moroccan independence, but actually to force a French climb-down and curb French expansion.

The question was whether Britain would back France or not. If not, the Entente Cordiale was obviously worthless. But if Britain did stand by the agreement, there was a risk of immediate European war. Somewhat to everyone's surprise, Britain did stand by the Entente, and at the Algeçiras Conference which finally settled the dispute (at the prompting of President Theodore Roosevelt of the United States) it was Germany that climbed down, stage by stage. Neither this result, nor any other part of the Tangier crisis were good for European peace; after it, the divisions of the continent hardened year by year. In 1906 Staff talks began between Britain and France to arrange military cooperation in the event of German aggression. In 1907 Britain reached agreement with France's ally, Russia; Britain and Russia had been near to conflict only two years earlier – but times had significantly changed. So now the Entente Cordiale turned into the Triple Entente, and in the same year – 1907 – Germany, Austria-Hungary and Italy formally renewed the Triple Alliance. These two blocs of powers, whose interests and policies increasingly conflicted, now dominated the European scene.

In this unhealthy political atmosphere every incident became a potential crisis, and in the new century crisis was no longer something for statesmen to handle in cool privacy. Crisis was unfolded like a drama to a growing audience of newspaper readers. Most of them cared nothing for the finesses of politics and diplomacy; they saw only the bright colours of contrast and conflict, never the softer shades of compromise. They saw the menacing posture of leaders, read the bravado of both sides, and added to these the fuel of their own emotions.

Britain, in particular, was affected by this new development. The number of popular newspapers, designed for mass readership, was increasing: the *Daily Express* was founded in 1900, the *Daily Mirror* in 1903, the *Daily Sketch* in 1909, the *Daily Herald* in 1911. Coloured by their various opinions, they involved the man in the street as never before in political developments. It was no accident that a newspaper interview given by the Kaiser to the *Daily Telegraph* in 1908 should become a stepping stone in the deterioration of relations between Britain and Germany. By ill-chosen phrases, unintended offence, the Kaiser conveyed a strong sense of German ill-will. It was no accident again, in the following year, that one of the most senseless scares of the period was worked up by newspapers: a base-

'A very large number of German officers made no secret of their longing for a war...' German officers, a drawing from *Simplicissimus* by E. Thony

'The only Asian country with a modern army and navy, based on modern industry'. A wood-block illustration from a book celebrating the Japanese victories in the Russo-Japanese war

帝國艦隊
浪速艦
高千穂艦
須ケ艦
明石艦
三笠艦

日露旅順口海戰
帝國海軍大勝利　萬歳

less dread that Germany was secretly outbuilding the Royal Navy in battleships. It was this that produced the famous slogan: 'We want eight and we won't wait!' Salutary in some ways, this form of agitation could produce a public hysteria very dangerous to the already explosive condition of Europe.

The rigid division of the great powers into blocs created new dangers and problems for the smaller states of Europe. These could either line up behind one of the blocs, or try to stay neutral – if the powers permitted. Scandinavia had for many years tried to maintain neutrality, chiefly neutrality between Russia and Britain, until recently the chief naval rivals in the Baltic. Now there was a new power factor in that sea: the German Navy. Furthermore, the strongest of the Scandinavian states, Sweden, was a diminished entity. Until 1905 Norway had been united to Sweden under a single crown; now Norway had separated and become an independent kingdom. The weakening of Sweden weakened Scandinavian neutrality itself, until it now really depended purely on German suffrance.

Belgian neutrality was of even more fragile fabric. Belgium has a frontier with Germany, and another with France. In terms of the century's first decade, that meant that she lay right in the most convenient path between those old enemies. Too small to defend herself alone, Belgium could only depend on the guarantees of neutrality made to her as far back as 1839 by five powers including France, Prussia and Britain. The formal name of this guarantee is the Treaty of London, but it is known to many by another title. Already in 1905 Field-Marshal von Schlieffen's plan for a lightning campaign against France embraced a massive turning movement by the German armies through Belgium. Because of the Schlieffen Plan, the Treaty of London would soon be called 'a scrap of paper'.

Neutrality, in fact, needed solider foundations than a narrow strip of water or a treaty; a great mountain barrier like the Alps or the Pyrenees could help to supply this need. Thus it was possible for Spain to follow an independent course; her land frontier was defensible, her long sea coast mostly uninviting to attack. Behind the Pyrenees, Spain could stand back from Europe's conflicts. In any case, she had conflicts of her own: the separatism of provinces with proud traditions – the Basque country and Catalonia; the almost perpetual state of internal revolt against the stifling and oppressive aspects of the monarchy and the Spanish branch of the Roman Catholic Church.

The small states of the Balkans, on the other hand, had no chance of avoiding the clash of great powers. All the Balkan states were trapped between three antagonistic empires: Russia, Austria-Hungary and Turkey. In 1908 Turkey's hand lay right across the Balkans. To Greeks or Slavs, conscious of different traditions, a different religion, Turkish rule was always alien and distasteful, though not necessarily always harshly tyrannical.

No, it had not been so bad. There was great freedom. The terrible thing was the insecurity. If you had a good horse, it would be stolen sooner or later by a Turkish officer. Justice was arbitrary and so weak that you had to be your own policeman. In those days, everyone had been armed.[3]

A hope of better times for the Balkan peoples under Turkish rule appeared in 1908: the revolt of the 'Young Turks' party against the autocracy of the Sultan Abdul Hamid. The Young Turks professed a liberal programme which was warmly greeted by the subject peoples. But they very soon found that they had only exchanged an inefficient despotism for an aggressively Turkish-nationalist and incomparably more efficient regime.

It was in its capacity as the Kingdom of Hungary that the Habsburg Empire chiefly affected the Slavs of the Balkans. Just over three quarters of a million Serbs and Croats came under Austrian rule; just under three million were ruled from Budapest. This was only one of many strange aspects of the Dual Monarchy which made it one of the curiosities of history, barely comprehensible even to its own people.

They were supposed to feel themselves to be Imperial and Royal Austro-Hungarian patriots, but simultaneously Royal Hungarians or Imperial-Royal Austrian patriots. Their not incomprehensible slogan in the face of such difficulties was 'United we stand!' In other words, vivibus unitis. But for this the Austrians needed to make a far stronger stand than the Hungarians, for the Hungarians were first and last only Hungarians and counted only incidentally, among people who did not understand their language, as Austro-Hungarians. The Austrians on the other hand were primarily nothing at all and in the view of those in power were supposed to feel themselves equally Austro-Hungarians and Austrian-Hungarians – for these was not even a proper word for it. And there was no such thing as Austria either. The two parts, Hungary and Austria, matched each other like a red, white and green jacket and black and yellow trousers. The jacket was an article in its own right; but the trousers were the remains of a no longer existent black and yellow suit the jacket of which had been unpicked in the year 1867. The Austrian trousers since then were officially known as the kingdoms and lands represented in the Council of the Imperial Realm; which naturally meant nothing at all, being a name made up of names; for these Kingdoms, for instance the entirely Shakespearian kingdoms of Lodomeria and Illyria no longer existed either and had not existed even at the time when there was still a black and yellow suit in existence. And so if one asked an Austrian what he was, he naturally could not answer 'I am from the non-existent kingdoms and lands represented in the Council of the Imperial Realm'. If only for this reason he preferred to say 'I'm a

Pole, a Czech, an Italian, a Friulian, a Lodin, a Slovene, a Croat, a Serb, a Slovak, a Ruthenian, a Wallachian'. And this was nationalism, so called. . . Since the earth existed no being has ever died for want of a name. All the same this is what happened to the Austrian and Austro-Hungarian Dual Monarchy: it perished of its own unutterability.[82]

The famous Parliament building beside the Danube at Budapest was often the forum where the insistent demands of Hungarian nationalism were ventilated. In 1906 these reached such a pitch that the Emperor sent soldiers to close the Parliament down; in accordance with imperial policy, the soldiers in question belonged to one of the Empire's many other races – in this case they were Rumanians. This was just one in the series of recurring constitutional crises of the unutterable Empire, one more example of its internal tensions. Often it seemed that only outside enmities held it together, and this was one of those times. The enemy was not far to seek: Serbia.

More famous for bad food, fleas and brigandage – and a notorious parade of vice on a minor scale in Belgrade – than for anything else, Serbia nevertheless cherished ambitions of her own. By general European standards, Serbia was only semi-civilised; her politics were never far removed from the brigandage of her mountains; assassination was a favourite method. In 1903, all Europe recoiled from the double murder, in shocking circumstances, of King Alexander I and Queen Draga, by a group of army officers. A new dynasty, the Karageorgevich, had been installed, but it had yet to find favour in Europe's eyes. Yet this rough little country of less than four million inhabitants was the repository of a large idea: Serbia's very existence represented South Slav independence. 'Yugo-slav' means simply 'South Slav'; there were many who saw in Serbia the beginning of independence for all South Slavs in a free Yugoslavia. As an observer said at the time: 'This little race of pig-keepers – the main industry of Serbia – surrounded by powerful neighbours, aimed high, and knew no fear.'[53]

Serbia was thus a thorn in the flesh of the Habsburg Empire, a continuing incitement to subversion and outrage. Powerful voices in Hungary and Austria, including that of a fire-eating Chief of Staff, Conrad von Hötzendorff, urged that Serbia should be crushed before more mischief occurred. The Emperor and the moderates, fearing the consequences of a general war, held back the 'forward party'. Nevertheless, in 1908 they were sufficiently in the ascendant to obtain the formal annexation of the two South Slav provinces, Bosnia and Herzegovina, which had been under Austro-Hungarian 'protection' since 1878. This abrupt act, deeply offensive to Russia, at once produced another European crisis. War was averted – narrowly – by diplomacy, but the fundamental danger of the situation increased. Russia proclaimed the Slav states of the Balkans to be under her protection; one more rash move in that direction, and the power blocs of Europe would certainly be at each others' throats.

It was in the two great power blocs that the greatest concentrations of Europe's military strength were to be seen. The outward forms of military power were, of course, what the Industrial Revolution had made them: mass armies drawn from Europe's increasing mass populations, equipped by the mass-products of modern industry, and moved by steam loco-motives across the complex networks of Europe's railways. It was the mass that was significant: at the time of the Russo-Japanese War, Russia could mobilise a total of three and a half million men. Her French ally, by desperate efforts, could mobilise about as many. Germany, with a larger population than France and a more efficient administration than Russia, could achieve about four million; Austria-Hungary about two and a quarter million. Four countries, over thirteen million men in arms: and this would only be a beginning. Never had such masses been available for war; never before had it been possible to commit such numbers to the manoeuvres of war. It was hard to predict what the outcome would be when they clashed, except that it was bound to be bloody.

Only Britain, sheltered behind the largest navy in the world, could dare to cling to a small army raised by voluntary recruiting, or, as some sarcastically called it, 'conscription by hunger'. Except in the excitement of war itself, the army was generally unpopular in pre-1914 Britain. Rudyard Kipling summed up a widespread attitude in his poem 'Tommy':

Yes, makin' a mock o' uniforms that guard you while you sleep
Is cheaper than them uniforms, an' they're starvation cheap;
An' hustlin' drunken soldiers when they're goin' large a bit
Is five times better business than paradin' in full kit.

Then it's Tommy this, an' Tommy that, an' 'Tommy 'ow's yer soul?'
But it's 'Thin red line of 'eroes' when the drums begin to roll –
The drums begin to roll, my boys, the drums begin to roll,
O it's 'Thin red line of 'eroes' when the drums begin to roll.[61]

The Army was called many unpleasant things; but as long as the Royal Navy remained supreme, and the soldiers were prepared to go on doing their duty, it didn't greatly matter what people called them. The drums were beginning to roll.

The armies of Europe fell into their ranks with a strange mixture of old and new paraphernalia in the first decade of the century. The French infantry wore uniforms almost unchanged since the days of Napoleon III; the cuirassiers looked almost exactly as they had done in the days of

Napoleon I. The German army, with all its modernity, also boasted its cuirassiers in breastplates, its 'Death's Head' Hussars, its Uhlans. The Austro-Hungarian army, with its pale blue and green and scarlet, made a fine display of nineteenth-century panache. And yet into the hands of all these strangely-dressed men modern industry was putting the weapons of a terrible future.

Already some hints of that future had been seen, but few took note of them. In South Africa, in 1899, the British had encountered one of the modern phenomena which was about to change the nature of war and the instruments of power. This was the 'empty battlefield', in which an enemy using smokeless powder and magazine rifles could remain practically invisible and very lethal at great distances. Old-fashioned formations – dense columns or rigid lines – were helpless in this situation (though the armies of Europe did not yet know it). The empty battlefields would require new tactics, and a new type of soldier which the mass populations might find it difficult to supply – a man who could think and act alone.

The Russo-Japanese War in 1905 had also displayed the unnerving impact of new styles of war. Modern artillery revealed its capacity for devastation; the Japanese fired no less than one and a half million shells into Port Arthur, including a large number of 11-in. calibre each weighing 550 lbs. A British observer said:

The great impression made on me by all I saw is that artillery is now the decisive arm and that all other arms are auxiliary to it . . . the side which has the best artillery will always win.[40]

Trench systems, protected by barbed wire, were used by both sides on a huge scale, and with them another modern weapon came into its own: the machine gun. A Japanese explained its working and effect:

[Its] belt is loaded into the chamber of the gun; it works like the film of a vitascope. And the sound it makes! Heard close by, it is a rapid succession of tap, tap, tap; but from a distance it sounds like a power loom heard late at night when everything else is hushed. It is a sickening, horrible sound! The Russians regarded this machine-gun as their best friend . . . Whenever an army attacked the enemy's position, it was invariably this machine-gun that made us suffer and damaged us most severely.[40]

These were just some of the new elements which would decide the fate of Europe's mass armies when power was put to the test.

It was not only land warfare that was changing: the nature of power also suffered a sea-change. In 1906 Britain, under the stimulus of alarm at the growth of the new German Navy, produced a battleship which made all previously existing types obsolete. This was the famous *Dreadnought*, and her launching had greatly accelerated the pace of the naval arms race, with Germany and Britain feverishly competing to send ever more powerful battleships down the slipways. But the ironic truth was that the real transformation of sea-power did not lie in these combinations of big guns and thick armour, no matter how impressive they looked. The menace to naval supremacy now lay under the surface of the sea itself: the submarine. For an island state, depending heavily on imports, this was a most alarming novelty.

It was not the only one. Technology could place Man's instruments of power under the sea – and over it. In July 1909 Louis Blériot flew his flimsy monoplane across the English Channel, bringing with him a message which was unmistakable. The *Daily Graphic* wrote (26 July 1909):

M. Blériot has guided an aeroplane in a given direction, and under not too favourable conditions, over the strip of water which makes England an island. There is no need to labour the point. The lesson is for all to read. What M. Blériot can do in 1909, a hundred, nay a thousand aeroplanes may be able to do in five years' time. When M. Farman flew a mile, it was possible to say that an ingenious toy had been invented. But a machine which can fly from Calais to Dover is not a toy, but an instrument of warfare of which soldiers and statesmen must take account.

In all these new contexts the international power game became more dangerous, more potentially destructive. And the game itself continued at a more feverish tempo. No sooner had Europe digested the Bosnian crisis than another, equally perilous, developed. Once more Germany decided to challenge France, and once more the arena would be Morocco. In 1911 Germany decided that the time had come to 'protect her interests'. The German gunboat *Panther* appeared in the harbour of Agadir, and immediately the nerve-ends of the European power system began to twitch.

The Agadir Crisis began as a matter between Germany and France; it very rapidly became a matter between Germany and Britain, France's Entente partner, a further stage in the now open hostility between the two nations. The British Government asked for explanations, and when these were slow in coming from Germany, the Chancellor of the Exchequer, Lloyd George, made a famous speech to the bankers of the City of London at the Mansion House:

I would make great sacrifices to preserve peace. I conceive that nothing would justify a disturbance of international goodwill except questions of the gravest national moment. But if a situation were to be forced upon us in which peace could only be preserved by the surrender of the great and beneficent position Britain has won by centuries of heroism and achievement, by allowing Britain to be treated, where her interests were vitally affected, as if she were of no account in the Cabinet of Nations, then I say emphatically that peace at that price would be a humiliation intolerable for a great country like ours to endure.[66]

Lloyd George's message sank home. Germany withdrew her demands in Morocco, and the Agadir Crisis died down – but its aftermath remained. Germans would not easily forget Lloyd George's speech. A Conservative leader said in the Reichstag:

When we hear a speech that we must consider as a threat, as a challenge, as a humiliating challenge, it is not so easy to pass it over as after-dinner speechifying. Such incidents like a flash in the dark show the German peoples where is the foe. The German people now knows, when it seeks foreign expansion and a place in the sun, such as is its right and destiny, where it has to look for permission. We Germans are not accustomed to that and cannot allow it and we shall know how to answer.[5]

After 1911 Europe's doom advanced with what now seem to be inexorable strides. The Bosnian crisis of 1909 had ended with the diplomatic defeat of Russia. The Agadir Crisis ended with the diplomatic defeat of Germany. Would either of these great powers, or the blocs to which they belonged, accept defeat again without trying the further test of war? If not, there could only be one result: a continental civil war, continental suicide. It would take a miracle to prevent it.

There was no miracle. National ambition and greed for empire continued to work their mischief. While the great powers were still embroiled in Agadir, Italy picked a quarrel with Turkey, in order to seize the great Turkish province of Tripoli (now called Libya). The Italians found the invasion of Tripoli more difficult than they expected; thirty years later they would find defending this province equally difficult. But in 1911 they managed to defeat the Turks, and so enlarged their empire, but in so doing they triggered off a more serious train of events.

The weakening of Turkish power was a signal to all her enemies, above all the Balkan states with their deep-seated hatred of the Turks. Now Serbia, Bulgaria and Greece (usually somewhat at loggerheads among themselves) combined to attack Turkey. The result staggered Europe. In seven weeks the Turkish grip on the Balkans which had lasted for five centuries was utterly smashed. And out of the ruin of the once-dreaded Ottoman Empire Serbia emerged as the strongest of the Balkan states, her territory practically doubled. This result was intolerable to the anti-Serb elements in the Austro-Hungarian Empire. The military party urged immediate war against Serbia. And now the perils of the power blocs, and the system of interlocking alliances by which Europe sought security, were clearly seen.

If Austria attacked Serbia, Russia would support the Serbs. If Russia attacked Austria, Germany would support the Austrians. If the Germans attacked Russia, France would be drawn in. If France was attacked, Britain would be drawn in. That was the meaning of the alliances: the intention was security, the reality was risk. As it turned out, in this moment of acute international danger, it was possible for the great powers – for the last time – to damp the fires. Germany and Italy calmed down Austrian excitement, while Britain and France worked to restrain Russia, and so a European war was staved off.

What prompted this peace-making? Was it dislike of being drawn into the quarrels of small and distant states? Was it last-minute dread of a calamity which would damage the whole continent? Or was it simply a fussy anxiety about not being quite ready, needing one more gaiter-button, one more clip of cartridges, the launching of one more warship? Whatever the reasons for this eleventh-hour hesitation, the fact remained that the Balkan Wars and their outcome increased Europe's already critical tension.

With each crisis the Emperor Franz Josef had a harder task to restrain the hotheads of the anti-Serb faction – and the Serbs themselves did little to help him. The Serbian press continued to voice loud demands for Slav unity; students and politicians spoke openly of a South Slav state, the Yugoslavia of the future, the most likely casus belli of the moment. Terrorist organisations helped the cause along with a series of outrages in the best Balkan style, which were much applauded by Serb patriots. Meanwhile Hungarian and Austrian patriots became angrier, and the pressures on the Emperor increased. He was now 84 years old, and his reign was drawing to an end in violence and desperate deeds as it had begun.

On 28 June 1914 the Archduke Franz Ferdinand, heir to the thrones of the Dual Monarchy, the Habsburg Empire, was in Sarajevo, capital of Bosnia, the province so provocatively annexed in 1809. When the visit was announced, a Serbian emigré journal in America issued this call:

Serbs, seize everything you can lay hands on – knives, rifles, bombs and dynamite. Take holy vengeance! Death to the Habsburg dynasty, eternal remembrance to the heroes who raise their hands against it![26]

The call was heard. Six young Bosnian students, armed and trained by the Serbian Black Hand Society, lay in wait for the Archduke in Sarajevo. They were not very efficient. A bomb missed him; opportunities were lost. But in the afternoon of 28 June one of them, nineteen-year-old Gavrilo Princip, succeeded in shooting both the Archduke and his wife Sophie, as they drove in an open car to the railway station.

The blood of the dead Archduke dried on his tunic, and remains encrusted there to this day, giving the garment the quality of a holy relic; well it may – this blood was the first drop in an ocean. For this was Austria's necessary pretext for war with Serbia. A diplomatic Note was despatched to Belgrade, and Austria began to mobilise. The consequences followed with precision, and this time there were no restraining hands:

28 July Austria declared war on Serbia;
30 July partial Russian mobilisation;
31 July full mobilisation in Russia and Austria;
1 August full mobilisation in Germany and France;
3 August war between Germany and France;
4 August war between Britain and Germany.

The great continental civil war had begun, and Sir Edward Grey, the British Foreign Secretary, watching the lamp-lighters going about their work in St James's Park, pronounced the obituary of the continent's mighty past: 'The lamps are going out all over Europe; we shall not see them lit again in our lifetime.'[112]

5   This generation has no future

August 1914 was a turning-point in the history of the world, a moment of transformation in the history of Europe, a moment of abrupt, enormous change. Tensions which had been mounting from the beginning of the twentieth century suddenly snapped. An American historian has found a particularly graphic image for what happened:

The nations of Europe were like a file of marching prisoners chained together by their ankles. And as the leader of the file took a step forward, so each of those behind him had to shuffle forward – prisoners of national pride and shackled together by treaty obligation. And willingly or unwillingly, they reached their ultimate destination – war.[117]

But this was to be more than a war; it became a trauma which enveloped not only that generation, but successive generations of Europeans ever since.

The war which broke out in August 1914 was like no previous human experience. This was twentieth-century war undiluted: war of masses. Human masses had never been numbered off like this before, like this vast, anonymous tide of men coming from all over Europe. When they reached the battlefronts, they were swallowed up in the interminable, anonymous complex of the trenches. Through the mud and clay and chalk of Belgium and France, 450 miles of trenches stretching from the sea to Switzerland, through the rock of the Alps and the Dolomites, through the sands and swamps of Eastern Europe, ran the battle-lines, and behind them the vast, anonymous camps of the soldiers sprouted across Europe like the sores of a wasting sickness.

Year by year, class by class, the conscripts of Europe put on their uniforms and marched off to the trenches. France called up, from beginning to end, eight million men, about one fifth of her entire population. In Germany the total reached thirteen million. Even liberal Britain was forced to conscript her soldiers; in the end she put over five million in the field, and the British Empire as a whole raised eight and a half million. There were 600,000 Canadians, 400,000 Australians, 120,000 New Zealanders, 130,000 South Africans. Most of them, sooner or later, found their way to

'The nations of Europe entered the war with strangely innocent enthusiasm'

French reservists mobilise
outside the Gare du Nord,
Paris, August 1914

Europe's battlefields. One and a half million Indians volunteered to serve under the British flag, and thousands of them, too, have left their bones in the soil of Europe.

The French Empire drew in large contingents of men from North and West Africa, Algerians, Moroccans, Senegalese, braving Europe's unfamiliar climate. Then, when Turkey entered the war, large areas of the Middle East became theatres of battle. Africa herself became one – the Cameroons, South-West Africa, German East Africa, scene of the longest campaign of all. Japan was at war with Germany from the beginning, and captured her great base in Asia, Tsing-tao. The United States of America declared war in April 1917; so Europe's war became the first war of the world, affecting every continent.

The numbers of the mass-armies grew from year to year. It seemed that there was no end to the columns of men in field-grey, horizon-blue, khaki – the drab livery of modern times. It seemed that no losses, no decimations could check the flow of identical human units from every country. These were the inflated populations of the Industrial Revolution, the anonymous masses from the anonymous industrial urban sprawls, now wearing anonymous uniforms, and all obeying identical compulsions. Horrified at this spectacle, D. H. Lawrence wrote of

the terrible, terrible war, made so fearful because in every country practically every man lost his head, and lost his centrality, his manly isolation in his own integrity, which alone keeps life real.[62]

It was not entirely so, of course; but it is easy to see why Lawrence thought it was so. Winston Churchill, from the standpoint of a different temperament, expressed the matter otherwise:

... nothing daunted the valiant heart of man. Son of the Stone Age, vanquisher of nature with all her trials and monsters, he met the awful and self-inflicted agony with new reserves of fortitude. Freed in the main by his intelligence from medieval fears, he marched to death with sombre dignity.[22]

In one element, unique to the twentieth century, the engulfing anonymity failed to operate. The air itself was now an arena of combat – and the style of that combat was both utterly new and curiously ancient. The new flying machines, products of the infant science of aeronautics, but precursors of human annihilation in the future, for a few years restored the oldest of all forms of war: single combat, such as the Greeks had offered under the walls of Troy.

The men who flew the machines and won their solitary victories in the sky were known as the Aces. The names of these young, dedicated, deadly

'The new flying machines . . . restored the oldest of all forms of war . . . single combat'

killers became household words. The most famous of them all was Germany's Baron Manfred von Richthofen; the sight of his bright red aeroplane spelt death to eighty British and French flyers before von Richthofen himself was killed at the age of 26. Ernst Udet was another notable German Ace who claimed sixty-two victims and survived the war to play a part in rebuilding the German Air Force twenty years later. At the head of the French list was René Fonck with seventy-five kills, but the most renowned of the French Aces was Georges Guynemer, of whom it was said that it was his vocation to become one of the illustrious dead – at the age of 23.

Edward Mannock headed the British list with seventy-three kills. Mannock dreaded being burnt to death, the commonest fate of a flyer in those days before parachutes, and always carried a loaded pistol to shoot himself with if his plane caught fire. But when his crashed aircraft was found it was burnt out, and Mannock's pistol had not been fired. Once again it was not the man with the most kills who won the greatest fame: in Britain that fell to Albert Ball. There was a personal magic about this ardent youth, killed before he was twenty-one years old, with forty-three victims to his score. In one of his last letters Ball wrote what many felt:

Oh, it was a good fight, and the Huns were fine sports. One tried to ram me, after he was hit, and only missed by inches. Am indeed looked after by God, but oh! I do get tired of living always to kill, and am really beginning to feel like a murderer. Shall be so pleased when I have finished.[15]

This international brotherhood of boy Aces mostly died in action. But while they lived these lieutenants, captains and majors enjoyed a personal fame and identity rarely permitted to those thousands of the same age and rank who fought the war of masses down below.

It was the Industrial Revolution which had produced the masses. It was the Industrial Revolution which made it possible to mobilise them, arm them, feed them, move them. This war, as no previous one, was dominated by technology. This was, above all, a war of fire-power: the fire-power of artillery, and the fire-power of the new automatic weapons – magazine rifles and machine guns. Fire-power filled the air and saturated the ground with projectiles and deadly fragments. To avoid them, men went underground into trenches, dug-outs and reinforced concrete 'pill-boxes'. To protect these, they placed 'aprons' of barbed wire – thousands of miles of it. And thus they created an obstacle which only more intense fire-power could destroy.

The guns became insatiable. In March 1918, for their great attack on the British armies which was intended to finish the war, the Germans used 6473 guns and 3532 mortars. At the end of the same year, counter-attacking against the Hindenburg Line, the British artillery was firing over

2,200,000 shells a week. French shell-production rose to 300,000 a day. The statistics are endless and incomprehensible. At Verdun, in one sector, one thousand shells fell on every square metre of ground. Who can envisage that? And these are only some of the fruits of the Industrial Revolution; there were many more.

In 1914 Germany's war-plan depended for its fulfilment on a network of strategic railways completed long before the war, and on a complex movement timetable which could not be altered without disaster. French mobilisation required 4278 special trains. British shipping (or ships under British control) transported during the war over 33 million people, $2\frac{1}{2}$ million horses and mules, over half a million vehicles, 49 million tons of stores and equipment. French industry during the whole war produced items as varied as 350,000 telephones and two million kilometres of cable, 30,000 radio sets, 180,000 aero engines and 35,000 aircraft, 5000 tanks.

In 1917 Winston Churchill became Minister of Munitions in Britain. By then, he says, 'the whole island was an arsenal'.[22] By November 1918, the power of his Ministry was enormous:

Nearly all the mines and workshops of Britain were in our hands. We controlled and were actually managing all the greatest industries. We regulated the supply of all their raw materials. We organised the whole distribution of their finished products. Nearly five million persons were directly under our orders, and we were interwoven on every side with every other sphere of the national economic life.[22]

So four and a half years of savage battle between the great capitalist powers brought about more practical socialism than seventy years of preaching since Karl Marx produced the Communist Manifesto.

This was the modern world's first experience of total war. To fill the ranks of the mass armies, and at the same time expand the industries on which they depended for their munitions, required the involvement of entire populations in the War. Distinctions between soldiers and civilians, between men and women, between old and young, became increasingly blurred. Conscription – for the forces and for industry – affected all; rationing affected all; shortages affected all; the peril of air bombardment affected all; the diminution of life's amenities affected all. The nations of Europe entered upon a new knowledge of life's cruelty.

They had entered the War with strangely innocent enthusiasm. In France, to the astonishment of almost everyone, all the fierce internal conflicts of the Third Republic vanished overnight. President Poincaré proclaimed in his message to the nation: 'France will be heroically defended by all her sons, whose sacred union in the face of the enemy nothing will

Paul Nash. 'We are making a
new world'

break. . . .' This was the 'union sacrée', and for a time it was the most important political reality in France, confounding all those – on the Right or on the Left – who had genuinely believed that the workers would rise up against capitalist war.

In Britain, until August, 1914 had been a year of fierce social strife, reaching the very brink of civil war. Then, on 4 August, the entire picture changed. The young poet Rupert Brooke, soon to die, expressed the mood which produced over a million volunteers in the remaining five months of 1914:

Now, God be thanked Who has matched us with His hour,
And caught our youth, and wakened us from sleeping,
With hand made sure, clear eye, and sharpened power,
To turn, as swimmers into cleanness leaping,
Glad from a world grown old and cold and weary . . .[16]

A similar spirit reigned in Germany; a neutral observer, the Swedish traveller Sven Hedin, wrote:

Germany at the present time is inhabited by a people which is at one with itself. Here we have but one party – that of the soldiers. Here everyone has but one goal, all have the same thoughts, all hold the same hopes and offer up the same prayers.[55]

The early innocence and enthusiasm of the European nations suffered hard and immediate knocks. From the very first, the brutal character of this modern style of war became apparent. In the five months remaining of 1914, France lost nearly a million men killed, wounded and captured. In 1915 the figure was nearly one and a half million. Then came 1916, the year of Verdun, the battle in which the German High Command intended that 'the forces of France will bleed to death'. In the event, the Germany Army bled almost exactly as much as the French. So far the British had come off relatively lightly, but 1916 was the year in which Britain's new mass army – the 'Kitchener Army' – began to play a major part. That part was called the Battle of the Somme; four and a half months later, when it ended, British casualties had reached a total of 415,000; 60,000 of them on the first day alone. German casualties in this battle were so heavy that they changed their method of announcing them to the German public, but nothing could change what the soldiers wrote in their letters:

We have had dreadful losses again. I shall not get leave I suppose until we have left the Somme, but with our losses what they are, this cannot be long or there will not be a single man left in the regiment.[53]

This was only the Western Front. In the East the experience of war was

'Fire power filled the air and saturated the ground
with projectiles . . . A British munitions factory

137

equally terrible. In the first month of the war Russia lost 300,000 men in East Prussia alone. In 1915 her losses have been estimated at two million. In the Caucasus during the first winter the Turks lost 75,000 men out of an army of 95,000, many of them frozen stiff as logs where they stood. The Austrians lost 350,000 in 1914 against Russia, and in 1915, when Italy joined the Entente, had to man a new front and face its attrition. Deep national antipathies made the Italian Front one of the bloodiest arenas of the War. Eleven successive battles in the region of the little River Isonzo cost Italy nearly a million casualties.

So, year by year, the manhood of Europe was consumed. Year by year, to their sorrow, the populations of Europe learned the meaning of total war. For a time their reaction to heavy losses, to material damage and personal privation, was redoubled rage against their enemies. From the first, in every country, hatred had been fostered as a necessary instrument of war by every means that existed of influencing public opinion. The Press, of course, was the chief of these, but all countries soon devised other forms of propaganda: posters, postcards, songs, stage shows and also – very effective – the new medium, the infant cinema.

Inflamed by the organs of propaganda, the hatreds of the continent ran their destructive course: Austrian hatred against Serbia, Italian hatred against Austria, French hatred against the German invaders of France. But no hatred was greater than that which the war produced between Britain and Germany. A German Privy Councillor told the correspondent of a New York paper:

It is a fight between England and Germany to the bitter end, to the last German if need be. We shall never ask England for mercy, and we shall extend no mercy to her. England and England alone has brought on this criminal war out of greed and envy to crush Germany, and now it is death, destruction and annihilation for one or other of the two nations. [*The Times,* 31 October 1914.]

This fine thought was echoed in the famous poem of Ernst Lissauer:

French and Russian they matter not,
A blow for a blow and a shot for a shot;
We love them not, we hate them not,
We hold the Vistula and Vosges-gate,
We have but one and only hate,
We love as one, we hate as one,
We have one foe and one alone . . .
England![53]

This was Germany's 'Hymn of Hate'; there were British counterparts:

'The war mounted
to a final paroxysm
of destruction'.
All that remained
of one of Germany's
proud Zeppelins

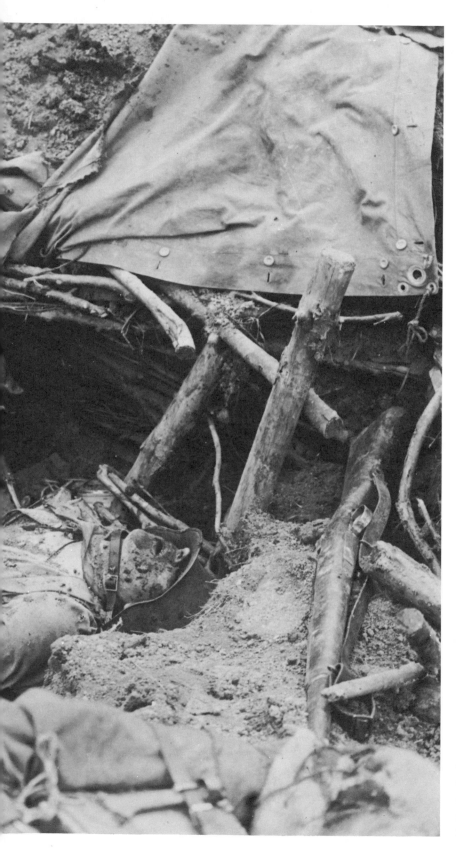

'With our losses
what they are there
will not be a single
man left in the
regiment'. 1917

By all the blood, that stained the Belgian waters,
By all the dead, that strewed the Belgian fields,
By children slain, by outraged wives and daughters,
We'll show no mercy, till the tyrant yields.
Down for ever down with the blood and iron culture,
Down for ever down with the Prussian Kaiser's pride,
Wring the eagle's neck – he's changed into a vulture,
Gorged with the flesh of the thousands who have died.[108]

As the war was drawing towards its end, one valiant hero of the British Home Front epitomised the hatreds it had bred in a letter to *The Times*:

At last . . . the view of Germany as she really is, is dawning on the British people. They are finding her to be a great heathen nation, ruthless, a worshipper of pure force, hacking her way with deeds of devilish cruelty and with a never-ending stream of lies and chicanery to what she hopes will be European hegemony. They are beginning to think that with a nation so polluted and polluting, whose ideals are so false and whose human feeling is so dead, no people acknowledging the morals of Christianity, or even of civilisation, ought, as it values its own soul, to have truck or dealing or even speech. . . . To the people the war is becoming a holy war – a war of right against wrong, of Heaven against Hell . . .[108]

It was not, of course, the heroes of the Home Front who had to fight the 'holy war'. Those who did have to fight it tended more and more to regard each other in a different light: as fellow-sufferers of the same grim fate. One English officer wrote:

England was beastly in 1918. . . . Envy, hatred, malice and all uncharitableness, fear and cruelty born of fear, seemed the dominant passions of the leaders of the nations in those days. Only in the trenches (on both sides of No Man's Land) were chivalry and sweet reasonableness to be found.[19]

A German soldier, at the end of 1916, spoke for millions on all the continental battle-fronts: 'Hans is dead. Fritz is dead. Wilhelm is dead. There are many others. I am now quite alone in the company . . . This is almost unendurable. If only peace would come!'[53]

How *could* peace come? Only in one of two ways: the victory of one side and defeat of the other, or by compromise. But how could the masses, whose passions were now fully roused, who were fighting for Heaven against Hell, be asked to compromise? In 1916 a British statesman, Lord Lansdowne, posed the question: 'What will be the blessings of peace to nations so exhausted that they can scarcely stretch out a hand with which to grasp them?' Amid the never-ending thunder of the guns the question was hardly heard and certainly not answered. The masses were in no mood for compromise.

It was even difficult now to remember how it had all begun, difficult to remind oneself that it had started as Austria's war of revenge upon Serbia – a product of the tensions and animosities of the Austro-Hungarian Empire. Now the head of that extraordinary institution lay dead. The Emperor Franz Josef, who had ruled the Habsburg domains for sixty-eight years, died in November 1916, and was succeeded by his great-nephew Karl.

Already the Empire had taken fearful punishment in the War. The great Russian offensive of 1916, under the command of General Brusilov, had inflicted terrible losses, nearly half a million Austro-Hungarian troops being taken prisoner. A high percentage of these were Czech or other Slav deserters, refusing now to go on fighting for the Habsburgs against men of their own kind. This was an omen more alarming than defeat in the field. And meanwhile the war of attrition with Italy ground on from one great fruitless, costly battle to the next. It is not surprising if the Empire was beginning to crumble; what is surprising is that an entity so politically and racially disunited could have stood up to such hammerings. Evidently it had not, at the outset, been the feeble thing it is often made out to be. But by the time of Franz Josef's death the war-weariness of the Empire was becoming plain.

The new Emperor was aware of this symptom, and what it might signify for himself and his dynasty. He tried, by the surreptitious means which alone were available to him, to extract his people from the war which they had begun in an evil day. But now he learned a bitter truth. In 1914 German staff officers had spoken of the Austrian alliance as being 'fettered to a corpse'. In 1917 the Austrians learned that the German alliance meant being fettered to an implacable war machine.

The partnership of Field-Marshal von Hindenburg and General Ludendorff had quickly become synonymous with German victory on the Eastern Front. In 1916 these two men took over the joint direction of all fronts and, indeed, of Germany herself. Both were determined to obtain a military solution to Germany's difficulties: military victory in the war. As Ludendorff said: 'I entered upon my duties with a sacred desire to do and think of nothing that did not contribute to bring the war to a victorious end. For this purpose alone had the Field-Marshal and I been called upon.'[67]

Now not only German strategy, but that of her weakening allies, would be governed by these two resolute soldiers. This was not an encouraging state of affairs; indeed, it 'demonstrated the inadequacy of the political machinery and talents of the German Empire in the face of so basic a political task as the planning and directing of a national struggle for survival.'[9] But this was how Germany would be guided during the next two years.

It was in 1916, also, that British Liberalism as a governing force finally passed away. At the end of that year Lloyd George replaced Asquith as Prime Minister, at the head of a National Government drawn from three parties: Liberal, Conservative and Labour. Shortly before his appointment Lloyd George declared:

There is neither clock nor calendar in the British Army today. Time is the least vital factor. Only the result counts – not the time consumed in achieving it. It took England twenty years to defeat Napoleon, and the first fifteen of those years were black with British defeat. It will not take twenty years to win this war, but whatever time is required, it will be done.[66]

This declaration became known as 'The Policy of the Knock-out Blow'. Lloyd George was wholly identified with it; his energy and determination would give new impetus and new efficiency to the British war effort.

Soon an even more implacable figure would join the leaders of the nations: Georges Clemenceau, whose political ruthlessness had won him the nickname of 'The Tiger'. Now, in a time of desperation, France called upon 'The Tiger' to become Prime Minister, and soon her enemies, within and without, would feel his claws. Asked in the Chamber of Deputies what his policy was, Clemenceau replied: 'I, messieurs, I wage war! In domestic policies, I wage war. In foreign policies, I wage war. Always, everywhere, I wage war. And I shall continue to wage war until the last quarter of an hour!'[117] The resolution of all these new leaders reflected the intransigent anger of their peoples. There would be no peace or compromise for these men – but there would be a price to pay for total war, and in 1917 the first instalment of the price was demanded.

The fate of Imperial Russia, and the fate of the Tsarist regime itself were particularly linked to the progress of the war. Russia was an autocracy, and the penalty of autocracy is that it is difficult to spread blame when things go wrong. A great deal had gone wrong, and yet the truth is that an always corrupt and inefficient system had actually performed wonders during this war. The Russian Army had sustained terrible losses, but its inexhaustible manpower was barely tapped; the Army in 1917 was stronger and better organised than ever before. Industrial production had greatly increased. Railway construction had been immense. Modernisation was happening – yet the sense of debilitating corruption and inefficiency remained. As Winston Churchill said:

Surely to no nation has Fate been more malignant than to Russia. Her ship went down in sight of port. She had actually weathered the storm when all was cast away. Every sacrifice had been made; the toil was achieved. Despair and Treachery usurped command at the very moment when the task was done.[22]

145

It was the bitter winter which gripped all Europe at the end of 1916 that demolished the Romanov Empire. Transport breakdowns due to heavy snow caused food shortages in Russia's towns. In March 1917 there were bread riots again. In Petrograd – the new name for St Petersburg – these swiftly turned to revolution, as in 1905. But this time the instruments of autocracy failed: the soldiers fraternised with the crowds. Authority was helpless; in just a week the Tsar was forced to abdicate. The largest of Europe's empires had ceased to exist.

The new Russian Provisional Government was constitutional and liberal, and intended to continue the war beside its democratic allies. They, for their part, greeted the March Revolution and the fall of the autocracy with approval. Many believed that Russia would be revived and strengthened by the change. They misunderstood the mood of the Russian people and the strength of the forces that were at work there. A month after the outbreak of revolution, Vladimir Ilich Lenin, together with G. E. Zinoviev, L. B. Kamenev and other Bolshevik leaders, returned from exile in Switzerland, passing through Germany in a sealed train by agreement with the German General Staff, the effective rulers of the state. The German object was simple: to make use of any instrument which would take Russia out of the War. And this was what the Bolsheviks firmly intended. Together with Trotsky, who also returned a month later, Lenin and his comrades played on the desire of the Russian people for bread and peace. Working through the Soviets – the Workers' and Soldiers' Councils – they undermined the Provisional Government. A second revolution, in October, established the Bolsheviks in full power. At once, under Trotsky's direction, they began peace negotiations with Germany.

So now, where there had been an empire with power, a significant factor in the European equation, there was a vacuum, a question mark. Facing the triumphant German and Austrian delegates across the table at the Peace Conference at Brest Litovsk, forced to accept the harsh terms they imposed, the new Soviet state seemed a very helpless thing. It was easy to grasp that power had departed, but difficult to perceive what power had been born; impossible to foresee that one not-far-distant day this new creation would dominate European affairs as the Tsars had never been able to do.

So the first of the drastic, unexpected changes in Europe's status was brought about by the war, and in the same breath the second also began to happen. In March 1917 the first Russian revolution; in April the United States of America declared war on Germany. This act marked the end of a tradition and the beginning of a new relationship. The tradition was that of the European refugees and emigrants who had made America – by deliber-

'The aftermath here was annihilation'. Ypres 1918

'Rationing affected all, shortages affected all'.
Coal queue at the Paris Opéra, February 1917

ately turning their backs on Europe, and, having done so, by remaining determinedly aloof from European affairs: it was the tradition of American Isolationism, which would never be the same again. Because now the new relationship was being forged, by American soldiers with European names but distinctly non-European attitudes, who were landing on European soil to fight and die in the greatest European war until that date. Never again would America be free of involvement in Europe.

The American build-up in France was slow at first – hampered by the material aid which America was already providing for the Allies – but it grew swiftly in 1918, until by November there were over two million United States troops in Europe. The first arrivals came in an angry mood, infuriated by Germany's unrestricted submarine campaign. The submarine and torpedo were no respecters of neutrality, and propaganda did not fail to make the most of the painful scenes provided by this new form of war. Like their European allies, the Americans were in no mood for compromise; they were pledged, in President Woodrow Wilson's words, to use 'force to the uttermost, force without stint or limit'.

The price of all this force mounted, and the bills were presented for payment. One empire had vanished already; others now began to crumble. The Turkish Empire was strained to its limits by the War, and just when the collapse of Russia offered the Turks some relief, they were faced with revolts of their Arab subjects backed by British forces. Turkey's position was becoming desperate. The Austro-Hungarian Empire also found the strain of war intense as the fourth year passed. Czech, South Slav and Polish nationalist groups living abroad proclaimed their independence of the Empire, and received the blessing of the Allied governments. Only the German alliance and hatred of Italy kept the embers of war fever alive in the Habsburg Empire.

The weariness, the sense of hopeless involvement in an endless tragedy, were not all on one side. By the beginning of 1917 France had sustained over 3,300,000 casualties – and the German armies remained as firmly lodged as ever on French soil. In May came catastrophe. Disillusioned by another failure, another disastrous offensive, a large part of the French Army on the Western Front mutinied, refused to obey its officers, refused to take part in any more attacks. During all these years the French Army had been the main instrument of the Entente's war on land; it would never be so again.

And this was only one of the miseries of the Allies in 1917. In four months' fighting earlier in the year the Italians had lost 346,000 men. The morale of the Italian Army, like the French, gave way under this unspeakable and apparently pointless slaughter. And now the example of the Rus-

SANGVE

ISLAM

LA FORTUNA DEL 1914
LA FORTUNE DE L'AN 1914

ALBERTO MARTINI

DANZA MACABRA EUROPEA 23

LIT. LONGO - TREVISO

'To the people the[
is becoming a hol[
A parody of Dür[
Great Fortune;
propaganda was [
bitter, and it wa[
the German natic[
(right), not just t[
German leaders, [
who were not to [
forgiven

sian Revolution lent strength to anti-war elements; the desire to have done with it all was increasing everywhere. When the Austrians and Germans attacked at Caporetto in October, the Italians collapsed in rout. Their armies retreated seventy miles; they lost 40,000 more men killed and wounded – but the significant figure was their enemies' claim of 275,000 prisoners. The Italian soldiers were losing their will to fight.

And still this was not the full story. All through the summer and autumn the British had been attacking at Ypres. In this low-lying country, where water was never far below the surface of the ground, artillery fire soon reduced it to a swamp. The shell-craters touched each other lip to lip. Pelting rain gave the soil the consistency of porridge. Tanks foundered; guns sank to their axles; the infantry struggled forward, up to their knees, their thighs, their waists. By the time the British captured the village of Passchendaele – just a brick-coloured stain on the ground – and the ridge on which it stood, they had lost a quarter of a million casualties. A War Correspondent wrote: 'For the first time the British Army lost its spirit of optimism.'[43] A German authority called this battle 'the greatest martyrdom of the War'.

1917 was a terrible year – one of the worst in Europe's history. Armies collapsed, nations collapsed – and yet the war went on, seemingly for ever. The reasons for this unbelievable ordeal were already fading in men's memories. New justifications for so much misery, so much brutality, so much ruin, were required. And this was particularly true in Britain and America – in Britain to avert war-weariness, in America to sustain the war-temper. Countries which had been invaded or feared invasion had at least those reasons for continuing to fight; the British and Americans had to have something else. In January 1918 Lloyd George was saying:

When men by the million are being called upon to suffer and face death and vast populations are being subjected to the sufferings and privations of war on a scale unprecedented in the history of the world, they are entitled to know for what cause or causes they are making the sacrifice. It is only the clearest, greatest and justest of causes that can justify the continuance even for one day of this unspeakable agony of the nations.[66]

'After all,' Lloyd George added, 'war is a relic of barbarism.' The alternative to barbarism could only be an international organisation to prevent war. This was the clear, great, just cause. It was a British concept, enthusiastically adopted by the American President, Woodrow Wilson. Wilson now gave his Peace programme to the American Congress. It comprised fourteen Points, which included 'open covenants of peace, openly arrived at', 'freedom of navigation upon the seas', 'equality of trade conditions', reduction of armaments, self-determination of colonial and subject peoples, and, finally, Point Fourteen: 'A general association of nations must be formed under specific covenants for the purpose of affording mutual guarantees of political independence and territorial integrity to great and small states alike.' In these cold, dry, formal words was enshrined humanity's new hope – that a League of Nations would truly make this war 'a war to end wars', and so the awful thing would be justified at last.

Meanwhile the war itself mounted to a final paroxysm of fury and destruction. Using all the newest and most sophisticated weapons available – tanks, flame-throwers and poison-gas on the battlefields, bombs on the cities behind them – the nations of Europe hurled themselves into the last frenzy of collective suicide. In six weeks, resisting massive German attacks, the British lost nearly a quarter of a million men. In just over three months Germany lost nearly 700,000. Spring, summer, autumn, the terrible battles of 1918 never stopped. France's casualties during this last year mounted to yet another million.

But now the overthrow of nations and empires was near completion. As Germany's strength ebbed, one by one her allies dropped away – first Bulgaria, then Turkey, then Austria-Hungary. The Emperor Karl was forced to abdicate, and when he did so six centuries of Habsburg rule in Central Europe came to an end. In Germany the Kaiser Wilhelm II was also forced to abdicate, and so, amid starvation, disease and revolution, two more empires vanished from the face of Europe.

At last it was over. On 11 November 1918, at 11 am, the first European catastrophe reached its close. The guns were silent at last. For this, at least, men could give legitimate thanks. Briefly, before they came to add up the reckoning, in the countries that claimed victory there was rejoicing – for those who felt able to rejoice. But many shared the mood of the British soldier-poet Robert Graves, when he heard of the Armistice at his home in Wales: 'The news sent me out walking alone along the dyke above the marshes of Rhuddlan, cursing and sobbing and thinking of the dead.'[47] Where the misery of war ended in the further blackness of defeat, the bitterness went even deeper. A German officer, Captain Rudolph Binding, wrote: 'This generation has no future, and deserves none. Anyone who belongs to it lives no more.'[11] Yet life would continue, despite it all. And the sanction of continuing life, as the guns fell silent, was the hope of a new and better world.

'This generation has no future'. These German prisoners-of-war survived to encounter all the hazards of peace

6

Are we making a good peace? Are we?

In 1914 the German armies had penetrated to only twenty miles from Paris, and in June 1918 they had been just as close again. The city had been bombed from the air, and bombarded by long-range guns. But now all that was over. The war was over, and Paris could breathe and hope again.

Hope, it need hardly be said, takes different shapes in the minds of different men. The President of the United States, Woodrow Wilson, was hoping for a peace based on high and just ideals. When Wilson came to Paris in the new year, he received a great welcome, which seemed to show that many Frenchmen shared his hope. Others were hoping for something rather less: to save their country from another catastrophe like the Great War, and to find some compensation for the damage it had done to her. And in one way or another these thoughts would be the preoccupation of Paris for the next few months. Not only Paris; in the words of Winston Churchill: 'To this immortal city, gay-tragic, haggard-triumphant, scarred and crowned, more than half mankind now looked for satisfaction or deliverance.'[22]

The peace-making proceedings which began in January 1919 are usually associated with Versailles, because that is where the chief of the resulting Treaties was signed. But almost all the work which produced the Treaties was carried out in Paris – and history's name for it is 'The Paris Peace Conference'. The centre of all the activity was the Quai d'Orsay, the French Foreign Ministry, a fine building looking out upon the Seine, and dating, like so much else that is handsome in Paris, from the reign of Napoleon III – or perhaps we should say the reign of Baron Haussmann.

The first thing the 1919 Peace Conference had to do was to take the measure of the catastrophe that had occurred. It was, above all, a European catastrophe. The European nations had borne the brunt of the war; it was in Europe that the most savage battles had taken place. No one, in 1919, could yet count the loss of European life – no one has ever been able to count it with certainty. Perhaps the military and naval dead amounted to twelve or thirteen millions – the vast majority of them Europeans. Perhaps the permanently disabled numbered as many again – the vast majority Europeans. Perhaps the civilian dead – by direct acts of war, by massacre,

Orpen. *Delegates to the Peace Conference, 1919*

157

'Two approaches, two very different sets of ideas . . .'
Lloyd George, Clemenceau and Woodrow Wilson
on their way to the signing of the Peace Treaty,
28 June 1919

by starvation, by disease – equalled the military; the majority again were Europeans. The economic cost can only be expressed in meaningless astronomic figures, which have to be translated as a man-made wilderness – in Europe.

The political face of Europe, of course, was already transformed. Four empires had vanished. The Tsar of all the Russias, the Supreme Autocrat, Nicholas II, together with his heir and the rest of his immediate family, was dead. The Romanovs were murdered in their prison exile, and their empire died with them. The last ruler of the House of Habsburg, the Emperor Karl, was in exile. The Habsburg Empire, once dominating the very heart of Europe, had disintegrated. The capital of the Turkish Empire, Constantinople, was occupied by enemy armies; the empire itself was a thing of the past. But above all, Imperial Germany, Europe's prewar powerhouse, had collapsed. The Kaiser Wilhelm II was in exile in Holland, and many clamoured that he should be tried and hung as a war criminal. The kings and princes of the German Empire had abdicated. Republics were proclaimed. Revolution – imitating the Russian Soviets – flared up in the cities; German democracy, under the name of the Weimar Republic, was born to the sound of cannon and machine guns.

So it came about that when the leaders of the nations assembled for the first meeting of the first World Peace Conference on 18 January 1919, they faced a map from which familiar lines were missing; they faced a scene from which familiar institutions were missing. They also faced a vast sum of human suffering. Out of all this they had to try to build something to match the world's hopes of a better order. But of course they faced also the familiar ingredients of political affairs: bitterness, vengefulness, ambition, greed. The war had not abolished Europe's old feuds and spites; in some cases it had sharpened them.

This conference was, in any case, dominated by the great victorious powers, France, Britain, Italy and America. The fact of victory was drummed in constantly by all the organs of their Press and by much crude oratory. And the victorious powers assembled to present their bills to the defeated: 'Squeeze them till the pips squeak' was the elegant demand of one eminent figure in Britain.

There was no ignoring the bills. How could France, for instance, ever lose sight of what had been done to her? For four and a half years great enemy armies had stood on French soil; for four and a half years the War had turned rich French provinces into battlefields whose mark was indelible. The battle-zone – now a wasteland – was a wide raw scar across the face of northern France, an area of devastation larger than the whole of Holland. From this zone two and a half million people had been driven out by the war. Gone from it also, as loot, or to feed the invading armies, were nearly a million head of cattle, and horses, pigs, sheep and goats in proportion. Hundreds of villages and small communities had simply vanished, some never to return, their sites marked only by memorials today. Three quarters of a million houses had been destroyed, 23,000 factories, 17,000 public buildings. Communications were at a standstill: 3000 miles of railway and 32,000 miles of road were wrecked. How could France forget this damage? How could she forget her 1,300,000 dead, almost all buried on French soil, their graves a daily reminder of the nation's suffering?

How could Belgium forget? For most of Belgium the aftermath of occupation was physical destruction where the armies had passed, but everywhere crops taken, factories stripped of machinery, money levies on towns and communes, hostages shot. In one small corner the scene darkened dramatically. Ypres was part of a battlefield – the famous Salient where over 200,000 men from the British Commonwealth, to say nothing of their allies and their enemies, lie buried. The aftermath here was annihilation. Today Ypres is once more, to all intents and purposes, the sixteenth-century Flemish town that the British Army admired in 1914. A superb effort of reconstruction has been made. But no reconstruction, no matter how faithful, could wipe out the memories of the years of barbarity. In February 1919 the Peace Conference was told: 'Hopes, without certainty, cannot suffice to Belgium, victim of her loyalty to her pledged word, punished for her loyalty by invasion, fire, pillage, rape and ruin.'

Italy's motives for entering the war had not been of the noblest: 'rushing to the aid of the victors' was how a sarcastic Frenchman described it. Italy entered the war because she had received promises from her allies – promises of gains after the war. And she felt that she had earned them. Italy's war had been fought mainly on Italy's soil; Italian towns and villages had felt the blast; and Italy's war had cost her nearly half a million dead – two thirds of Britain's total. Italy came to the Peace Conference to present a bill, to settle an account.

No part of Britain had been occupied by the enemy; no British town had suffered the fate of Ypres. But Britain had lost three-quarters of a million dead; one and a half million more had been wounded, many of them maimed for life. There was a War Debt amounting to over £1,300,000,000. And above all there was the transformation of a way of life: British security had been pierced by air bombardment; British stomachs had tightened under submarine blockade; British liberty had accepted conscription; British liberalism had given way to State control; British toleration had flown out of the window. A General Election at the end of 1918 showed the

British mood towards the beaten enemy. The Prime Minister, Lloyd George, now received his mandate for the Peace Conference which he would shortly attend; Winston Churchill wrote:

He reached the Conference somewhat dishevelled by the vulgarities and blatancies of the recent General Election. Pinned to his coat-tails were the posters, 'Hang the Kaiser', 'Search their Pockets', 'Make them Pay'; and this sensibly detracted from the dignity of his entrance upon the scene.[22]

And so, with mixed motives, the Conference began: seventy plenipotentiaries, 1037 delegates from thirty-two countries; armies of advisers, stenographers, assistants of all kinds, deployed, as Churchill said, in fifty-eight Commissions 'great and small, upon objects wise and foolish'. The drama of making a new world unfolded in solemn settings:

A high room: domed ceiling: heavy chandelier: dado of modern oak: doric panelling: electric light: Catherine de Medici tapestries all round the room: fine Aubusson carpet with a magnificent swan border; régence table at which Clemenceau sits . . . secretaries and experts on little gilt chairs. . . . The lights are turned on one by one as the day fades behind the green silk curtains. . . . Silence – very warm – people walking about with muffled feet – secretaries handling maps gingerly . . .[86]

The sessions were secret; it was only later that the world learned what had happened in these rooms. Two approaches, two very different sets of ideas about the task in hand, focussed around the personalities of two men, two leaders. On the one hand there was President Woodrow Wilson, warmly supported on at least one important issue by Lloyd George. Wilson had proclaimed his most cherished desire before the Conference opened: 'I wish we could enter into a great league and covenant for the world, declaring ourselves the friends of mankind, and uniting to maintain the right.' A League of Nations which would abolish war and international injustice: British and American thinking met on this ground. Harold Nicolson wrote: 'We were preparing not Peace only, but Eternal Peace. There was about us the halo of some divine mission. We must be alert, stern, righteous and ascetic. For we were bent on doing great, permanent and noble things.'[86] This was the language of idealism, expressing an Anglo-American attitude – the attitude of countries which had not been invaded.

The language of reality, on the other hand, was rather different. The French Prime Minister, M. Clemenceau (who was also President of the Conference), was a realist. 'Hopes without certainty', said the French Memorandum, 'cannot suffice to those who suffered the aggression of 1914.' For France, for Clemenceau, only one thing could suffice: security against any repetition of that aggression. The gulf between Clemenceau and Wilson – papered over for public view – was fundamental; in Clemen-

'Are we making a good peace? Are we?'
The signing of the Peace Treaty in the
Hall of Mirrors at Versailles

ceau's words: 'Mr Wilson has lived in a world that has been fairly safe for Democracy; I have lived in a world where it was good form to shoot a Democrat.'[13] For Clemenceau, a new world might be a fine thing, a League of Nations a fine thing, democracy a fine thing; security was everything. But President Wilson was the most powerful individual in the world, and for the time being his wishes prevailed.

Because of his authority as America's Head of State – and also because the Conference, by an astonishing oversight, had never agreed its agenda – Woodrow Wilson was able to obtain all priority for his great idea. The drafting of a Covenant for the League of Nations was pressed forward, and by remarkable efforts it was completed by 14 February. The President then presented it to the assembled delegates with great satisfaction, and just over a month later it was adopted. Certainly this was an achievement – but at a cost; Winston Churchill wrote:

Three months had now passed since the firing stopped and so far no agreement had been reached on any of the definite and all-important issues upon which the immediate peace and recovery of Europe depended. . . . A heavy price in blood and privations was in the end to be paid by helpless and distracted peoples for the long delay.[22]

Power, for the time being, remained with the great states whose leaders dominated the Peace Conference. Their armies stood on German soil: the French in Mainz, the British in Cologne, the Americans in Koblenz. Their blockade of Germany, Austria and Hungary was still in force and causing much hardship. But under the outward appearance of unassailable Allied strength, a different reality was asserting itself. Spurred on by the Press, the British Government was dismantling its forces at breakneck speed: by mid-January over half a million demobilised; by mid-March over two millions; by mid-April two and a half million. The United States did likewise. Already France was beginning to find herself militarily alone again.

And so, with a growing sense of ebbing power, but an even greater sense of ebbing time, the Peace Conference continued its business. The lack of an agreed procedure was showing itself to be a fatal defect; because of it another of President Wilson's pet themes was allowed to do mischief. The famous Fourteen Points for Peace, presented by the President to the United States Congress on 8 January 1918, were almost all that the Allies possessed by way of a Peace programme. A central proposition of the Fourteen Points was Self-determination, holy writ for the peacemakers in 1919: Italians under Austrian rule were to be reunited with Italy; there was to be autonomous development for all Austria-Hungary's subject races; autonomous development for the subjects of Turkey; an independent Polish state was to be restored. These were the promises, the declared intentions of the Allies. And now everyone who thought he had a claim based on these promises, or which might be based on them, or twisted to fit them, had his say in Paris.

There was Signor Orlando, the Italian Prime Minister, insisting on Italy's right to what had been promised her at Austria's expense. But the Austrian Empire had gone, and new nations stood on what had once been Austro-Hungarian territory. Signor Orlando's claims soon brought him into conflict with M. Pasič – representative of the new independent Yugoslavia. There was M. Bratianu of Rumania, with claims to press against Hungary, against Bulgaria, and against Russia. There was M. Beneš of the new Czechoslovakia, 'full of professions of moderation, modesty and restraint', but with claims which brought conflicts, among others, with Hungary and Poland – the latter now represented by the world-famous pianist, Paderewski. The question of Poland's new frontiers brought conflicts with all her neighbours. Then there was M. Venizelos, arguing the historic rights of Greece against Turkey. The Emir Feisal of Arabia had similar rights to assert, equally historic.

The only voices that were not heard at the Paris Peace Conference were German, Austrian, Hungarian, Bulgarian and Turkish, the voices of those whose territories were being claimed from them and whose future was now being decided. As the arguments swung to and fro, expediency and compromise displacing the early idealism, more than one delegate voiced misgivings. Harold Nicolson wrote in his diary for 8 March: 'Very tired, dispirited and uneasy. *Are* we making a good peace? Are we? Are we?'[86]

Amidst all the uncertainties, one unpalatable truth was already becoming clear: the degree to which real power had departed from Europe. In Paris real power was daily seen to lie with the President of the United States, whose agreement was vital for every decision. But was that really where power lay? President Wilson was a Democrat; in the Congressional Elections of November 1918 it was the Republicans who gained control. Wilson did nothing to gain Republican support for his policies in Paris; no Republican Senator formed part of the American Delegation. This was to be Wilson's undoing; in Churchill's words:

It was as a Party and not as a National leader that he sought to rule the United States and lecture Europe. His native foundations broke beneath him. While his arm was lifted in rebuke of the embarrassed and respectful governments of the old world he was unceremoniously hauled out of the pulpit by his hefty Party opponents at home.[22]

This serious error was also to be the undoing of European security. This ultimate dependence on American domestic quarrels in distant Washing-

'The idea of communism seemed to be marching swiftly'.
Lenin and Krupskaya, Red Square, Moscow, 1 May 1919

ton was a bitter fruit of the war – and a foretaste of greater dependence in the future.

And Europe herself was a diminished entity now. From all the deliberations in Paris there was a conspicuous absentee: Russia. President Wilson's Fourteen Points had promised that Russia would 'be more than welcome in the League of Nations under institutions of her own choosing'. But that was in January 1918; now things looked somewhat different. In 1919 British, French, American and Japanese troops were standing on Russian soil. Their original purpose had been to keep an Eastern Front alive against Germany after the collapse of Russia in 1918. But relations with the new Bolshevik Government had deteriorated, and soon the Allied contingents were drawn into the civil war which now flared across Russia. The Allies were not yet officially at war with the Bolsheviks, yet there was frequent sharp fighting between Allied and Bolshevik troops, a situation not easy to resolve.

The Russian Civil War itself was a ferocious affair, with abominable atrocities on both sides, breeding a malice which would linger for more than half a century. Meanwhile Russia, as a state, was null: a vacuum, to be filled by who knew what? And yet, strangely enough, as a force in world affairs this apparently helpless country had never been so powerful. In March 1919 the Third International, better known as the Comintern, was founded. Russian Bolshevism and World Revolution were now seen as twin brothers. Their very existence gave rise to understandable hysteria at the Paris Conference.

The export of revolution looked like good business at that time. It was, after all, only three weeks after the setting up of the Comintern that a Soviet government appeared in Hungary, and only a fortnight later another in Bavaria. The idea of Communism seemed to be marching swiftly westwards, and neither frontiers nor physical barriers can halt ideas. And so, under the threat of Bolshevism spreading from the East, and under the spur of idealism from Virginia – personified in President Wilson – the Peace Conference struggled towards a new world – of sorts. Unfortunately, the Conference never asked itself what sort of Germany, what sort of Austria – or even what sort of Europe – it was trying to create. It allowed the principle of self-determination to supply that answer, and in so doing the principle became somewhat bent.

New states, based on old national entities and aspirations, now acquired form and substance. Out of the fringes of old imperial Russia came an independent Finland and the three Baltic States: Estonia, Latvia and Lithuania. From the western marches Poland was reborn. Poland had last existed as an independent nation in 1772, and it was the vision of that

167

kingdom of 150 years earlier that inspired the Poles in 1919. But the fulfilment of the vision brought her into natural conflict with all her neighbours – Russia first, and with most immediate danger, but also Germany and the two other new creations, Lithuania and Czechoslovakia. In order to give Poland access to the sea, the famous 'Polish Corridor' was established, splitting East Prussia from the rest of the German Fatherland. A monument facing the Corridor on the German side bore the inscription: 'Never forget, Germans, of what blind hatred robbed you!' The great French soldier, Marshal Foch, said of the Corridor: 'There lies the root of the next war.'

A new state of Czechoslovakia had been recognised by the Allies in the autumn of 1918. Its first president was Thomas Masaryk, one of Europe's most famous democratic patriots. Masaryk said: 'We restored our state in the name of democratic freedom, and we shall only be able to preserve it through freedom increasingly perfected. In home affairs as in foreign, democracy must be our aim.'[76] But the new Czechoslovakia, founded in Paris on the principle of self-determination, was really only a Habsburg Empire in miniature. It contained Hungarians, Ruthenes, Poles, Rumanians – and over three million Germans. No amount of internal democracy could eliminate the anger of all these people – over one third of the population of the state – at being incorporated in what they considered an alien and artificial entity.

Self-determination for Rumania produced similar strange and unexpected results. By the terms of the Peace Treaties, Rumania more than doubled her territory and population – by the incorporation of strong and resentful Hungarian, Bulgarian and Ukrainian minorities. The new kingdom of Yugoslavia contained nine nationalities. Their conflicts were deep-rooted and bitter, intensified by language and alphabet (Cyrillic and Latin were both used) and by religion – this country contained not only Greek Orthodox and Roman Catholic Christians, but also Muslims. In such a scene parliamentary democracy was impossible. In effect, Yugoslavia was held together internally by Serbian domination and political dictatorship; externally, it faced the jealousies and hates of Italy, Bulgaria and Hungary.

Such were the curious products of idealism in 1919. When the time came to pull together all that had been done in the fifty-eight committees of the Peace Conference and embody these efforts in actual treaties, strange results were seen. The map-changers had evidently had some difficulty in reading maps. In the name of self-determination the Habsburg Empire had been abolished: now there were frontiers and customs barriers where there had been economic unity; industries were cut off from their raw materials and their markets; cities were separated from the agricultural regions which fed them; frontiers ran down the main streets of villages. Austria, once the centre of a great empire, was reduced to a population of seven million – two million being in Vienna, a capital without a country, where starvation walked the streets.

What was perhaps worst of all was that once-oppressed nationalities now became oppressors. It was argued that in prewar Europe there had been some forty-five million people living under foreign domination; after 1919 this figure was reduced to about seventeen million. But in the small and relatively powerless states which now filled so much of the map, seventeen million dissidents could be a much more explosive force than forty-five million under the repressive shadow of the departed empires.

The day came, 28 April 1919, when German delegates arrived at the Peace Conference. It was too late now – or it seemed too late – to confer with them, to discuss the Treaties; they came to sign – or take the consequences. When they heard the terms, the German delegates were appalled. These men were not representatives of the Kaiser's Germany, which had fought the war; they were representatives of a new Germany, trying to become a democracy – the Weimar Republic. The President of the Republic was Friedrich Ebert, an ex-saddler and a prominent Socialist. His Head of Government was Philipp Scheidemann, also a leading Socialist. Under these men the Weimar Republic was struggling for its life against Right-wing extremists, who did not believe in democracy at all, and Communists, who only desired Russian-style Soviets. Beset by these internal pressures, the Republic now discovered that the Peace Treaty would force it also to pay for the sins of the old Germany which it had repudiated.

These were some of the main provisions of the Treaty drawn up in Paris: to France Germany ceded the provinces of Alsace and Lorraine, taken from France in 1871. This was painful, but expected; it was a clause written into the Fourteen Points, and in any case many of the people of Alsace and Lorraine had never ceased to consider themselves French. Germany also lost land to Belgium and to Denmark, but worst of all was the 17,800 square miles which went to Poland. All in all, eight million Germans would now be living under foreign rule. The German fleet, whose construction had so sharpened the rivalries of the two nations before the war, had surrendered to Britain, and was anchored in captivity. By the terms of the Treaty Germany would only be allowed to have thirty-six warships. All her merchant ships over 1600 tons were also to be surrendered. Her overseas colonies were stripped from her. Her army was to be reduced to 100,000 men. She would have no Air Force. Her disarmament would be supervised by Allied commissions. Germany would pay repara-

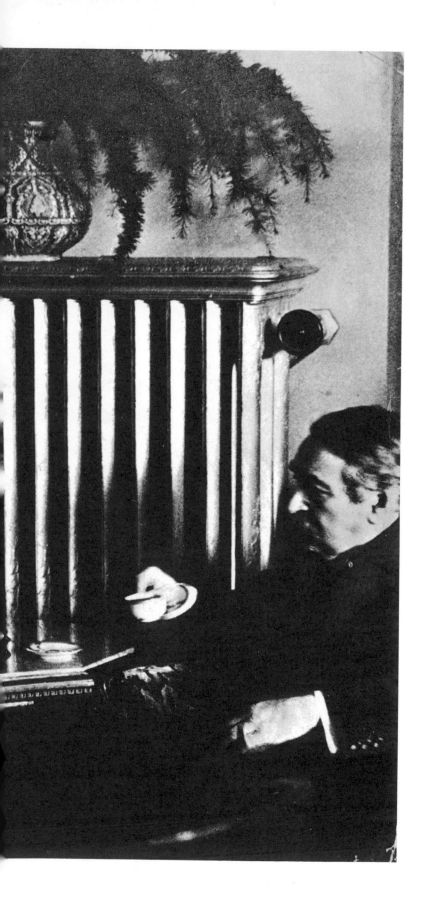

'We have the right to
speak of a European idea'.
Gustav Stresemann (centre)
with Sir Austen Chamberlain
and Aristide Briand in 1928

tions for all damage done to the Allies during the course of the war; she would supply coal to France, Belgium and Italy; she would build merchant ships to order of the Allies; she would give up horses, cattle, sheep; she would pay £1000 million on account by 1921; she would pay the costs of Allied Occupation.

This was punishment – not much doubt about it. To rub home the lesson of helplessness (especially for Austrians, who now had a country without an economy) Germany and Austria were forbidden ever to unite. Yet all this might have been accepted; what neither the old Germany nor the new Germany could accept was Article 231:

Germany accepts responsibility for causing all the loss and damage to which the Allied and Associated Governments and their nationals have been subjected as a consequence of the War imposed upon them by the aggression of Germany and her Allies.

This was the 'War Guilt' clause: a stigma on an entire nation. This was a moral judgment which an entire nation felt entitled to resent. Scheidemann resigned, exclaiming: 'May the hand wither that signs this Treaty!'[48] But there was nothing for it; Germany was powerless; sign she must. Her Foreign Minister, Brockdorff-Rantzau, who led the German delegation in Paris, perhaps saw a little further into the future (though not far enough) when he softened the blow by saying:

By not insisting on dictating terms to us in Berlin and by inviting us to Versailles instead, the Allies have given the government a chance of playing down the extent of the defeat to the Germans at home. . . . We shall win the final battle.[48]

And so Germany, in the person of two nonentities, two relatively unknown members of the Weimar Government, Herr Müller and Dr Bell, signed under protest, on 28 June 1919. A thousand people, four hundred of them members of the Press, watched the ceremony take place in the Hall of Mirrors at the Palace of Versailles, where forty-eight years earlier, on 18 January 1871, the German Empire had been proclaimed. A wheel had revolved in history.

The wheel did not stop, however, with the signing of the Treaty of Versailles. Now came the supreme irony. President Wilson, the prime mover of the League of Nations, the man of power in Paris, returned to his own country in July, and laid his Treaty (incorporating the Covenant of the League) before the Senate. This was the Republican Senate, whose cooperation he had scorned. Their hostility was evident, and to counteract it the President set off on a tour of America, to urge support for the League. He spared himself nothing; he made speech after speech at meet-

'. . . disenchantment with the war bred distrust
of all things military . . .':
an international peace meeting in the 1920's

ing after meeting, amid scenes sometimes of immense excitement. And then came the fall: after three weeks of campaigning, President Wilson collapsed, stricken by a paralysis from which he never recovered and which would shortly end his life. The Senate rejected the Treaty, and with it the League of Nations.

This was the resumption of American Isolationism; its wider implications were obvious — as Churchill put it: 'Europe was to be left to scramble out of the world disaster as best she could.'[22] For France, above all, the effect of this American reaction was shattering. The French, obsessed, as well they might be after the experiences of 1870 and 1914, with security, had wanted an even harsher treaty with Germany. Wilson, to overcome their fears, had offered a treaty of assistance, promising that America would defend France against unprovoked aggression. Britain promised the same — subject to ratification by Congress. But now the Senate refused to commit America to Wilson's promise; the British excused themselves on the grounds of America's refusal; and France stood alone again after all — alone and very much embittered. A large number of Frenchmen saw what Churchill saw as the result of these proceedings: 'Germany, beaten and disarmed upon the field of battle, defenceless before her outraged conquerors, rises the largest and incomparably the strongest racial mass in Europe.'[22] Such was the amazing product of idealism and expediency, self-determination and aggrandisement. But it would take a little time before Europe understood.

The world of the Versailles Treaty was generally a world of disillusion. The war had ended; war continued. There was war between Poland and her Soviet neighbour, with the Red Army penetrating to the gates of Warsaw before the Poles threw it back. There was war in Hungary, against the Czechs and Rumanians; 'Red Terror' under the short-lived Communist regime of Bela Kun had given way to 'White Terror' under Admiral Horthy, and an embittered nationalism that would continue to trouble Europe. There was war between Greece and Turkey, arising out of M. Venizelos's successful canvassing in Paris, but ending in a disastrous defeat for Greece and a new, rejuvenated Turkey under Kemal Ataturk, strong enough to reject her Peace Treaty and demand another. There was war in Ireland, leading to the creation of yet another new nation in Europe, the Irish Free State. There was no security; no true sense of peace. The feuds of Europe ran as deep as ever.

It was not until 1925 that the sense of real peace returned. It was in that year that, in Churchill's words, 'by the waters of a calm lake, the four great Western democracies plighted their solemn troth to keep the peace among themselves in all circumstances.'[22] He was speaking of the Treaties of Locarno, signed in 1925. Their details are not important now; what *is* important, historically, because it seemed so hopeful at the time, is the fact that Germany, for the first time since the war, took part in the discussions as an equal partner of France, Italy and Britain, the powers which had defeated her. At last it seemed that a new spirit, a spirit of genuine reconciliation, had been born in Europe. The British Foreign Secretary, Austen Chamberlain, who received a Nobel Prize for his work at Locarno, said: '[Locarno] was the real dividing line between the years of war and the years of peace.'[60] The German Foreign Minister, Gustav Stresemann, also received a Nobel Prize. Stresemann said: 'Let each one of us first be a citizen of Europe linked together by the great conception of civilisation which imbues our Continent. . . . we have the right to speak of a European idea.'[60] The French Foreign Minister, Aristide Briand, said: 'At Locarno we spoke European. It is a new language that we certainly ought to learn.'[60]

These were the silver voices of idealism, still able to make themselves heard after much rough treatment. In the mid-twenties they expressed what men had hoped for as a decent outcome of the War, what they had expected from the Treaty of Versailles, and what they continued to hope for from Peace. Unfortunately, the hard world of reality was not yet ready to 'speak European'. Churchill called the Locarno signatories 'the four great Western democracies'; while they remained democracies, even vestigially, the Treaties of Locarno might bear fruit; but if democracy disintegrated, the very foundation of the Treaties would disappear.

7

The hope of Mankind

The High Contracting Parties,
In order to promote international co-operation and to achieve international peace and security;
By the acceptance of obligations not to resort to war;
By the prescription of open, just and honourable relations between nations...
Agree to this Covenant of the League of Nations...

In June 1919 the Treaty of Versailles formally ended the Great War. The ink of the signatures on the Treaty was scarcely dry when men began to voice their doubts about what had been done and their fears for what the result of it might be. A British Civil Servant said at the time: 'One might indeed despair, were it not that the League of Nations has emerged. To it we must look as the future hope of mankind.'[121]

The League of Nations effectively came into existence in the moment of signing the Treaty of Versailles. Already the Swiss Government had said that it would be honoured if the League would make its headquarters at Geneva, and the offer had been gratefully accepted. So Geneva, with its long tradition of neutrality and sanctuary for refugees of all persuasions, from Calvin to Lenin – the town which Joseph Conrad rather unkindly called 'comely without grace, and hospitable without sympathy' – industrious, immaculate, peaceful Geneva now became the focus of a fervent hope and a pious activity.

As it turned out against expectation, Geneva was not, perhaps, the best choice for the new League's home. In 1919 the city did not have the accommodation required by a large international organisation. There was no building large enough to house the League Secretariat, and the first Assemblies had to be crowded into the little Salle de la Réformation. There were not enough international telegraph or telephone facilities; all these things came later. To begin with, the League and its various national delegations had to make do in hotels and meeting rooms. The Beau Rivage Hotel, looking out across the Lake to Geneva's famous water-spout, was the home of the British delegation. At the Beau Rivage Foreign Secretaries like Austen Chamberlain, Arthur Henderson and Anthony Eden worked and entertained. There Britain's first Socialist Prime Minister, Ramsay MacDonald,

'We wish to glorify War – the only health-giver of the world'. Severini. *Armoured train in action*

177

who occupied himself a great deal with foreign affairs, would charm the delegates with sanguine speeches and bask in their applause. Conservative or Labour, remembered or forgotten, all these men (like their European colleagues) were committed to the idea that nations could regulate their affairs in cooperation, not antagonism; that an international organisation would be able to prevent future wars; that Internationalism, not Nationalism, was the true hope of mankind.

The idea of a new world order captured the imagination of many people in many lands. League of Nations Associations and Unions were formed to promote the League's policies; they held enthusiastic demonstrations and rallies – where they were permitted to do so. In the democracies, above all, belief in the League was the accepted thing; few and far between were those who did not pay it some form of lip-service. Its publications kept people informed of its activities, optimistically reported its daily progress towards the new order of peace and goodwill. 'World Opinion', it was widely thought and often said, would be the ultimate force which would bring the new order about. In the words of Lord Robert Cecil (one of the League's chief founders) at the First Assembly, which opened on 14 December 1920:

By far the most powerful weapon at the command of the League of Nations is not the economic weapon or the military weapon or any other weapon of material force. By far the strongest weapon we have is the weapon of public opinion.

Public Opinion did indeed, in the 1920s, seem to be a more tangible and forcible factor in world affairs than ever before, possessing new sources of information and new modes of expression. The Cinema had made rapid strides during the War (in Britain alone serving an audience of about twenty million a week, compared with about four million today). All over the world people became accustomed to seeing events actually unfolding, not with the immediacy which television brought later but, thanks to increasingly swift newsreel techniques, often surprisingly close to immediacy. This marked a new and definite stage in the involvement of whole populations in the processes that ruled them: they could actually *see* the famous people walking and gesturing in Geneva – or, elsewhere. Soon, of course, the new medium would provide means of working up political passions and exerting political pressures, and the consequences of that would be disastrous.

Even more immediate than film, but without the benefit of vision, was the medium of radio. The British Broadcasting Company began transmitting programmes from Marconi House on 2L0 in 1922; by 1924 1,129,000 wireless receivers were licensed in Britain. Radio now brought news while

'. . . committed to the idea that an international organisation would prevent future wars . . .': Ramsay MacDonald and Stanley Baldwin, Prime Ministers of the 1920s (Salomon)

it was hot; it was a pity that so little of it was good news. Radio brought the voices of Kings,* Presidents, Prime Ministers, Dictators, some cultivating the arts of surrounding bad news with soothing words, some quite frankly blustering and threatening. Radio, as it developed, enabled nation to speak unto nation, an achievement warmly approved by those who did not think it important to enquire whether the recipient might not wish to hear the message. And it was against this background of more continuous communication and heightened awareness that the League of Nations operated.

The original membership of the League was only eighteen countries; in the course of 1920 this rose to forty-five, and ultimately, at one time or another, fifty-nine countries became members of the League. For those who were impressed by shows of hands and counting heads, this roll-call certainly looked imposing. But nothing could disguise, even from the League's most enthusiastic supporters, certain very serious weaknesses. There were, for example, some conspicuous absentees. It had been the energy and resolution of an American President that had forced through the actual creation of the League in such a short time in 1919, and yet – miserable irony! – America was not, and never would be, a member. The absence of the great democracy across the Atlantic was the most serious weakness of all; but it was not the only irony.

When President Wilson had enunciated his Fourteen Points for peace in 1918, Point Six laid down:

The evacuation of all Russian territory and such a settlement of all questions affecting Russia as will secure the best and freest cooperation of the other nations of the world in obtaining for her an unhampered and unembarrassed opportunity for the independent determination of her own political development and national policy and assure her of a sincere welcome into the society of free nations under institutions of her own choosing; and, more than a welcome, assistance also of every kind that she may need and may herself desire. The treatment accorded Russia by her sister nations in the months to come will be the acid test of their goodwill, of their comprehension of her needs as distinguished from their own interests, and of their intelligent and unselfish sympathy.

But that was in 1918, when the Bolshevik Revolution was still a fresh and undigested fact. Since then, there had been Intervention, with fighting between the Bolsheviks and Russia's one-time allies, and there was civil war, which produced a flow of terrible stories. A British journalist, Sir Philip Gibbs, who visited Russia in 1921, wrote: 'Perhaps there were

*Between six and seven million people heard the voice of their monarch for the first time in 1924, when George V's speech opening the Empire Exhibition at Wembley was broadcast.

happy people in Russia, but for the most part I only met those who told tragic tales of imprisonments, executions, death and misery.'[44]

The 'Socialist Sixth of the World' did not look a promising candidate for the League of Nations, with its high ideals. Nor did the Russian Communists desire to join it; to them the League was simply a capitalist club which they always referred to with abuse and scorn. But the Soviet Union contained 136 million people, and their non-representation at Geneva was a bad business – bad for them, and bad for the League's credibility.

The stark truth, which many people found quite unpalatable, was that the effectiveness of the League of Nations really depended on the three great European democracies which had won the war: Britain, France and Italy. United, they might have held the League together and given it the power of useful political intervention; but they were not united, and very soon one of them ceased to be a democracy.

It was in 1909 that the Italian poet Marinetti launched the Art movement known as Futurism with his amazing manifesto: 'We wish to glorify War – the only health-giver of the world!' (see p. 104). In 1915 he joined forces with the ex-Socialist newspaper editor Benito Mussolini and the playwright Gabriele D'Annunzio, who proclaimed: 'If it is a crime to incite citizens to violence, I shall boast of this crime.'[120] All three advocated Italy's entry into the war. All three were wounded in the war. All three became more, not less, nationalistic as a consequence of the war. And the climate of opinion in 1919 greatly stimulated that sentiment, for Italy, although ostensibly victorious, felt as frustrated and cheated by the peace as any of her ex-enemies.

In 1919 violent solutions seemed the only answer to Italy's problems, real or imagined. While D'Annunzio seized the port of Fiume on the Dalmatian coast (once Austrian, but now claimed by Yugoslavia), Mussolini and Marinetti founded the Fasci Italiani di Combattimento – the Fascist Party.* This modelled itself on D'Annunzio's example in Fiume, where he held his brief dictatorship by balcony demagogy, extreme nationalist propaganda, and squads of black-shirted intimidators. In 1920 he was ejected from Fiume, but Fascism in Italy continued to grow. It clashed violently with the Communists and Socialists. These were years of inflation, food shortages and industrial agitation in Italy; they were also years when the example of the Russian Revolution was very near and compelling. Peasants seized land; workers occupied factories. There was extremism at work on both sides of Italian politics, but it was Mussolini's Fascists, using knuckle-dusters, clubs and caster oil, who finally prevailed. In three years

*Fascio di Combattimento means Union of Ex-Servicemen, the prop of the Movement.

181

D'Annunzio, on board the warship given
him by the Italian Government

the Fascists are thought to have killed some 3000 of their political opponents; this is a small enough number, by the standards of other later brutalities, but with the police, the army and authority in general looking on with approval, it was enough.

In 1922 the Fascists came to power. First they seized control in the industrial centres of Bologna and Milan. Their more adventurous spirits demanded a 'march on Rome', but this was not altogether to Mussolini's liking. He took care to prepare the way for this particular 'heroic act' by secret negotiation with a frightened Government. When his followers did converge on Rome, in October 1922, Mussolini remained in Milan; his own 'march' was almost entirely conducted in a sleeping-car. Nevertheless, this theatrical escapade gave him what he wanted. He was offered the premiership of Italy, with very wide powers. In 1925 he was able to convert these into outright dictatorship; he became 'Il Duce' – the leader.

So the first Fascist State came into existence. There were many Europeans who liked the look of it: tourists were gratified to find that the Italian trains now ran on time; economists admired the draining of the Pontine marshes for agriculture; architects approved the new modern buildings constructed under the regime. It all had a very fresh look, but the truth was that Mussolini's allegedly new state was a complex of accommodations: accommodation with capitalism, for economic reasons; accommodation with the monarchy, to emphasise constitutionalism; accommodation with the Vatican, for practical reasons in a deeply Catholic country. Fascism called itself a 'Corporate State', attempting to regulate every aspect of communal life: trade unions, education, the Press, radio, films, leisure. It never entirely succeeded, despite its boasts; but it set a pattern of totalitarianism that others would imitate and improve upon.

Whatever else it may have been, or failed to be, Fascism was a regime which extolled violence and militarism. The discontented ex-servicemen who gave it its first recruits became the Blackshirts, an official militia, clamping fascist rule upon the nation. But the armed forces were always in the forefront: a large army with modern weapons, which required a doubling of iron and steel production, a modern navy and an air force to advertise Italy's new-found strength. The promise of grandeur and expansion was constantly held before the Italian people – and before Europe. 'Imperialism', said Mussolini, 'is the eternal and immutable law of life.' Announcing the conditions for the fulfilment of the 'Corporate State', he said: 'The ultimate and the most important condition is to live in a period of high tension of idealism. . . . Our own Fascist period is one of high tension of idealism.'[83]

All this, of course, was a very long way indeed from the ideas of peaceful

'. . . how deep the roots of Nationalism were . . .'
Mussolini and his Foreign Minister Count Grandi
conferring with the German chancellor Dr Brüning,
shortly to be overthrown by nationalism

cooperation between nations which were being proclaimed day by day at Geneva. Italy remained a member of the League of Nations, but Mussolini made it clear that he detested the League and all it stood for; he could never bring himself to visit Geneva as other national leaders were accustomed to do. In fact, the entire spiritual drift of his fascist system was anti-League, and sooner or later the question would arise which way Europe was to go – the way of the League, or the way of national dictatorship. Even the most high-minded idealists began to realise what a tender plant Internationalism was, and how deep the roots of Nationalism were, even without the stimulus of Italian-style Fascism.

Nowhere were national ambitions and hatreds more passionately alive than in Hungary. The Hungarian Peace Treaty – the Treaty of Trianon – was signed in June 1920, and Hungarians of all persuasions loathed it. The journalist John Gunther later wrote:

Hungarian nationalism has fed ever since 1919 on the open wounds made by the peace treaties which, in their comparative iniquitousness, reached in the Treaty of Trianon the most iniquitous point. Hungary lost, after the War, no less than 68·5% of its territory – 191,756 square kilometres out of a former total area of 282,879 square kilometres. Hungary lost no less than 58·2% of its population – 10,782,560 people out of 18,264,500. Hungary lost all its gold, silver, copper, salt, and mercury; it lost its best collieries, 85% of its forests, 65% of its vineyards. It lost 56% of its horses, 69% of its cattle, 52% of its factories, 57% of its arable land, and 52% of its total wheat production.[49]

Gunther points out that of the 'lost' ten and three-quarter million people, over six million belonged to non-Magyar minorities which had been repressed in pre-1918 Hungary. But such were the curiosities of Wilsonian 'self-determination' that now some three million Magyars were incorporated in Rumania, Yugoslavia and Czechoslovakia. It was not surprising, then, if 'the sole basis of Hungarian foreign policy since the War has been revisionism – to change the treaties in order to get its lost territory back.'[49] Nor was it surprising, in view of this anger and resentment, that nationalist secret societies should flourish in Hungary. They had different and strange-sounding names – 'Huns of the Magyar Blood', 'Love of Fatherland', 'National League', 'The Blood-League of the Apostolic Double Cross', and so on – but their central aim was the same: revision of the Peace Treaty. In September 1922 Hungary joined the League of Nations; this act helped to disguise, but did not lessen, Hungarian bitterness and the danger of conflicts.

This dangerous brand of nationalism, so much out of tune with the ideals of Geneva, was not confined to Hungary. Poland – product of the Treaty of Versailles – existed in constant friction with her neighbours:

Russia, with whom she had been at war; Lithuania, from whom she had seized the ancient capital, Vilna; Czechoslovakia, with whom she had a rankling grievance over the loss of Teschen; and above all Germany, divided by the Polish Corridor. Yugoslavia, full of internal discords, was also in a state of continuous quarrel with her neighbours, Italy, Hungary, Bulgaria and Albania. The unpalatable truth was that peace-making had created as many new causes of strife in Europe as it had dismissed old ones. The question now was, would the League be able to resolve them?

With Italy becoming increasingly totalitarian and warlike, America and Russia always absent, what the League could or could not do depended in reality entirely on Britain and France. In the last resort, the League's authority, its capacity to enforce its decisions in international disputes, rested on sanctions – economic sanctions, or even military sanctions. And it would not be countries like New Zealand or Belgium or Peru that would make those sanctions effective. It could only be the two great European democracies, Britain and France. At rock bottom it could be said that the only real force that the League ever possessed was the French Army and the British Navy, and it behoved true peace-lovers to make both as strong as possible. But this, of course, was the very thing that peace-lovers were *not* prepared to do. Professor Gilbert Murray, one of the League's most prominent supporters in Britain, faced with this very proposition, said: 'The sort of man who thinks that is the sort of man who ought never to be allowed to touch international affairs.'[8] Partly through the influence of those who thought like Gilbert Murray, but largely through blindness and folly, both Britain and France drifted steadily into weakness. What was even worse was that they also drifted into almost outright hostility towards each other. The problem that divided them was Germany.

What France wanted from Germany, after two damaging invasions in fifty years, was above all security. As M. Clemenceau had told the Peace Conference in January 1919: 'If a new war should take place, Germany would not throw all her forces upon Cuba or upon Honduras, but upon France; it would always be upon France.'[22] Security, in the minds of men like Clemenceau or Poincaré, did not consist in having the goodwill of small nations; it consisted quite simply in having stronger forces than Germany and strategic advantages.

France also desired compensation for the damage done to her during the War: reparations. And reparations, to a great many of the French, meant Germany actually handing over money and goods. There were practical difficulties about this, as the French discovered and the British were not slow to point out, and these difficulties were suddenly intensified by a fearful and unforeseen thing that was happening in Germany. It was one

186

'A famine which is believed to have killed
two million people'. Russia shortly after the Revolution

more irony, after all the destruction that had taken place, that Germany's means of production, in 1919, were intact, undamaged by the war. Potentially she remained what she had been before – Europe's most powerful economic unit. Yet in 1922 the German economy was in ruins.

The war – the actual conduct of war – had cost Germany 164 milliard marks; this was a debt outstanding against the national revenue. In May 1921 Germany was forced to accept a further reparations debt of 132 milliard marks. To meet the double strain, the Weimar Republic, afraid to increase taxes, printed paper money – and as it did so Germany's finances collapsed. In 1914 the American dollar had been worth 4·20 marks; in June 1920 it was worth 40 marks; by November 1923 it was worth 4,200,000,000,000 marks. This was the famous – or infamous – inflation. The effect inside Germany was shattering:

The saving, investing middle class, everywhere the pillar of stability and respectability, was in any case newer in Germany than in France and England – hence the instability of German policy even before 1914; it was now utterly destroyed, and Germany thus deprived of her solid, cautious keel.[104]

In the international field, the inflation naturally made nonsense of reparations. Conference after conference on the subject broke down. France became more and more impatient with Germany – and Britain became more impatient with France. When M. Poincaré, France's wartime President, became Prime Minister in 1922, he decided to adopt strong measures, to seize what was owing by force, as he was entitled to do by the Treaty of Versailles. This marked the parting of the ways with Britain. Bonar Law, the British Prime Minister, told Poincaré:

You can try to get your money, and a small amount it will be in any case. You can try by seizing what you can get your hand on now, but you cannot do the two things. You cannot at the same time seize what you can get and leave German credit a chance of recovery.[60]

Poincaré nevertheless determined to go ahead, even though neither Britain nor America supported him. On 11 January 1923 French and Belgian troops entered the Ruhr, where 80% of Germany's coal, steel and pig-iron were produced and 10% of her population lived. The Germans responded with passive resistance and a situation bordering upon guerilla warfare ensued. But the French were in no mood for trifling, the pressure of the German economy became intolerable, and in September the German Government accepted again its obligation to pay reparations – somehow. So the Ruhr occupation ended with an apparent French victory, but in fact it was a defeat on several counts. The franc dropped from 63 to 90 to the £; the British alliance was ruptured; the Weimar Republic fatally injured by association with another humiliation.

Only five years had passed since the end of the war, and once more there was discord on all sides, as well as economic depression to make life miserable for millions all over Europe. In the Soviet Union, in 1921, there was a famine which is believed to have ultimately killed two million people. In the same year, in London, there was an unemployed demonstration which turned into what history has called (perhaps somewhat excitedly) 'The Battle of Downing Street'. Unemployment was becoming a regular part of the social scene, unacceptable – but accepted. In 1922 came the first 'Hunger March' of the unemployed, from Glasgow to London. They recurred throughout the decade, reaching a climax in 1929 when marchers converged from all over the country upon the capital.

Yet these years were called the 'Gay Twenties'; it is hard to see why. For an upper crust, a wealthy few, the forms of gaiety undoubtedly expanded, with American novelties coming into European use one after another: nightclubs and cabaret, cocktails, the American mixed drink mania adorned with amazing names – Sidecars, Manhattans, Gimlets, Horses' Necks, Fallen Angels, Satan's Whiskers, and so on. But cocktails were not for the many: for millions and millions the twenties were far from gay. In fact, they were bitterly disappointing; the brave new world that had been promised was obviously not forthcoming. Every kind of escapist rubbish was forthcoming: juicy crimes and scandals; the new cult of the supermen and superwomen, the film stars; bouncy jazz music to make people forget their troubles (in the sixties troubles had to be invented, so a lot of popular music became very sad); new sports like car-racing, dirt-track racing, greyhound racing, the Schneider Trophy air race; some old sports, like football, were elevated practically into a religion. But there was no brave new world.

It was in the very midst of the twenties, when world affairs looked grim and cynics found all too much scope, that one part at least of the expected brave new world did come to life and look as though it might fulfil the hope of mankind. In 1924 there was suddenly a new climate of international opinion which produced the hey-day of the League of Nations. In Britain Labour came to power for the first time, with Ramsay MacDonald – vain, woolly-minded, sentimental, sincerely pacifist Ramsay MacDonald – as Prime Minister and Foreign Secretary. When his Government fell less than ten months later, he was succeeded as Foreign Secretary by Sir Austen Chamberlain. In France Edouard Herriot was Prime Minister, and the great internationalist Aristide Briand was Foreign Secretary, later to become Premier. These were the champions of the League, its true believers, and they were fortunate enough to meet in Gustav Stresemann, the German Chancellor and Foreign Minister, another man who firmly believed in reconciliation.

The first fruits of reconciliation policies were the Treaties of Locarno in 1925. After Locarno, wrote Winston Churchill, 'hope rests on a surer foundation'. Then, in 1926, a further step towards world – above all, European – settlement was taken. In September of that year Germany was admitted to the League. At last it seemed that all was forgiveness and fresh hope. Aristide Briand's speech of welcome to the Germans was, according to one who heard it,

. . . the finest speech the Assembly has ever listened to. His rich and beautiful voice dropped at times almost to a whisper as he pleaded for peace on earth, and then rose again to a clarion note as he proclaimed the birth of a new era. . . . That superb orator could play like a master on the heart-strings of his audience and none of them could remain unmoved. As we went out again into the bright sunlight of Geneva, we felt that we had witnessed one of the great turning points of history.[106]

This was a bright moment for the hope of mankind, and only two years later there was another. In 1928 sixty-five nations signed the Kellogg Pact, which condemned war as a solution to international disputes, and renounced it as an instrument of policy. Internationalists everywhere rejoiced, and even the man in the street, tearing his eyes with some difficulty from the football and greyhound results, must have thought this was good news, although every other page of his newspaper displayed the sort of peace which passeth understanding.

The man in the street in Britain was an important fellow; his opinions counted. And he was in a state of shock – indeed, in two states of shock at the same time, which is a serious condition. Protected in his island behind his famous 'white cliffs' for centuries, it had been a fearful shock to discover what total war was really like. Now it was another shock to relearn that Peace has its calamities, no less renowned than war. Britain had been promised a 'land fit for heroes to live in'. What she got was two million unemployed by 1921, dropping to 1,200,000 in 1929, but then rapidly increasing again. Mass unemployment is never a pretty picture; when hundreds of thousands of the unemployed are men who have recently offered their lives to their country, it is unbearable.

A mood of disillusionment and disgust began to be felt very soon after the war. One ex-soldier wrote to *The Times* on Armistice Day 1919:

I have today given two minutes praying for our dead and two hours regretting I am not one of them. They 'live' in a world where no bread is needed; I am condemned to 'exist' in a land which threatens to starve me.

The fruits of 'victory' in war, in the early twenties, seemed to be merely disappointment and impoverishment. The reasons for this were various, some avoidable, some not. As a trading nation, Britain had inevitably suf-

'The disarmament of Germany had been written into the Treaty of Versailles'.
A Nuremberg student, 1928
(August Sander)

'Hitler's programme was flat rejection
of the Treaty of Versailles'.
Hitler in front of the Landsberg city gate
after his release from the fortress in 1924

fered by the loss of shipping and overseas markets through the war. At the same time, however, she had profited by a long-overdue industrial revival, an important step towards a second industrial revolution.

New industries had been created by the war, and were here to stay: chemicals, aircraft and aero-engines, the refining of non-ferrous metals. Electrical generating capacity had doubled. Electric bulb production had quadrupled. Ball-bearing production had doubled. Optical glass production had increased sixty times. All these were valuable gains, and with them had gone a great modernisation and reorganisation of existing industries, with large measures of state control. The question was whether these gains would be maintained and carried forward in peace; the answer, soon given, was that they would not. Orthodox economic theory, belief in Free Trade and Laissez-faire, dislike of state control, lack of enterprise among industrialists, all these helped to account for a sense of poverty which was not entirely justified by fact. But justified or not, its consequences were far-reaching.

In the twenties economic depression bred disillusionment with the peace; disillusionment with the peace bred disenchantment with the war; disenchantment with the war bred distrust of all things military. Disarmament – the 'general limitation of the armaments of all nations' envisaged in the Treaty of Versailles – became the great quest of the postwar years, and nowhere was it pursued more wholeheartedly than in Britain, where dread of military commitment was linked to dread of military expenditure, and both were excused by constant reference to the 'futility of war'.

Year by year, relying on 'collective security' through the League of Nations with general popular approval, British governments dismantled British power. In 1919 the Royal Navy had regained a supremacy unequalled since the Napoleonic Wars. In 1922, at the fatal Washington Naval Conference, Britain accepted battleship parity with the United States; she agreed to scrap older battleships, stop current building, and build no more battleships for ten years. So the Navy, once the nation's pride, was allowed to slide into numerical weakness and technical obsolescence. The Royal Air Force similarly: in 1919 the RAF was the most powerful in the world, with 22,000 operational aircraft; by 1922 it had sunk to one tenth of the size of the French Air Force. As for the Army, it was not to be compared with the efficient and well-equipped Expeditionary Force of 1914. But no one seemed to mind (except the Chiefs of Staff, whose noses were increasingly rubbed into the consequences); Ramsay MacDonald expressed a widespread belief when he told the Fifth Assembly of the League of Nations:

Our interests for peace are far greater than our interests in creating a machinery of defence. A machinery of defence is easy to create, but beware lest in creating it you destroy the chance of peace.[60]

In the thirties the dangers of this manner of thinking began to become clear, though the dedicated internationalists resolutely refused to see them. The disarmament of Germany had been specifically written into the Treaty of Versailles as a guarantee of peace, and with the pious hope that it would lead to general disarmament. Of course it had done no such thing; many Germans were correspondingly all the more disgusted with the Treaty, and the desire to thwart it grew. In 1931 this desire expressed itself in an alarming fashion. The Treaty had laid down strict limits to German naval building, but with astonishing technical ingenuity the Germans overcame them; the result was the so-called 'pocket-battleship' *Deutschland*, a ship whose tonnage was within the Treaty limits, but which was as fast as a cruiser and as powerful as a battleship. The British and French Admiralties were naturally deeply alarmed, and made plans to counter this threat – while well-meaning internationalists and pacifists continued to call for disarmament.

Even pocket-battleships might not have been all that serious if democracy had survived in Germany, but the Weimar Republic was nearing the end of its road. The Republic had never been forgiven by many Germans for the signing of the Versailles Treaty; inflation had done it more damage, by destroying the middle class; then came the humiliation of the French march into the Ruhr and Germany's climb-down; finally there was the Depression, which produced nearly five million unemployed in Germany in 1931. This marked the finish of the Weimar Republic.

Now Adolf Hitler's National-Socialist Party,* born in the Munich Bier Kellers in the violent times just after the War, prepared to take power. Hitler's programme was flat rejection of the Treaty of Versailles and the reunion of all Germans in a pan-German state; it was, in fact, stark nationalism, with anti-Semitism, totalitarianism and a special cult of violence added for full flavour. Imitating Mussolini's Fascists, the Nazis fought and won 'the battle of the streets' – intimidation by thuggery, but far more savage than anything seen in Italy. The Stresemann period in the mid-twenties, when the doctrine of 'reconciliation' seemed to hold sway, had been a bad time for the Nazis, but in 1930 they became the second largest party in the Reichstag. In July 1932 they became the largest party, polling thirteen and three-quarter million votes, about 40% of the total electorate. German democracy had signed its own death-warrant.

The shadows might darken in the world outside, but millions of people

*NSDAP: in translation, National-Socialist German Workers' Party.

still looked to the League of Nations as their only hope, and in Geneva hope always shone brightly. The League was the first of the great permanent international organisations which we now take for granted, and whose expense we accept as just one more of the burdens of modern living. These organisations evolve a life of their own, which sometimes seems totally detached from the real world. The League had its permanent Secretariat, its periodical Assemblies, its Committees and Sub-committees and Agencies. It was immensely busy, and to all those who were caught up in this unending business it was unthinkable that so much well-meant activity might be purposeless – indeed irrelevant.

The League, as the thirties opened, did, after all, have achievements to boast about. It had settled international disputes – between Poland and Germany in 1921, between Albania and Yugoslavia in 1924, between Greece and Bulgaria in 1925. It administered the Saar and the Free City of Danzig. It had set up a Court of International Justice at the Hague, and an International Labour Organisation, for the improvement of working conditions, in Geneva. It had made progress against slavery, epidemics, malnutrition; it helped backward countries in matters of finance, health and education. The enthusiasts did not like to be reminded that whenever the sovereignty of great powers was in question, the League was always helpless.

There were disturbing symptoms within the member-states of the League itself. Not merely in Italy and Germany, but right through Europe, totalitarianism was expanding, democracy was on the wane. In 1923 a military dictatorship was established in Spain under General Primo de Rivera. King Alfonso XIII referred to him as 'my Mussolini', and for a few more years the Spanish monarchy sheltered behind his strong rule. But when de Rivera died in 1930, the monarchy's last prop vanished. King Alfonso was exiled in the following year, and a Spanish Republic came into being, with the dark forces of anarchism and communism stirring restlessly in the background.

Poland also soon became a dictatorship. Her geographical position between Germany and Soviet Russia, and the artificiality of her frontiers with both, spelt serious political weakness for the new Poland. In 1926 there was a coup-d'état, led by Marshal Józef Pilsudski, the hero of the struggle for national revival who had defeated the Russians in 1920. Under Pilsudski, Polish nationalism became a powerful factor; Poland's determination to hold frontiers seized by the sword, and even expand them, was another danger to European peace and League of Nations idealism.

The pattern repeated itself elsewhere. The next dictator was royal: King Alexander of Yugoslavia. His country – the long-awaited land of the

South Slavs – was made up of no less than nine nationalities. It should have been a federation, but in fact it was ruthlessly dominated by the Serbs (who accounted for just over half the population). None resented this more than the Croats, who firmly believed that they – not the arrogant Serbs – were the true creators of South Slav independence. In 1928 the world was shocked once more by Balkan violence: a Serb deputy in the Yugoslav parliament pulled out a revolver, shot the Croat leaders one by one, killing two and wounding three more, and then walked out unmolested. Croats began to say that they had been better off under the Habsburgs. To prevent his state from falling apart amidst this dissension, King Alexander resorted to direct personal rule. The Yugoslav kingdom was reprieved, but violent men with violent thoughts remained at large.

Hope in Geneva nevertheless lingered on, hope for peace through collective security and disarmament, *both at once,* and nowhere was this conflict of good intention more acute than in Britain. In 1930 Britain again had a Labour Government, again headed by Ramsay MacDonald, but this time the Foreign Secretary was Arthur Henderson. It has been said that

the League of Nations at Geneva provided the perfect habitat for Henderson. '. . . the moral climate at once elevated and rather dowdy was entirely congenial. Here was a place dedicated expressly to high purposes in which he believed.' In turn, Henderson was exactly the kind of man to please Geneva. . . . His patent integrity and the massive strength of his personality inspired the League delegations with his own confidence in the League's future. It was a form of faith-healing. It was in doing so much to encourage the League to believe in itself that Henderson probably rendered the greatest disservice to the world on which he wished to confer the blessings of eternal peace.[52]

Henderson was one of many who believed that it was armaments themselves which produced international fear and tension, rather than vice versa. It thus seemed like the crown on a life's work when, in February 1932, he became Chairman of the World Disarmament Conference.

The Disarmament Conference, thought Henderson, like other internationalists, would provide the final and necessary step in the construction of the new international order. But a succession of horrible ironies now defeated him and all who thought like him. Japan and China were both members of the League of Nations, yet in the previous year Japan had carried out a blatant act of aggression against China in Manchuria. Now, only five days before the 1932 Disarmament Conference opened, the Japanese attacked the port of Shanghai, and China appealed directly to the League for help. It turned out that all the League had to offer was an International Commission of Investigation, and dissertations of high moral tone. The Japanese smiled and bowed and prevaricated at Geneva, and went on with their aggression in China. Once more it was proved that against a great power the League had no power. And it was also proved that Disarmament itself, the great peace hope of the postwar years, was actually dangerous to peace.

The Disarmament Conference was fated. It broke up in July 1932, having accomplished nothing except delusion. The following year, only three days before the Conference reconvened on 2 February, Hitler became Chancellor of Germany. In October, despite earlier proclamations of peaceful intent, he took Germany out of the Conference, and out of the League of Nations. Soon he was openly admitting – indeed, boasting – that Germany was rearming, in flat contravention of the Treaty of Versailles. But nothing, it seemed, would ever convince the high-minded, the really dedicated internationalists, particularly the British variety.

Conscription was reintroduced in Germany in March 1935; June of that year witnessed a remarkable demonstration of the confusion of British public opinion. The League of Nations Union published the results of a poll which it had organised, known then and ever since as the 'Peace Ballot'. In response to certain unhappily-worded questions it transpired (not surprisingly) that ten and a half million people were in favour of remaining in the League. Rather less understandable was the fact that ten million of them were still prepared to vote for all-round reduction of armaments – despite Japan, despite Hitler, despite Mussolini. Utterly unintelligible was the simultaneous vote of seven million of these same people for preventing aggression by military measures. But this was the year when one Member of Parliament received a letter from a constituent, asking: 'Can you assure me that you stand for the League of Nations and Collective Security and will oppose any entanglements in Europe?'[84] British public opinion in 1935 was lost in confusion, ripe for any defeat, and defeat was not slow in coming.

It was in October 1935, just four months after the publication of the Peace Ballot results, that Italy, a founder member of the League of Nations, attacked Abyssinia, also a member of the League. This was the acid test. Suddenly the British internationalists were the ones who demanded strong measures, even military measures. Lord Allen, a notable pacifist and supporter of the League, said, 'Collective Security today is the key that opens all the doors to peace.'[8] Professor Gilbert Murray said, 'The League of Nations is enormously strong. Such weakness as it shows is the weakness of timidity not lack of strength.'[8] Anthony Eden, soon to be Foreign Secretary, told Mussolini: 'His Majesty's Government is irrevocably committed to the League.'[8] But collective security was a myth. France, under the premiership of Pierre Laval, was all too conscious of Germany's grow-

'The grey world
after the war'.
Wigan 1930s

ing strength, and had no intention of antagonising Italy. Britain, after years of military run-down, was in no condition to fight alone, and the small nations had nothing to offer. The League proclaimed economic sanctions against Italy, and enthusiasts announced that in that hour 'the League was born!' But the sanctions were ineffective. Collective security, without military strength behind it, was seen to be an illusion. The Emperor of Abyssinia, Haile Selassie, made a moving appeal to the League, but in vain; there was nothing more the League could do for him. Italy's aggression against Abyssinia marched to its triumphant conclusion, and in that hour the League died.

The organisation lingered on, and, with a final irony, it was now that it assumed the outward shape that is generally associated with it. The Palace of the Nations, begun in 1929, was finished in 1936, just in time to become a mausoleum. Here at last were the necessary offices, 700 of them, and the fitting conference rooms for the words that no longer meant anything. There was a floor of Finnish granite, walls and pillars faced with Swedish marble, enigmatic and forbidding murals, depicting Technical Progress, Medical Progress, Social Progress, the Abolition of War, and so on, by the Catalan artist José Maria Sert. Under their sombre painted sermons the Assemblies still met and passed their resolutions; everyone was still very busy. But underneath it all the mainspring was broken. Malcolm Muggeridge, who as a journalist had seen the League's hey-day and watched its fall, wrote its epitaph:

Twinkling lights of Geneva, noisy, smoky cafés of Geneva, Lake of Geneva beside which men walk unfolding newspapers in the wind – newspapers which tell of such a speech, such a resolution, such exchange rates and stock prices; conversation of Geneva, ebbing and flowing like the sea's tide but never abating – this was a kingdom, once flourishing, now decayed and scarcely existent.[81]

The end of the League: bad luck for the hope of mankind.

'A Cause was about to appear'.
Spanish Civil War: Loyalist soldiers
at the front, 1936 (David Seymour)

8   Form! Riflemen form!

When Europe seemed to be threatened by the rise of a military dictator in the nineteenth century, the Poet Laureate, Lord Tennyson, sounded an alarm call to the British people:

There is a sound of thunder afar,
Storm in the South that darkens the day,
Storm of battle and thunder of war,
Well, if it do not roll our way.
Storm! storm! Riflemen form!
Ready, be ready to meet the storm!
Riflemen, riflemen, riflemen form![107]

The 1930s were such a time again. Only fifteen years after a savage war which had almost torn the mighty continent to pieces, dictatorship was on the march, men were dividing into factions and taking sides again. But taking sides, in the 1930s, was no longer the simple matter that it once had been.

The 1914-18 War had displayed violence and social disruption on an unimagined scale. Millions were killed. Immense material damage was done. European culture was brutally assaulted. The very sense of Europeanism itself was assaulted by this attempted suicide of a continent. Nightmare landscapes appeared in once fertile regions; nightmare landscapes sprouted in men's minds and expanded there, long after the war was over:

What are the roots that clutch, what branches grow
Out of this stony rubbish? Son of man,
You cannot say, or guess, for you know only
A heap of broken images, where the sun beats,
And the dead tree gives no shelter, the cricket no relief,
And the dry stone no sound of water . . .[37]

In the Waste Land of the mind after the War, all manner of images lay broken or decayed. Patriotism was mocked by too many dead soldiers. Victory was mocked by the insecurity of peace. The novelist Richard Aldington gave these words to one of his characters: 'You, the war dead,

*The poem refers to Napoleon III's war with Austria in 1859.

201

I think you died in vain, I think you died for nothing, for a blast of wind, a blather, a humbug, a newspaper stunt, a politicians' ramp. But at least you died.'[1]

In the Waste Land of the mind, morality was mocked by mass murder. Monarchy was mocked by the overthrow of kings. Democracy was mocked by ineffectiveness. Humanity itself was mocked by the triumph of machines. As for faith, that was mocked above all: religion had fought too hard on both sides in the war, and the results were not pretty. Paul Nash, the painter, wrote: 'Evil and the incarnate fiend alone can be the master of this war, and no glimmer of God's hand is seen anywhere.'[74]

It was just as difficult to perceive the glimmer of God's hand in the grey world after the war, the world of unemployment and the dole. In Britain in 1930 there were almost two million unemployed, in Germany over three million, and this was only a beginning of the Great Depression. Soon the figures would rise to two and three-quarter million in Britain, six million in Germany. It was hard, indeed, to see the hand of God in this. Increasingly, the sound of church bells, so loud in Europe at the beginning of the century, was drowned by the blast of engines and the blare of gramophones. Another emptiness was created, with malign forces waiting to fill it.

In January 1933 Adolf Hitler became Chancellor of Germany. A general election quickly confirmed his rise to power: over seventeen million votes were cast for the NSDAP, the Nazi Party, giving it by far the largest number of seats in the Reichstag. In 1934 Hitler completed his long march from the Bier Kellers of Munich to supremacy in the Wilhelmstrasse: he became the Führer, leader and absolute ruler of Germany. So now the Third Reich came into existence, the new German empire which the Nazis boasted would last for a thousand years.

The nature of the Third Reich soon revealed itself to anyone who cared to take note. The crude violence of the SA,* the Brownshirts, in the 'battle of the streets' reached a peak in the last 'free' election which was a true sign of things to come. This was a state in which all political parties except the National-Socialists were suppressed. Trade Unions were suppressed. The Nazi Party apparatus regulated the life of Germany's sixty-five million people at every level. The arts, literature and theatre, the press, radio and cinema, were all subject to Dr Joseph Goebbels's Ministry of Propaganda. Its function was to stamp out independent thought at the roots. If it failed, there was the Gestapo,† the secret state police, under Heinrich Himmler, to seek out, punish or 'liquidate' all the enemies of the Reich, real or supposed.

Concentration camps (a half-forgotten phrase now given entirely new

*Sturm-Abteilung: the Storm-troopers.
†Geheime Staatspolizei.

meaning) were the ultimate sanction of the Nazi dictatorship. They appeared immediately in 1933, and soon their network was spreading across the country. In these camps savagery ran amok under the cynical sign 'Arbeit macht frei' ('Work makes one free'). Hundreds of thousands of Germans entered these corners of hell on earth, mostly never to return. Their first victims were Communists, Social Democrats, pacifists, Jehovah's Witnesses – and Jews. In 1933 there were half a million Jews in Germany; by 1939 there were less than a quarter of a million. Most had fled; the concentration camps destroyed the rest.

It is too easy to say that Germany 'had gone back to the Middle Ages'. This was the twentieth century; Germany was a modern nation with a modern economy; what she was doing she did in twentieth-century style. When Hitler came to power, the German economy was in chaos, with some six million unemployed and industry stagnant. By 1938 Germany had achieved virtually full employment and her industry was outwardly flourishing, though orthodox economists questioned whether this could continue. Yet Germany had all the appearance of thriving in the thirties under Hitler, and her people knew it: the names of fourteen million Germans – two out of every three male adults – were registered as members of the Nazi Party or one of its affiliated organisations. A spirit of excitement and anticipation spread through the country sweeping away the fog and gloom of the Depression. Now there seemed to be something to live for again, a new German destiny, a greater Germany.

One thing was quite clear: Hitler's Germany, Nazi Germany, was essentially military. Industrialists were happy to support Hitler's policy of rearmament, which in turn played a large part in economic recovery. Forbidden weapons reappeared: in 1935 the German Air Force (the Luftwaffe) was formally reborn, with Hermann Goering, the First World War fighter 'ace', as its commander. He boasted that his Air Force already possessed nearly 2000 aircraft – a formidable show of power. In that same year conscription was reintroduced, and the target of an army of thirty-six divisions, equipped with tanks and heavy artillery, was proclaimed. In the German shipyards U-boats were being built again.

So German militarism now reappeared on the European scene. Under the Nazi slogan, 'Ein Reich, Ein Volk, Ein Führer' ('One state, one folk, one leader'), this militarism was openly dedicated to the unification and expansion of the German race. Eight million Germans had been separated from their Fatherland by the terms of the Treaty of Versailles, which Hitler endlessly denounced. They, too, heard that Nazi slogan.

Adolf Hitler himself was an Austrian, born in 1889 at Braunau on the River Inn, which marked the frontier between Austria and Germany. He

In 1934 Hitler completed
his long march.
The Nazi Party rally
at Nuremberg

believed his country's fate to be indissolubly linked to Germany's, but by the terms of the Treaty of Versailles Austria was specifically cut off from Germany; union between the two was strictly forbidden. And since Austria, now with only seven million people, was also cut off from the economic resources on which she had once depended, her position was more hopeless than that of any other German land. Nazi agitation found plenty of material to work with.

It was yet one more ironic paradox in a continent full of such things that those Austrians who wanted to preserve their independence could only look in one direction for real support: to Italy – hated Italy. A quarter of a million Austrians in the Tyrol had been swallowed up by Italy in 1919, and were harshly treated by Mussolini's Fascist regime. But Italian troops stood on the Brenner Pass, and in 1935 it was the threat of Italian divisions crossing the Brenner that saved Austria from Hitler. If Mussolini changed sides, Austria was doomed, and if Hitler gained Austria, what else might he not gain?

In 1935 the cry 'Riflemen form!' resounded through Europe, but Europeans, looking for a cause, a side to join, found much to confuse, little to inspire them. Only the new, aggressive, totalitarian regimes seemed to offer a clear line; even in the democracies their example led men into temptation. In France the tradition of a violent Right was familiar: the nationalist, anti-semitic, anti-democratic 'Action française' had existed since 1899; now it found allies and imitators in Colonel de la Roque's 'Croix de Feu', M. Coty's 'Solidarité Française', and others. In February 1934 these groups marched on the Chamber of Deputies; the police had to open fire and fourteen demonstrators were killed, but the Government was forced to resign. In June of the same year Sir Oswald Mosley addressed a mass meeting of his British Union of Fascists at Olympia. Even a small country like Belgium had its Fascists, called Rexists, led by Léon Degrelle and linked to nationalist extremist groups.

Italian Fascism was still a model: it had given Italy an unusual appearance of order, efficiency and strength. Fascism had always worn military costume and played up national feeling. Until 1935 there was rivalry, even the possibility of open conflict, between Fascists and Nazis, Italian and German nationalism. But 1935 was a turning-point, a year in which old relationships expired and ominous new ones were born. It was in October of that year, when Italy invaded Abyssinia, that European peace began to disintegrate. Britain and France, the only European countries with the power to deter Italy, could not agree on a policy, and this disagreement was disastrous for Europe. What they did succeed in doing was making an enemy of Mussolini by invoking ineffective sanctions, and thus driving

'The man in the street in Britain was in a state of shock'. Watching the Coronation procession in 1937 (Cartier-Bresson)

'How unpleasant of Winston Churchill to say "We have suffered a total and unmitigated defeat"'. Churchill at dinner during the appeasement period

him towards alliance with Hitler. In 1936 the totalitarian power bloc – the Rome-Berlin Axis, as Mussolini called it – became a new factor in European affairs, making its appeal to men of many countries.

What else was there for Europeans to cling to or turn to? What was there for Austrians, who might dislike Hitlerism, but could only see survival in unity with Germany? Or for Czechs, proud of their new democratic state – which nevertheless contained three and a quarter million Germans? For Dutch and Belgians, who had been the cockpit of Europe too often? For the British, struggling to emerge from economic depression, struggling to save the last remnants of Victorian liberalism in a hostile world? For Frenchmen, who wanted to preserve their great Republic, and at the same time continue to practise its vigorous, sometimes destructive habits of democracy? Could the answer be Communism, another form of totalitarianism, although the declared enemy of the Fascists and Nazis?

Communism existed at two levels: as a political idea, and as a political reality. As an idea it had already suffered serious setbacks: the large, apparently powerful Communist Parties of Italy and Germany had been suppressed. Elsewhere, in the democracies, Communists were generally at loggerheads with Social-Democratic parties, which it pleased them to call 'Social Fascist', and so the working-class movement was split. Communism, as an idea in the 1930s, despite the crispness of some of its slogans, offered only another confusion.

No less confusing was Communism as a reality. The Soviet Union, the 'Socialist Sixth of the World' as its admirers called it, was now under the firm grip of Joseph Stalin, and reflected his enigmatic personality. Communists and fellow-travellers everywhere extolled the 'Workers' Fatherland'; it could do no wrong. A stream of well-meaning non-Communist visitors poured into the USSR – writers like André Gide and Bernard Shaw, economists like Sydney and Beatrice Webb, scientists like Professor Julian Huxley, even millionaires like Lady Astor. They performed their carefully guided tours, uttered their words of rapture, and came home to report the economic and social miracles they thought they had seen, to give, as one Moscow reporter of the period says, 'a blanket endorsement of what they would not understand'.[68]

A vast literature supported them; in Britain 1935 was the year in which the publisher Victor Gollancz founded the Left Book Club, a large part of whose output was pro-Soviet propaganda. The Soviet Union was now a member of the League of Nations, represented by Maxim Litvinov, who 'spoke the Geneva language to perfection'. Litvinov proclaimed Soviet willingness to live in peace and trade with any country, which was exactly what many people wished to hear. Those who questioned the Soviet one-party state, the absence of the right to strike, the muzzled press, the forced-labour camps, the arbitrary arrests, the brutality of forcible collectivisation, the continuing grinding poverty of the Soviet masses, were dismissed as 'Fascist reactionaries'. But the truth was that terrible things were happening, and worse about to happen, in the Socialist fatherland.

It was in 1935 that the Second Five-Year Plan began to bear fruit. Soviet heavy industry greatly expanded, light industry developed, consumer goods began to come into the shops, grain rationing was abolished. Posters in Moscow announced: 'Now, comrades, life is better, life is brighter.' And propaganda made the most of these successes. But it was in this very year that the long series of political and military purges began. 'Purge' is the soft name for torture and murder; in the history of the Soviet Union 'purge' signifies that the Communist form of totalitarianism can be as cruel as the Fascist form. Now, while propaganda dwelt on the splendours of the Moscow Underground, improved transport or new housing projects, the prisons and forced-labour camps filled to overflowing. By 1938 it has been estimated that some twelve million people had been arrested; about a million had been executed, and about two million more had died.

The 'Old Bolsheviks', the men who had helped Lenin to make the Revolution in 1917, great names in Soviet history like Kamenev, Zinoviev, Bukharin and Radek, were swept away. Accused of conspiring with the exiled Trotsky, spying for foreign powers, anti-Party activities, being 'enemies of the people', one by one they made their confessions and were shot. The purge spread to the armed forces, and by 1938 had practically crippled them. Out of fifteen Army commanders, two survived. Fifty-seven out of eighty-five Corps commanders were shot, 110 out of 195 divisional commanders. In all, between a quarter and a half of the officers of the Soviet armed forces were caught up in the purges. Once more, in the words of one of the old Socialist Revolutionaries who had struggled against the autocracy of the Tsars, the Russia of the people had become 'this great martyr of history'.

One thing was clear: Communism would not supply the cause that men of good will in Europe needed. There would have to be something else, another banner, to make the riflemen form against the various menaces of totalitarianism. As luck would have it, such a cause was about to appear: a cause which would sweep away disenchantments, unite unlikely bedfellows, and bring to an end a peace which had now gone stale.

Spain was not yet a tourist paradise. In early 1936 there were not many visitors, by today's standards, but there were some, and a few, like Louis MacNeice, heard or sensed the rumble of imminent eruption behind their holiday pleasures.

And next day took the boat
For home, forgetting Spain, not realising
That Spain would soon denote
Our grief, our aspirations;
Not knowing that our blunt
Ideals would find their whetstone, that our spirit
Would find its frontier on the Spanish front,
Its body in a rag-tag army.[70]

In July 1936 what might have seemed just another Spanish uprising in a long sequence of such events took place: this time a military revolt against the Republic which had replaced the monarchy in 1931. Spaniards themselves regarded the Civil War that followed as their own affair. Their memorial to it stands in what is called the Valle de los Caidos – The Valley of the Fallen – in the foothills of the Sierra Guadarrama outside Madrid. It is dedicated to all the Spaniards who fell in the Civil War. As the official guide-book puts it:

Our heroes are united in the humanist value of faith, brotherhood and love of the country for which they laid down their lives, and the great outstretched arms of the Cross embrace all Spaniards, without invidious distinctions, in its slender uprightness, like a lighthouse of faith, in memory of all those who lived up to their ideals in the name of Spain.[90]

The Civil War was a crisis in the various deep-seated antagonisms of Spanish society in 1936: antagonism of deeply-felt religious and anti-religious sentiments; antagonism of Spanish peasants and workers, living in crushing poverty, to rich landowners and bourgeoisie; antagonism of proud regional groups – Catalans and Basques – to any central Spanish government. These were all Spain's private business; but suddenly, in 1936, the world made Spain *its* business. Neither the Republican Government nor the group of Army officers (calling themselves the Nationalists) who had risen against it possessed the resources to defeat the other side quickly. This meant that the Civil War was bound to be a long one, and that it would take a heavy toll in human life: in the event, about a half a million dead. It also meant that both sides would have to look for outside help – and so the embroilment of Europe in Spain began.

Hitler and Mussolini soon saw in Spanish Nationalism under General Franco a potential ally; they supplied him with bombers and transport aircraft which performed a valuable service for him in bringing the army of Morocco over into Spain, despite the Government's command of the sea. After the machines came men to handle them. Italy's so-called volunteers in Spain rose to a maximum of 50,000; in reality they were members of the

'Goering's young Luftwaffe pilots found excellent training'. An air-raid in Spain, 1938 (Robert Capa)

Fascist militia. The Italian Air Force and the Italian Navy also gave considerable aid to General Franco. The German contribution rose to a maximum of about 10,000, including the famous Condor Legion, in which Goering's young Luftwaffe pilots found excellent training. So Germany and Italy fell into line beside each other in Spain. It was in November 1936 that their friendship was cemented in the proclamation of the 'Rome-Berlin Axis', which later became a formal treaty known as the 'Pact of Steel'. So the taking of sides, the forming of camps began, carrying Europe a further stage back towards the power blocs of 1914.

On a score of battlefields whose names were to become famous chapter-headings in European history, the Republic fought back against its enemies. The fighting was fierce and costly, and the Republic needed help – but where was that to come from? At first France supplied aircraft and some other weapons, but then both France and Britain became involved in the pious farce of 'non-intervention', an exercise of committees and paper agreements which was flouted at every point. While the democracies indulged in high-mindedness and cant, Hitler and Mussolini continued to pour arms and soldiers into Spain.

The Soviet dictator, Stalin, was not dissatisfied to see the Spanish Civil War continuing. It absorbed the attention of the Nazis and the Fascists, with the added attraction that it might also bring them into outright conflict with the democracies. So Stalin sold the Republic aircraft, tanks, guns and trucks, and sent 'advisers', men with names that would be heard again: Malinovsky, Rokossovsky, Konev. The Comintern threw all its propaganda weight behind the Republic, and at the same time manipulated Soviet aid as a lever for Communist control. The price of the Soviet help received was high (ultimately it would be fatal to the Popular Front Republic) – but where else would the Government find any help at all?

The answer lay in an extraordinary phenomenon: the riflemen of Europe, forming at last into what Louis MacNeice called in his poem 'a rag-tag army' – the International Brigades. These were Europe's Popular Front in action. Admittedly, they were organised by the Comintern, and always largely Communist, but they did represent all shades of the Left (and some of the Centre) – political parties, trade unions, students, individuals – who recognised the need to fight Fascism with something more than words. The forming of the International Brigades marked a turning-point for Europe's Left, a realisation that Fascism would not be deflected by pacifist idealism or talk of disarmament. Anti-Fascists needed arms. It was a painful moment of truth. Cecil Day-Lewis, who would many years later become England's Poet Laureate, expressed the compulsions of the International Brigadiers in 'The Volunteer':

Tell them in England, if they ask
What brought us to these wars,
To this plateau beneath the night's
Grave manifold of stars –
It was not fraud or foolishness,
Glory, revenge, or pay:
We came because our open eyes
Could see no other way.[30]

So the riflemen of Europe came to Spain – about 10,000 of them from France, 5000 from Germany and Austria, over 3000 from Italy, 1500 from Yugoslavia, 1000 from Hungary; altogether, something like 40,000 of them, from fifty-four countries. There was a 'Nine Nations Battalion'; there were two American battalions (so knocked about in the Battle of Brunete in 1937 that they had to be amalgamated). Some battalions took the names of national heroes: Garibaldi, Lincoln, Washington, Rakosi, Masaryk. A company of the British Battalion was called the Attlee Company, after the Leader of the Labour Party, later Prime Minister. The over-all commander of the Brigades was André Marty, a leading French Communist. Two Italians held key staff posts. An important military commander was a Rumanian, Lazar Stern, known in Spain as General Kléber.

Looking back, there is something tragic, even sickening, about that sudden international display of enthusiasm over Spain. Seventeen years of the League of Nations had produced no such solidarity. Seventeen years of Left-wing anti-militarism had done much to weaken the forces of international order, and so make the rise of the totalitarians possible. Seventeen years of general high-mindedness meant that the gesture came too late, and that these riflemen of Europe would have precious little except their rifles to oppose to totalitarian tanks and bombers. Yet, rightly or wrongly, nobly or absurdly, this microcosm of Europe in Spain was the outlet of enormous passions.

The Brigaders comprised all sorts. There were the politicals: Josip Broz, later better known as Marshal Tito, an International Brigade organiser at base in Paris; Willy Brandt, later Chancellor of West Germany, went as a reporter; Walter Ulbricht, later President of East Germany, went to 'investigate' Trotskyists; Clement Gottwald, later President of Czecho-slovakia, was a political adviser; Laszlo Rajk, Secretary-General of the Hungarian Communist Party, purged and executed in 1949, was there; so was Pietro Nenni, President of the Italian Socialist Party. There were the intellectuals: Arthur Koestler, the Hungarian-born Communist who later denounced Soviet Communism; Antoine de Saint-Exupéry, the French flyer and novelist who hated dictatorship, and would one day die fighting

215

'What Spain had meant for Europe had long been lost'.
Republicans fleeing into France in 1939 (Robert Capa)

it; George Orwell, the English writer who fought among the Trotskyists in Spain, and exposed Communist treachery towards them; André Malraux, writer, anti-Fascist, individualist, who later became Minister for Cultural Affairs in the Fifth French Republic. The roll-call of what is now called 'commitment' might take an hour to read. Perhaps the attitude of all these predominantly Left-wing intellectuals was best summed up by W. H. Auden in his famous poem, 'Spain, 1937':

Tomorrow for the young poets exploding like bombs,
The walks by the lake, the weeks of perfect communion;
Tomorrow the bicycle races
Through the suburbs on summer evenings. But today the struggle.*[4]

Today the struggle; and it was bitter indeed. The bloody epics multiplied: the defence of Madrid by the Republic, under the slogan 'No Pasaran!' – 'They shall not pass!'; the defence of the Alcazar at Toledo by the Nationalists, under the slogan 'Arriba España' – 'Long live Spain!' These were the great symbolic battlegrounds of the war, but there were many others as fiercely fought: Guadalajara, Brunete, the Ebro, Santander. And always the final ebb of battle favoured the Nationalists; steadily the Republic lost ground and strength, and outside Spain the enemies of the Republic and democracy prospered.

Indeed, democracy and its associated ideas of peaceful internationalism were now in total disarray. In Britain a new Prime Minister, Neville Chamberlain, made himself the embodiment of a policy of 'appeasement' which – whatever its motives – amounted simply to surrender to the dictators at every stage. On the other side there was also a significant change, a shift of power. The Italian 'volunteers' did not greatly distinguish themselves in Spain; Mussolini's bombast suffered its first deflation, and from being Hitler's mentor, he now sank to junior partner.

The muscular vigour of Hitler's Germany now loomed over the entire continent. Physical fitness was a Nazi fetish, and European newsreels and magazines regularly displayed bronzed young Germans cultivating 'strength through joy' – camping, climbing, walking, and generally singing what were unmistakably army marching songs. This image of youthful energy matched Hitler's forcible policies; already he was stirring up new threats of danger in Europe's tender places: the Polish Corridor, Czechoslovakia, Austria. It was Austria's fate to become the first victim of appeasement: in March 1938 she was absorbed, without a champion and without a struggle, into the German Reich. Disillusioned with democracy,

*Quoted by Hugh Thomas,[110] who points out that Auden later altered some of his writing on Spain in the thirties.

abandoned by all, the Viennese greeted with hysterical raptures the Austrian who always hated Vienna, now returned to be their absolute and terrible ruler.

In Spain the bombs still fell, the machine guns chattered, fresh blood smoked on the dry sierras, the martyrdom continued. In 1938 a shift in Soviet policy inevitably brought a shift in Comintern policy; in November the International Brigades withdrew from Spain. Dolores Ibarruri, the fiery Spanish Communist leader known as 'La Pasionaria', told them: 'You can go proudly. You are history. You are legend. . . .' So, indeed, they were: the legendary riflemen of Europe, returning, some to cherish undying memories of their epic days, others to the bitter disillusion which is so often the reverse side of a legend.

The Republic continued to shrink, the Nationalists continued to win, and Hitler and Mussolini continued to rejoice. In 1938 every Nationalist victory seemed to spell doom to democracy, but future years would show that the alliance of General Franco's Spain with Nazi Germany and Fascist Italy was more apparent than real. In any case, it was no longer in Spain that the crisis of Europe was now unfolding. The hot breath of Hitler's hatred now blew upon Czechoslovakia, the unfortunate child of Versailles, self-determination and high ideals. For a short – very short – time it looked as if democracy might stand firm beside the Czechs, and the sound of gunfire not only be heard in Spain. Men faced again the prospect of going to war for a small country threatened by aggression. They came to the idea with special consternation born of the years of disenchantment and mockery; in the words of Louis MacNeice:

. . . we who have been brought up to think of 'Gallant Belgium'
As so much blague
Are now preparing again to essay good through evil
For the sake of Prague . . .[70]

But nobody essayed anything for the sake of Prague. Democracy's muscles were still flabby, its nerves jangled. Instead of a fight there was farce: Berchtesgaden, Godesberg, Munich, confrontation of the umbrella and the cosh, appeasement's masterpiece. Czechoslovakia, not yet twenty years old, was dismembered. What was awful was the joy, the absolutely genuine joy of so many people in the West. War had seemed so close. The unthinkable, the unspeakable, the thing to be averted by all means – by disarmament, by conferences, by pacts and pledges – had been once again imminent, on today's agenda. And then, miraculously, instead Mr Chamberlain had produced 'Peace in our time' – with a piece of paper to prove it. The relief was enormous; Malcolm Muggeridge records:

Chamberlain dolls were offered for sale, and sugar umbrellas; in Scandinavia there was a movement to present him with a trout stream, in Portugal and France it was proposed to name streets after him.[81]

How ungracious, how unpleasant of Winston Churchill to say to the House of Commons: 'We have suffered a total and unmitigated defeat.'

The euphoria of Munich was short-lived, as Churchill's words came fearfully, speedily true: defeat after defeat for democracy. Now Spain was already receding from men's mind. On 15 March 1939 Hitler swallowed the remains of Czechoslovakia; German troops entered Prague, in derision of appeasement. Thirteen days later the Nationalists took Madrid, and the Spanish Civil War was virtually over. It was no longer important for Europe; what Spain had meant for Europe had long been lost. All that mattered was the symbol: the march of the Nationalists through the capital where so much of Europe's blood had been spilt resisting them seemed to many a clear and grievous sign of things to come. As though to underline the point, only ten days later Mussolini attacked Albania, and once more the Democracies were helpless to prevent aggression – indeed, they scarcely seemed to notice it.

Now all that could be asked was a little time – time to regain the lost years of trust in fine phrases and high ideals without the strength to uphold them. But time had run out. Britain and France looked belatedly to their weak armouries and took the inventory of all they lacked, the tally of lost power. And Hitler looked to his final tilt against the Europe of Versailles: his baleful eye was on Poland.

The few remaining months of peace between the fall of Prague and the attack on Warsaw passed like a bad dream. The entire Nazi propaganda apparatus was now directed ostensibly to the return of the free city of Danzig (administered by the League of Nations) to the Reich, but actually Hitler's object was nothing less than the destruction of Poland. Now, if past events seemed unbelievable, what followed was more so: the Democracies stiffened their fibres, and gave guarantees to Poland. But how could they fulfil them, at the opposite end of Europe? Only the Soviet Union could help Poland, and Poland refused Soviet aid. Yet Poland, unlike Czechoslovakia, meant to fight, with or without aid, if necessary with only her own outdated forces.

The Democracies reluctantly negotiated with the Soviet Union to form a joint front against Hitler, but Stalin had other ideas; he believed he had found a better offer. On 23 August the supremely unbelievable took place: a Non-aggression Pact between Nazi Germany and the Soviet Union. Supremely unbelievable, supremely cynical, this signature spelt the doom of Poland, the doom of peace. Nine days later the blitzkrieg on Poland

'Nobody essayed anything for
the sake of Prague'.
German soldiers entering Prague,
Spring 1939

opened, and for the second time in the century the mighty continent prepared for suicide.

It scarcely seemed possible; only twenty-one years had passed since the 'war to end wars'. Only twenty-one years since Lloyd George had greeted the coming of peace with the words:

I want to so build that when we are forgotten dust, in ages to come, men will look back and say of the men and women of this generation: 'They builded well.'

Indeed, they had tried, many of them, to build well; but in their search for good they had forgotten the power of evil.

Yet the human spirit is not easily quenched. Louis MacNeice uttered the message of surviving hope for Europe in 1939:

To-night we sleep
On the banks of Rubicon – the die is cast;
There will be time to audit
The accounts later, there will be sunlight later
And the equation will come out at last.[70]

'. . . to stamp out independent thought at the roots . . .' Max Beckmann. *Fastnacht Paris.* One of the 'decadent' painters persecuted by the Nazis

'The battle was fought in the summer skies'.
Paul Nash. *Battle of Britain 1941*

226

9 With hardship their garment

It is a rare thing, in history, to encounter a man as profoundly bad as his detractors say he is. It is hard to doubt that Adolf Hitler was such a man. For six quaking years Hitler held the threat of violence over Europe, sometimes bluffing, sometimes not. On 1 September 1939 all doubts were removed; the violence ceased to be a threat, it became reality. And it proved to be a violence unparalleled, a violence inconceivable.

On that Friday, 1 September, Hitler launched his tanks and Stuka dive-bombers against Poland. Less than three weeks later all organised Polish resistance had collapsed; Poland was a conquered country. Europe had seen, with amazement, a new style of war: lightning war – Blitzkrieg. The shock was all the greater because from 1914 to 1918 the Western Front had planted its static image in men's minds. Tedium and frustration had been major ingredients of that war:

Soldiers manned the same trenches for months – sometimes years – on end; took spells out of the line, and returned to the same dug-outs, the same saps, the same corpses, the same smells and dirt; they went on leave . . . and came back again to the old billet, the old mud, the old shelling and the old comrades, with a few more faces missing since they went away.[109]

That was the war: expedient after expedient failed, attack after attack withered in front of the interminable trench-lines that never seemed to move. And now, as though by magic, one single crushing onslaught by tanks and mechanical forces had overthrown a nation; Blitzkrieg spelt the return of speed to war.

Blitzkrieg also spelt destruction. In the First World War terrible damage had been done in the battle zones. A traveller in the first post-war train from Paris to Berlin described one of the shattered cities:

Street after street of ruined houses, at right angles to the line, ran radiating past us, and each street sparkled white in the moonlight with splinters of shivered glass or gleamed grey with the pallor of crumbling masonry. The ruins were wrapped in a winding sheet of mortar, fine as dust, but where the wind had winnowed in the deserted streets the mortar lay in drifts against the walls as thick as sand heaps. . . . Nothing moved in that wilderness of stone and dust, nor did any living thing appear. Even the rats had deserted it.[80]

Now air power turned whole countries into battle zones; any city, anywhere, could share this fate. It soon transpired that one average air raid, even in 1939, could be more devastating than weeks of First World War gunfire; villages were obliterated, cities crumbled quickly under this form of attack. When the Germans entered Warsaw on 28 September, one of their officers wrote:

I was shocked at what had become of the beautiful city I had known – ruined and burnt-out houses, starving and grieving people. The nights were already unpleasantly chilly and a pall of dust and smoke hung over the city, and everywhere there was the sweetish smell of burnt flesh. There was no running water anywhere. In one or two streets isolated resistance by Polish nationalist bands was being continued. Elsewhere everything was quiet. Warsaw was a dead city.[50]

The first of Europe's dead cities; the first of many.

In 1940 the Blitzkrieg was repeated – on an even larger scale. First Denmark and Norway were overrun; feeble British and French aid to Norway was brushed aside. Then the attack was aimed against France and Britain themselves and, as in 1914, it was launched through neutral countries – this time not only Belgium but Holland also was caught in the net of invasion. Now another city learned the brutal weight of modern war: to hasten Dutch collapse, the centre of Rotterdam was devastated by bombing. Holland's resistance lasted precisely four days. Then it was Belgium's turn; she lasted eighteen days.

Next came the turn of France, supposedly Europe's greatest military power, with an army of over five million men. But the French Army was a 1918-style army with 1918 ideas; it fought bravely enough, but it could not withstand the new weapons and the new methods of 1939. The Blitzkrieg burst out of the Ardennes, and down through northern France, sweeping across the battle zone where the First World War had stuck for four years in a matter of days, or even hours. The French Government fled to Bordeaux, and Paris was declared an open city, not to be defended. On 14 June, just five weeks from the beginning of their great offensive in the West, the Germans entered Paris while the world stood aghast, and one week later France surrendered. The German triumph – a specially personal triumph for Germany's Führer, Adolf Hitler – was apparently complete.

The unbelievable had now, with awful suddenness, become fact: Hitler was the master of most of Europe. The whole seaboard facing Britain was in his hands: Norway, Denmark, Holland, Belgium, the French Channel and Atlantic coasts were all occupied by German forces. He had conquered Poland, Italy was his ally; it seemed that nothing could stop him, if he wished to go on – and no one doubted that he did so wish. Yet he *was* stopped, at the narrow waters of the English Channel, which became the

'With hardship their garment'. Survivors of a bombing raid in Germany

228

new arena of European resistance, with long-range guns firing across it, and a decisive struggle being fought in the skies above.

The British, barring a few defeatists and a few home-grown Fascists, never contemplated giving in. Their strategic position, their military resources, their economic resources were alike hopeless. But fortunately, as Sir Basil Liddell Hart said, 'the British were instinctively stubborn and strategically ignorant'. Also, they had found a leader and a voice. Winston Churchill made the British declaration of intent on 4 June 1940, even before France fell; neither he nor his countrymen ever departed from it:

We shall defend our island, whatever the cost may be, we shall fight on the beaches, we shall fight on the landing grounds, we shall fight in the fields and in the streets, we shall fight in the hills; we shall never surrender . . .[23]

In the event, the battle was not fought on beaches, nor in streets nor hills; it was fought in the summer skies, chiefly over south-eastern England. The result, once more to the world's amazement, was the first defeat sustained by Germany in the war – defeat by a narrow margin, certainly, but defeat nevertheless. The failure of the Luftwaffe to destroy the Royal Air Force in the Battle of Britain, and the costly repulse of its daylight attacks on British targets, brought a gleam of hope to the conquered peoples of Europe. To the British themselves it brought at first a splendid, incredulous exhilaration, and then a grim ordeal.

September 15 was the peak day of the Battle of Britain; the next morning the British people read in their papers that RAF Fighter Command had shot down 185 German aircraft on that day. The cold reappraisal of history has since reduced the real figure to sixty[33] but coming at the end of two months' very hard fighting, sixty on one day was enough to bring about a decisive change of German strategy. The Luftwaffe now concentrated on night attacks on British cities, above all London. One by one the cities of Britain learned to share the fate of Warsaw and Rotterdam: Liverpool, the Clydeside, Coventry, Birmingham – the list was long, but always it was London that bore the chief brunt of this offensive.

By the end of 1941, over 40,000 British civilians had been killed, over 50,000 injured, and immense material damage had been done, to say nothing of the sad loss of architectural and other treasures. But the British, in Churchill's words, 'fought on with hardship their garment',[23] and in so doing gave new courage to Europe under Hitler's heel. And London had now become not simply the embattled capital of the British Empire, but also a microcosm of Europe's hope of freedom. To London, to share the bombs and all the beastliness, came those Europeans who refused to submit and found the means to escape the Nazi tyranny: Czechs, Poles, Norwegians, Dutch, Belgians and French. By radio from London, on the European

Service of the BBC, these exiles brought fresh hope and a new determination to fight to their less fortunate fellow-countrymen at home.

Now, at last, France also found a leader and a voice – though in June 1940 anyone might be forgiven for not perceiving that these were the roles that General Charles de Gaulle would more than adequately fill.

He himself at this stage, was unknown and virtually alone. He had no following and no organisation. He lacked all prestige. Indeed, apart from his will and his character, his only assets lay in the receptiveness of his British hosts to the improbable proposition that France, in his person, should be given an opportunity to fight on.[28]

On 18 June, four days before the French surrender, General de Gaulle addressed the people of France from a BBC studio:

Has the last word been said? Must we abandon all hope? Is our defeat final and irremediable? To those questions I answer – No! Speaking in full knowledge of the facts, I ask you to believe me when I say that the cause of France is not lost . . . Whatever happens, the flame of French resistance must not and shall not die.[31]

Brave words apart, for the time being the Nazi-Fascist Axis was evidently in the ascendant. In October 1940 Mussolini, having already helped to deliver the *coup de grâce* to France, attacked Greece. But Italy's much-vaunted military power, having displayed serious weaknesses in Spain, now proved to be a hollow sham; in Greece, as on other battlefields, the Italians met humiliating defeats. On this occasion Hitler was able to rescue them from their difficulties; in April 1941 another Blitzkrieg swept through Yugoslavia and on into Greece. In just over three weeks the Greek forces were smashed, despite British help, and two more countries were added to the string of Hitler's conquests.

Nazi Germany seemed invincible. All Western Europe as far as the Pyrenees (except for Switzerland) was under Hitler's domination; all Scandinavia except for Sweden and Finland (defeated and dominated by the USSR); all south-eastern Europe, because Hungary, Rumania and Bulgaria now became his allies. And yet, under this appearance of utter supremacy, there were signs of bad omen for the Nazis. Their conquest of Yugoslavia had been too easy; it was the Government which had capitulated so readily, not the people.

The peoples of Yugoslavia had so far known little of unity among themselves, but they began to find it in resisting the German and Italian invaders of their country. Fierce national and ideological dissensions split the Yugoslav resistance: the Chetniks, led by General Mihailovič, were supporters of the monarchy and largely Serbs; they were opposed by Partisans, left-wing groups led by the Communist and one-time International Brigade organiser, Josip Broz, based chiefly in Montenegro and

Bosnia. The Partisans proved to be the stronger, and Broz, under the name of Marshal Tito, built up Europe's most effective resistance movement, an army rising to about 200,000 men, a permanent drain on Germany's military strength. Mihailovič was in due course executed by the triumphant Partisans, but first pronounced for himself an obituary which could apply to millions of Europeans: 'I was caught in the storm of the world.'

With the first significant mutters of rebellion rising in the lands he had conquered, and with Britain still unconquered at his back, Hitler performed his most lunatic act: on 22 June 1941 he invaded the Soviet Union. It was now that the Second World War took on its aspect of unlimited savagery. All that had already happened – brutalities in Poland, destruction in Western Europe or the Balkans, the bombing of Britain – paled into insignificance beside the loss of life and the damage that was to come. The scale of the war suddenly expanded almost beyond comprehension: vast distances, vast numbers of men, vast masses of equipment – and vast casualties – became commonplace. On 22 June some three million German troops crossed the Soviet border along a front of over 1200 miles, backed by 2000 aircraft and over 3500 tanks. The Red Army faced this onslaught with four and three-quarter million men and over 10,000 tanks – less modern, but still a powerful force. Clearly the coming battles were going to see Blitzkrieg at its highest level.

The German objectives in their first thrust lay deep inside Soviet territory: Kiev and the Ukraine in the south, first Smolensk then Moscow in the centre, and Leningrad in the north. Everywhere the battles were bitter: in the five remaining months of 1941 the Germans admitted to losing 750,000 men, four times their rate of loss in the 'blood-bath' of Verdun in 1916; in the first year of the war the Soviet Union lost four and a half million. That was one third of the entire losses of all belligerents in the First World War: and there were three more years to go.

Leningrad symbolises Russian resistance to Hitler; here army and people together struggled to slow down the German advance. Nearly a million people of all professions came out to help in constructing defences; they dug 15,875 miles of trenches, 340 miles of anti-tank ditches, and laid down 400 miles of barbed wire. These certainly helped to prevent the Germans from rushing the city, but by September it was cut off from the rest of the Soviet Union by encircling armies. And now Leningrad became a fortress defended by soldiers and civilians alike; they built 4000 concrete pill-boxes in the outskirts and in the streets; they made 17,000 reinforced firing points inside houses; they put up fifteen miles of barricades across the streets. And so, by great courage and resolution, the Germans were stopped at last.

'Hitler performed his most lunatic act'. German tanks approaching Moscow, November 1941

The Germans were stopped, but three million people were trapped inside Leningrad for the winter. By November, famine had set in, and with it a serious fuel shortage. In December 52,000 people died; in January they were dying at the rate of 3500 – 4000 every day. The final total of the dead of Leningrad will probably never be precisely known; the official figure is 632,000, but the composer Dmitri Shostakovich, who was in the city during the siege and wrote a symphony to commemorate it, told Alexander Werth that 900,000 people had died.[118] Their memorial carries the inscription:

'We shall never forget anyone,
We shall never forget their deeds.'

This was total war as it had never been seen before – with an extra ingredient of horror. The invaders brought to this war in the Soviet Union all the cruelty and vileness of Nazi racial theories. Wherever their armies went their policy was to extinguish national culture; they tried to crush Russian thought and Russian life. Hitler ordered Leningrad to be 'wiped off the face of the earth', as though the sheer grandeur of this Russian city too contemptuously rebutted his idea of the Slavs as 'sub-human'. In the event, some forty per cent of Leningrad's homes were damaged in the siege, and 3000 buildings totally destroyed; the splendid imperial palaces near the city, Tsarskoye Selo, Pavlovsk and Peterhof, were reduced to filth and ruin. Now the ruins have been cleared and the buildings restored by loving hands, and the city of Peter the Great lives on.

In 1941 Europe's catastrophe became, as it had done in 1914-18, the catastrophe of the world. Already nations all over the world were drawn in: Canadians mustering in Britain, Australians, New Zealanders, South Africans and Indians gathering on the Mediterranean fronts. The Atlantic Ocean gave its name to a battle for Britain's very survival. In the Battle of the Atlantic over 3000 Allied ships and nearly 800 U-boats went to the bottom: all that ingenuity, all that skill, all that work, all those valuable cargoes, all those lives – just another part of the tally of destruction.

It was in December 1941 that Japan attacked America, so turning Southeast Asia and the Pacific Ocean into new battle arenas, but also – more significantly – releasing the mighty energies of America for full participation in Europe's war as well. Under President Roosevelt's guidance, America gave first priority, not to defeating Japan, as many Americans expected and desired, but to liberating Europe from Hitler. And this was just as well, because neither British nor Soviet industry (heavily damaged by the invasion), nor both together, could compete with the combined economic resources of Europe mobilised by Hitler. Only American production could offset that advantage – American production at a level that even took

'. . . a land full of treasures, now terribly vulnerable . . .'
American troops advancing in Sicily, 1943 (Robert Capa)

American breaths away. The US weapons programme for 1942 was: 45,000 aircraft, 45,000 tanks; 20,000 AA guns. For 1943: 100,000 aircraft; 75,000 tanks; 35,000 AA guns. Such a scale of production would transform the war – and the world after the war. In 1941 these astonishing figures were a wonderful omen, and yet, as Churchill perceived: 'Many dark and weary months of defeat and loss must be endured before the light would come again.'[23]

The expansion of American productivity was swift, yet over a year and a half went by before the equipment and forces were ready to begin the liberation of Europe from Hitler. The beginning was made in July 1943, with the Anglo-American landings in Sicily; the immediate result of this operation was the fall of the first of the dictators, Mussolini, the defection of Italy from the Axis, and in October her declaration of war on Germany. The Germans, however, continued to hold Italy, which now paid for the change of heart by becoming a battleground. As the Allies forced their way up towards Rome, through a land teeming with reminders of Europe's past, a land full of treasures, now terribly vulnerable, a new kind of dilemma faced them. The destruction of great cities, with their material wealth and industry, was all-too-familiar; but in Italy almost every little town, every village church, every hillside palazzo might contain some priceless or venerated object, some work of art whose loss could never be repaired.

The Abbey of Monte Cassino was such a place: a cradle of Western civilisation. It was founded by St Benedict in AD 529, and here the famous Benedictine Order was born. Here, during the Dark Ages, ancient literature was lovingly copied and preserved, linking Europe's classical past to her medieval and modern future. Twice the Abbey was destroyed by human hands: by the Lombards when it was only fifty years old, and by the Saracens 300 years later. Five centuries after that it was wrecked by an earthquake. But always it was carefully rebuilt, and new splendours added. Great craftsmen decorated it; its cathedral became an architectural wonder. In 1943 the hill of Monte Cassino, the Abbey on top of it, and the bustling market town at its foot, together became a key point in the German defence of the Italian peninsula. A Dark Age had returned, and the Battle of Monte Cassino would now reveal the price of Europe's liberation in modern currency. The Abbey, in particular, took on a significance that would have surprised its founder. A British soldier wrote:

Everybody has experienced the sensation, when walking alone past a house, that invisible eyes were watching from a darkened interior. Hostile eyes can be sensed without being seen, and the soldier develops an exceptional awareness of this. Monte Cassino projected this feeling over an entire valley, and the feeling was being substantiated all the time by gunfire that could only have been so accurate and so swiftly opportunist through being directed by quite exceptionally positioned observers. . . . To the soldiers dying at its feet, the Monastery had itself become in a sense the enemy.[72]

It was an irony that the German officer commanding the Cassino sector, General von Senger und Etterlin, was himself a devout Catholic. It was an irony that the Germans had, in fact, 'neutralised' the Abbey as the battle began. Von Senger says:

On our side it was the considered tactical opinion that so conspicuous a landmark would be quite unsuitable as an observation post, since we could expect it to be put out of action by heavy fire very soon after the big battle had started. It was the German practice to place the artillery observers half way up the hills in a concealed position with a camouflaged background.[98]

It was one of the most cosmopolitan of Allied armies that stood in front of Monte Cassino. There were Poles, fighting furiously to avenge their conquered country – at a cost of nearly 4000 officers and men, a third of them killed; there were Americans, British and Indians, French, Algerians, and Moroccans, Canadians and New Zealanders. With one voice they demanded the elimination of the Abbey. In the words of General Kippenberger, commanding the New Zealand Division:

It was impossible to ask troops to storm a hill surmounted by an intact building such as this, capable of sheltering several hundred infantry in perfect security from shellfire and ready at the critical moment to emerge and counter-attack. I was in touch with our own troops and they were very definitely of the opinion that the Abbey must be destroyed before anyone was asked to storm the hill.[72]

The pressures mounted, and the Supreme Allied Commander, General Sir Harold Alexander, found himself faced with a critical decision. In his Memoirs seventeen years later he wrote:

. . . when soldiers are fighting for a just cause and are prepared to suffer death and mutilation in the process, bricks and mortar, no matter how venerable, cannot be allowed to weigh against human lives . . . the commanding general must make it absolutely clear to his troops that they go into action under the most favourable conditions he has the power to order. . . . The monastery had to be destroyed.[2]

Accordingly, on 15 February 1944, the Abbey of Monte Cassino was pounded for several hours by Allied heavy and medium bombers. Fortunately the movable treasures had gone, taken to safety by the Germans. Fortunately the abbot, the monks and the refugees inside the Abbey acted on the warning they received and left in time. Fortunately, by a miracle, the tomb of St Benedict was undamaged. But this great building, spanning fourteen hundred years of European history, was reduced to a vast heap of broken stones. And – final irony – the military gain was nil; General von

Senger wrote: 'Now we could occupy the Abbey without scruple, especially as ruins are better for defence than intact buildings.'[98]

This, then, was a part of the price of liberation. When General Alexander took his hard decision to allow the bombing of the Abbey, there was little hope and certainly no guarantee that any of Monte Cassino's splendours could ever be recreated. In fact, a magnificent effort of restoration has been made, and St Benedict's legacy survives as it survived the Saracens and the Lombards. But in 1944 the dilemma was very real, and the questions were cruel: how much destruction would liberation require? How many more Monte Cassinos would be needed? How many could Europe afford?

The hope – the sole hope – of liberation for Europe lay in the Grand Alliance (the highly unlikely and often unhappy alliance, in which Hitler could never bring himself to believe) between Britain, the United States and the Soviet Union. Nazi Germany remained to be defeated, and the policy of the Grand Alliance towards Nazi Germany was contained in one grim phrase: 'Unconditional Surrender'. That phrase conveyed detestation of Hitler, detestation of Nazism in all its aspects, and determination to overthrow both the man and the system he had made. But it conveyed little of hope for Germans who also hated Hitler, and it promised a great deal more destruction in Europe.

By now the Allied Air Forces were striking at Germany herself. Already in May 1942 there had been a sign of what was to come when 1074 RAF bombers raided Cologne – the first of the thousand-bomber raids. In 1943 the Strategic Air Offensive approached its zenith: American Flying Fortresses and Liberators by day, and British Lancasters, Halifaxes and Wellingtons by night, brought to the cities of Germany the message of Warsaw, Rotterdam, London, Belgrade, Leningrad.

In July 1943 the RAF launched two successive attacks on the port of Hamburg, and it was these raids that introduced the awful phenomenon of the fire-storm. A deluge of incendiaries heated the air in the city which, as it swirled up, created gales mounting to a force of 150 miles per hour; as these swept through the streets, in turn they fanned the flames to furnace heat. The Hamburg Police President wrote in his report:

Escape from the sea of flame seemed already impossible. . . . The fire had become a hurricane which made it impossible in most cases to reach the open . . . to cover long distances in the red-hot streets of leaping flames was impossible. . . . The destruction was so immense that of many people literally nothing remains . . .[115]

Seventy per cent of the total area of Hamburg (6200 acres) were laid waste; 40,000 people were killed, and nearly a million rendered homeless. General Galland, famous fighter pilot, then commanding the German Air Defences, wrote:

238

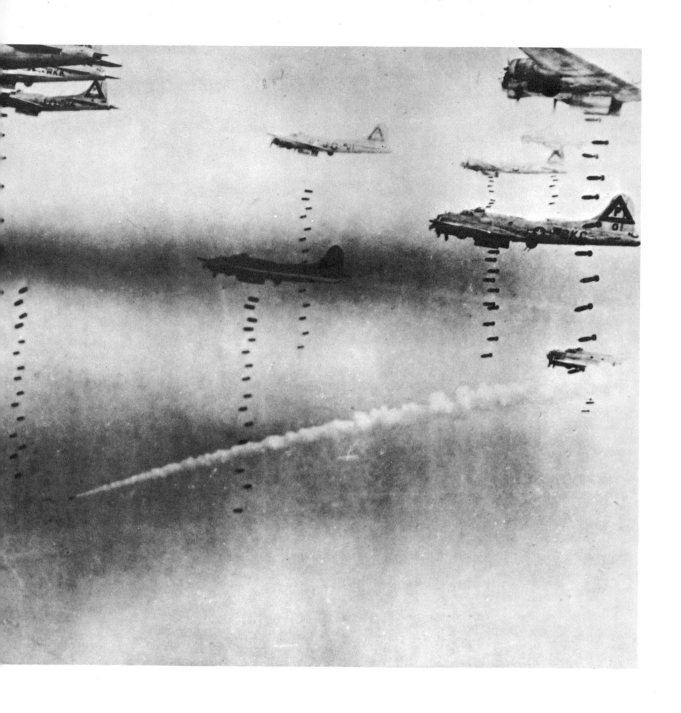

'He who has forgotten how to weep, learns again at
Dresden's ruin'. Allied bombers over Dresden, 13 February 1945

A wave of terror radiated from the suffering city and spread through Germany. Appalling details of the great fire were recounted. The glow of fires could be seen for days from a distance of 120 miles. A stream of haggard, terrified refugees flowed into the neighbouring provinces. In every large town people said: 'What happened to Hamburg yesterday can happen to us tomorrow'. . . . Psychologically the war at that moment had perhaps reached its most critical point. . . . After Hamburg in a wide circle of the political and military command could be heard the words: 'The war is lost'.[41]

The cities of the Ruhr, the German industrial centres, the oil-producing plants, the capital, one by one they sustained the impact of the air offensive. The roll-call swelled: Cologne, Essen, Düsseldorf, Nuremberg, Mannheim, Stuttgart, Munich, Berlin – and Berlin again and again in costly assaults through the winter of 1943-44. The climax of this strategy of destruction came with the devastation of Dresden in February 1945. The poet Gerhart Hauptmann watched Dresden burning for five days, and wrote: 'He who has forgotten how to weep, learns again at Dresden's ruin.'

The world was not yet ready to weep in 1944; it was still a time of anger. For Europe it was also a time of mounting destruction, in Italy, in Austria, in Germany, in Britain and in France. For now the moment was approaching for the great Anglo-American re-entry into North-West Europe, and the way was being prepared by bombs. On the German side, the secret V-weapons were reaching readiness: soon V-1 'flying-bombs' and V-2 rockets, directed at England, would add their quota to the general wreckage. The invasion itself would have something more to add.

Behind the massive fortifications of Hitler's 'Fortress Europe', men awaited the coming of the Allies with mixed emotions. The state of the war had now completely changed: Germany, hammered from the air, was also being hammered on the Eastern Front. The disaster of Stalingrad had cost an entire army, and after Stalingrad one Russian offensive after another forced the Germans back towards their Fatherland. With the pressures on the Nazi system mounting everywhere, a heavy blow in the West could be decisive. It was for this reason that the coasts of Belgium and north-western France were protected by the elaborate defences known as the Atlantic Wall, built by slave labour under the direction of the Todt Organisation. In these batteries and bunkers the Germans waited with apprehension, and beyond those ramparts the peoples of Occupied Europe waited with mounting hope.

The blow fell on 6 June 1944: D-Day. Everywhere there was the immediate sense of what one of its American historians has called a 'mighty endeavour'.[69] But it was only much later that the full details of all the technical ingenuity and organisational skill that had made the landings possible

'It was still a time of anger'. A Soviet soldier surrenders to the Germans

were revealed. There was, to begin with, the invasion armada itself: nearly 5000 ships and landing craft of all descriptions, protected by about 900 warships. There was the sheer audacity of planning to land 150,000 men and 1500 tanks in the first 48 hours. There was PLUTO, the Pipe Line Under The Ocean which was to bring in the flood of petrol that the armies would need in order to fight and then advance into Europe. But above all there was the almost impertinent stroke of imagination which produced that astonishing construction, the Mulberry Harbour.

It was calculated that once ashore the Allies would need to bring in 12,000 tons of stores and 2500 vehicles every day. How could this be done? All past experience and fresh knowledge indicated that it would be a long time before they captured – and cleared – a French port large enough to handle this traffic. So the idea was evolved of bringing their ports with them, towing the monstrous breakwaters and floating quays across the Channel. In the event, they brought two Mulberries, each making a port about the size of Dover. It was only intended that the Mulberries should be used for three summer months; in fact, the British Mulberry was in use for eight months. Its American counterpart, further to the west, was destroyed in a terrible gale only a fortnight after D-Day, so the British harbour had to do double duty. In the course of its active life, two and a half million men, half a million vehicles and four million tons of supplies were landed through it, figures which give some idea of the irresistible material strength at the disposal of the Allied Supreme Commander, General Eisenhower.

Now there was a stirring of hope and action throughout Occupied Europe. Directed by radio from London, to the sound of the famous 'V' signal, the European resistance movements rose for the long-prepared battle against the Nazi oppressors. The resistance groups ambushed convoys, disrupted communications, attacked headquarters and destroyed supplies. Their activities helped to complicate the already difficult problems of the German command, and, as always, the Germans undertook savage reprisals against the civilian population.

At Oradour-sur-Glane, a quiet village near Limoges, on a dreadful Saturday afternoon only four days after D-Day, troops of the SS 'Das Reich' Division carried out an appalling and senseless massacre. The SS men arrived without warning, and without explanation they ordered all the women and children they could find into Oradour's church, and all the men into a number of barns. They then proceeded to shoot them all down, and set fire to the buildings. One woman survived, and five men; 642 men, women and children were murdered. And Oradour had never been a resistance centre. Perhaps it was all a mistake, but a mistake of a kind that

'The message of Warsaw, Rotterdam, London, Belgrade, Leningrad'.
Henry Moore. Shelter drawing. 1941

can only be made by an abominable regime based on an abominable philosophy.

Fittingly, the great triumph of the French Resistance was Paris. In June 1940 Paris had fallen without a fight; in August 1944 it was the proud boast that 'Paris liberated herself'. It was not quite true: General Leclerc's Free French armoured division had a substantial part to play. But it is true (and important) that Paris was liberated by Frenchmen, and their memorials are scattered through the streets where they fought for freedom. A new France was arising, and on 25 August 1944 Paris became acquainted with France's new leader, General de Gaulle, whose name and person were living denials of defeat, surrender and collaboration. New nation and new leader would not always be on the best of terms, but in 1944 the enemy was still entrenched on French soil, and that was enough to unite Frenchmen; victory over Germany was all that mattered.

And victory seemed to be approaching rapidly. In September Brussels was liberated. Soon the great port of Antwerp would be cleared. The Allies advanced into Holland (and the name of Arnhem became a new, sad battle honour of the British airborne troops). Strasbourg was freed by the French. The Russians were all over Eastern Europe and already fighting on German soil. It was evident that the end of the second European catastrophe was not far off. In the West one large obstacle remained: the Rhine, the great river whose name is woven into German patriotic legends and songs:

'Who'll guard the Rhine, the German Rhine,
To whom shall we the task assign?'
Dear Fatherland, no fear be thine,
Firm stand thy sons to guard the Rhine.[96]

But in March 1945 the Watch on the Rhine faltered. At Remagen the Americans crossed the river by a railway bridge which the demolition charges failed to destroy, and further north the British poured across in an amphibious operation as elaborate as a sea-crossing. The Rhine barrier was breached in the West; the Russians were threatening Berlin itself. Hitler's vaunted 'Thousand-Year Reich' was shrinking visibly each day.

In April, both Americans and British made terrible discoveries about the nature of their enemy. On 11 April the Americans reached the concentration camp of Buchenwald; four days later the British reached Belsen. Richard Dimbleby, BBC War Correspondent, reported:

I've seen many terrible sights in the last five years, but nothing, nothing approaching the dreadful interior of this hut in Belsen. The dead and the dying lay close together. I picked my way over corpse after corpse in the gloom. . . . Down

Belsen, 1945

the passage and in the hut there were the convulsive movements of dying people too weak to raise themselves from the floor. They were crawling with lice and smeared with filth. They'd had no food for days, for the Germans sent it down into the camp en bloc and only those strong enough to come out of the huts could get it. The rest of them lay there in the shadows growing weaker and weaker. There was no one to take the bodies away when they died, and I had to look hard to see who was alive and who was dead. . . . Some of the poor starved creatures whose bodies were there looked so utterly unreal and inhuman that I could have imagined that they had never lived at all. They were like polished skeletons, the skeletons that medical students like to play practical jokes with . . .[35]

Now all the world – including Germany – had to recognise the truth about the Nazi regime – a truth already discovered by the Russians at Auschwitz, Maidanek and other camps in the East, but still widely disbelieved in the West. There was no disbelieving Belsen. There the British Army found 10,000 unburied corpses in April 1945, and 40,000 starving and disease-ridden survivors, many of whom would also shortly die. This was only a sample, by no means the worst of what was now to be revealed in Germany. The network of concentration camps (over 300 of them) ran right across the Nazi empire, and their tragic inmates were collected from every part of it. These camps were the true symbol of Hitler's Reich, and of its twin foundations, bigotry and brutality.

It is indeed a rare thing in history to find a man as truly bad as his detractors say he is. The man who, by the projection of his own personality, created the state, the system of government based upon the concentration camps was Adolf Hitler, now fifty-six years old. This method of rule (which we may choose to call maniacal) was always implicit in Hitler's philosophy. As early as the 1920s, when he was presenting himself to the German people as a simple patriot and reformer, the hideous idea was in his mind: the idea of racial extermination. There were always two opposite images of Hitler visible – for those who cared to look. One the one hand, there was the man who loved children, dogs, young people, the simple life; on the other, there was the seam of sadistic violence which inspired the formation of the Brownshirts, the Nazi Storm Troops who won 'the battle of the streets' by intimidation, beating and murder. A very large number of Germans thought of Hitler as a good German comrade, but to many others he was no comrade at all. Several hundred thousand Germans – a small percentage of the population, but a significant number of human beings – were sent to concentration camps, men as various as the Social Democrat Kurt Schumacher, the aristocrat Prince Leopold of Prussia, or the churchman Pastor Niemöller. In a steady stream those who opposed or were suspected of opposing Hitler's regime passed through the

'The man who loved children, dogs, young people'

gateways of the camps. Few returned; thousands died in horrible conditions.

The Brownshirts gave Hitler his victory, and thought that they would be the future rulers of Germany. They were mistaken. In June 1934 Hitler had the Storm Troop leader, Röhm, and many of his associates killed. The SA was broken, and real authority inside the system was transferred to the SS* under Heinrich Himmler. This was a man as fanatical and demented as Hitler himself, and fully sharing his racial theories. To Himmler and the SS fell the task of wiping out Europe's 'lesser races', above all the Jews. This was Himmler's doctrine, as later propounded to the SS leaders:

Anti-semitism is exactly the same as delousing. Getting rid of lice is not a question of ideology, it is a matter of cleanliness. In just the same way, anti-semitism for us had not been a question of ideology but a matter of cleanliness which now will soon have to be dealt with. We shall soon be deloused. We have only 20,000 lice left, and then the matter is finished off within the whole of Germany.[25]

The chief extermination camp for Jews in Nazi-occupied Europe was Auschwitz in Poland. The camp commandant, Rudolph Höss, estimated that two and a half million Jews from all over Europe were gassed and burnt there, while another half million died of starvation and disease. Altogether some four million Jews were murdered in concentration camps, and another two million by mobile SS execution squads. This was just one aspect of Hitler's 'New Order'.

It is a fact that, unlike 1914, Germany did not enter the war with enthusiasm in 1939. But the quick, easy victories of the early days, the triumphs of the Blitzkrieg, were Hitler's vindication, and after the fall of France he became a national hero indeed. There seemed to be nothing that he and Germany could not do together. The German race would be truly a 'master race' under this infallible leader, and there were many who relished this prospect. For the other races of Europe, particularly in the East, the German victories meant unlimited horror. Hundreds of thousands of Russian and Polish prisoners of war and civilians were marched off, contrary to all international convention, to slavery. Himmler explained his attitude to this policy for the benefit of SS generals in 1942:

One basic principle must be the absolute rule for the SS man: we must be honest, decent, loyal and comradely to members of our own blood and to nobody else. What happens to a Russian, to a Czech, does not interest me in the slightest. . . . Whether nations live in prosperity or starve to death interests me only in so far as we need them as slaves for our Kultur; otherwise it is of no interest to me. Whether 10,000 Russian females fall down from exhaustion while digging an

*Schutz Staffeln (Protective Squads)

248

anti-tank ditch interests me only in so far as the anti-tank ditch for Germany is finished.[25]

From France, from Belgium, from Holland, Norway, Yugoslavia, people were snatched away for forced slave labour inside Germany. By 1945 there were some seven million slaves working in German industry and agriculture. Some classes of deportees were marked as available to be worked to death, and were indeed worked to death without mercy. Not even the barbarian invasions of the Dark Ages, nor the cruelties of the Thirty Years War exceeded this.

Now the end of the nightmare was in sight. In the last days of April 1945 Hitler's empire had shrunk to a few streets. He himself had also shrunk; no longer a semi-divinity in the eyes of the German people, he was also diminished physically (and even more mentally) by the attempt on his life by a few brave Army officers in July 1944. He resisted still, in his bomb-proof bunker in Berlin, but the 'Thousand Year Reich' had now only a matter of days to go, and Hitler's life-span was ebbing with it. His is not a story for pity. All the loss of life in Europe since 1939, all the damage, the irretrievable destruction of a culture, the deaths of cities, the devastation of whole countries, had this for their justification: the wiping out, utterly, of Hitler's horrible regime. This, for millions and millions of people in 1945, was the only thing to live for. This was what Liberation had to mean, and no price was too high.

'The Germans have been punished, but
not enough'. A German officer, 1945

Human rights and fundamental freedoms

In 1919 a nation had been reborn. The Kingdom of Poland had vanished from the map of Europe in 1795, partitioned between her three greedy and ruthless neighbours, the Russian Empire, the Austro-Hungarian Empire and the Kingdom of Prussia. The Treaty of Versailles brought Poland back to life, amid much rejoicing. But the new state, the focus of great hope and enthusiasm, only lasted twenty years. In 1939 Poland was partitioned again, between the conquering Germans and Soviet Russia.

Half of Poland was now occupied by the Soviet Union, which took back everything that had once belonged to Imperial Russia – and a little more besides. Soviet rule under Stalin surpassed the oppression of the Tsars which had previously kept Poland in a state of continual ferment. About one and a half million Poles were now deported from the Soviet Zone of occupation, many of them to forced labour, some to a worse fate. Among those deported in this way were between twelve and fifteen thousand officers and NCOs of the Polish Army who had surrendered to the Russians. These men vanished completely; it was impossible to discover what had become of them: the Soviet Government denied all knowledge of their existence or whereabouts. But much later, in 1943, mass graves were discovered by the Germans in the Forest of Katyn, near Smolensk. Naturally, Nazi propaganda seized upon this discovery as a chance to mask the brutalities of Nazi conquest itself; but making all due allowances on that score, there remain clear indications that these graves did contain the bodies of several thousand Polish officers who had been murdered (whether deliberately or through inhuman error) by the Soviet Secret Police.

For twenty-one months the Poles endured the tyranny of two invaders. Then, in June 1941, the Nazis turned on their Soviet allies. The Russians were expelled from Poland and driven back deep into their own territory. At first, overwhelmed by defeat after defeat, it seemed unlikely that the Soviet Union itself would survive, let alone recover the strength to reassert its domination over Poland. Yet the day might come . . .

And sure enough, the day did come: in July 1944 once more Russian armies arrived on Polish soil, this time in hot pursuit of the defeated Germans. It was high time the Germans were driven out; Poland's sufferings, since that dreadful moment of Nazi occupation in 1939, had been terrible.

Hitler, in the earliest days of his invasion, explained his policy for Poland to his lieutenants:

There should be one master only for the Poles – the German: two masters side by side cannot and must not exist and therefore all representatives of Polish intelligentsia are to be exterminated. This sounds cruel but such is the law of life.[25]

Part of Poland was accordingly annexed to Germany, and about one and a half million of its inhabitants were deported as slave labour. Both in this zone and in the 'Government-General', the Nazi name for the rest of Poland, which they treated as a kind of colony without rights, millions of Poles were murdered. Their property was always liable to confiscation. They were regarded as 'sub-human'.

The spirit of Poland, however, could not be crushed; in the very hour of defeat, a resistance movement came to life. This took its political orders from the Government in exile in London, headed first by General Sikorski (until his death in September 1943) and afterwards by Stanislaw Mikolajcyk. The military side of Polish resistance took two forms: regularly-constituted Polish air, land and sea units fighting beside the Western allies, and an underground force in Poland itself called the Home Army, also taking its orders from London. Secret factories made arms and ammunition for the Home Army. Clandestine radio receivers and transmitters and underground newspapers kept Poles in touch with the outside world. So the Polish spirit was sustained, waiting for its day, waiting for Liberation, which, in July 1944, seemed to be at hand.

By the end of July the leading Russian units were on the Vistula within sight of Warsaw. During the next few days they established three bridgeheads over the river close to the city; their nearest airfield was no more than twenty minutes' flying time away. The Germans, at this stage, appeared to be in total disorganisation. And precisely at this juncture – on 29 July – a Soviet broadcast in Polish was recorded by the BBC Monitoring Service at Caversham:

No doubt Warsaw already hears the guns of the battle, which is soon going to bring her liberation. Those who have never bowed their heads to the Hitlerite power will again, as in 1939, join battle with the Germans, this time for decisive action. . . . Poles, the time of liberation is at hand. Poles, to arms! There is not a moment to lose.[103]

This seemed to be the cue for the Polish Resistance to rise against the invader in Warsaw as the French Resistance was to do in Paris later that very month. Accordingly, on 1 August, the Home Army, some 40,000 strong, sprang into action; the battle for Warsaw was on. From the first it was a hopelessly uneven fight. Even against weakened German forces in

'It was high time the Germans were
driven out'. An SS raid in Warsaw

253

retreat, the Poles, lacking heavy weapons and supplies of all descriptions, would have been at a disadvantage that only immediate Russian help could redress. But now the Germans made an unexpected rally. They rushed tank divisions to Warsaw, counter-attacked the Russians with great vigour, and mercilessly set about reducing the city.

The Polish Government appealed to Stalin for Russian aid. Winston Churchill and President Roosevelt appealed to Stalin on behalf of the hard-pressed Home Army. But no Russian help appeared. Perhaps, as Marshal Rokossovsky told the BBC Correspondent Alexander Werth, it was because 'even the Red Army gets tired after a while'. Perhaps, as the Marshal admitted, some Soviet correspondents and propagandists had been far too optimistic at the end of July. Perhaps there was more to it. At any rate, on 16 August, after a bloody fortnight in Warsaw, Stalin told Churchill: 'The Soviet Command has come to the conclusion that it must dissociate itself from the Warsaw adventure, as it cannot take either direct or indirect responsibility for the Warsaw action.'[23]

The rest of August passed, and, unbelievably, the battle continued through September. Above ground, and finally in the sewers, the fight to the death went on. But Warsaw was doomed, and Stalin wept no tears at that.

Sooner or later [he said] the truth about the group of criminals who have embarked on the Warsaw adventure in order to seize power will become known to everybody. These people have exploited the good faith of the inhabitants of Warsaw.[23]

The Russians would not even allow Allied aircraft to use Soviet airfields for supply drops into Warsaw until the battle was almost over. Marshal Rokossovsky told Alexander Werth: 'We just don't want any British and American planes mucking around here just at the moment.'[118] And so at last, on 2 October, after two heroic and tragic months, the few survivors of the Home Army were forced to surrender.

The immediate reckoning of the Rising in 1944 was about a quarter of a million people killed in Warsaw. Hitler, in a rage, ordered the utter destruction of the city; he wanted it to be wiped off the map. The remaining population was removed; nine-tenths of the city was demolished. And Stalin knew that buried under the rubble was the last hope of opposition to the new Soviet conquest of Poland.

It was in the months of the Warsaw Rising that the gates of Eastern Europe were opened to the Russians by a bold act in an unexpected quarter. Rumania, under a semi-Fascist government, had been the most active of Hitler's allies on the Eastern Front. Half a million Rumanians became casualties, fighting for the Germans; but by August 1944 Rumania had

had enough. And suddenly the young King Michael stepped out from the wings of the political stage, arrested the Government leaders, and ordered the Army to cease fire. Two days later Rumania changed sides and declared war on Germany. For these services King Michael was awarded the highest Soviet decoration, the Order of Victory. Rumania now became the launching-pad for a series of Russian drives into South-east and Central Europe. The first stage was Bulgaria, another ally of Hitler, but never officially at war with the Soviet Union. This awkward formality was soon attended to: on 5 September the Soviet Union declared war on Bulgaria, Bulgaria surrendered at once, and on 6 September declared war on Germany. Political matters are not often arranged so easily.

The Russian advance continued irresistibly into Yugoslavia. Here the situation was different – and outwardly even more favourable for the expansion of Soviet power. The Communist-directed Partisan Movement, led by that redoubtable Comintern veteran, Marshal Tito, was a powerful military force which had already succeeded in liberating large areas from German occupation. When Belgrade was freed in October, Red Army and Partisans marched through the Yugoslav capital together. The full significance of this sharing of the honours was not immediately apparent; at the time all that was obvious was that Soviet power had spread right across the Balkans.

Already Soviet imperialism under Stalin had achieved more than generations of Russian Imperial statesman had even dared to contemplate. But in the days of the Tsars, of course, there had always been a solid counter-weight to Russian influence in South-eastern Europe: the Habsburg Empire. When that empire ceased to exist, both Austria and Hungary were very much reduced by the Peace Treaties, and three million Hungarians found themselves living under foreign rule – a fertile source of grievance between the wars. In 1939 the Government of Admiral Horthy joined the Anti-Comintern Pact and threw in its lot with Hitler's Germany. Hungary received some of her lost territory back – but at a price. The Hungarians were to discover that while it was not too bad to be Hitler's ally when Germany was winning, when the tide turned they would be expected to share the sacrifices. Their Second Army was wiped out beside von Paulus's Sixth Army at Stalingrad, and altogether Hungary lost 150,000 men on Hitler's behalf. By the end of 1944 the Hungarians would have been well pleased to opt out of the whole business, speedily if not gracefully, as the Rumanians and Bulgarians had done; but that was not permitted. The Germans had to make a stand somewhere, and Hungary was the appointed place.

As the Russians advanced into Hungary fierce battles took place all over the country; Budapest itself became the scene of one of the fiercest of all. The Soviet Army arrived on the outskirts of the city in December 1944, and began to fight its way into Pest, advancing towards the Danube in bitter street fighting whose progress was measured street by street, sometimes house by house. Across the Danube, in the old fortress-town of Buda, German SS troops and some Hungarian supporters put up a bitter resistance for two months. By the end of that time much of Pest was badly damaged, all the Danube bridges were down, and historic old Buda was practically destroyed. Today's city is yet another of Eastern Europe's miraculous, faithful reconstructions, not yet completed, but already beginning to acquire a little of the patina of age.

Western Europe knew little about the sufferings of Hungary in 1945, and cared less. The Russians were still thought of as gallant allies. There was deep admiration for their hard fight against the invasion in 1941 and 1942, and for the wonderful recovery after Stalingrad which was now carrying them from one victory to another. The names of a new galaxy of Soviet marshals – Zhukov, Rokossovsky, Malinovsky, Tolbukhin, Vatutin, Vasilevsky and the rest – became familiar far beyond the confines of their profession. Europe had not seen such a blaze of military talent since Napoleon's marshals had carried the French eagles to Austerlitz and beyond. There was a state of euphoria in the West in early 1945; Europeans were delighted to hear of the Soviet victories and not yet ready to think seriously about what the aftermath might be, when Soviet military power became an immovable, permanent reality in Eastern and Central Europe.

It was in February 1945 that the Allied leaders met at Yalta in the Crimea. Under the well-polished surface of ambiguous communiqués and amiable poses, the Yalta Conference concealed serious discords. In after years it would be compared with Munich. At Yalta the unhappy fate of Poland was decided: she would be abandoned to Stalin's tender mercy by Britain and America. (How tender this mercy would be was soon seen, in March, when seventeen non-Communist Polish leaders, travelling under a Soviet safe conduct, were arrested and imprisoned in Moscow where some of them died.) At Yalta fatal understandings about 'spheres of influence' in Eastern Europe were reached, and the wide gap which was developing in the 'special relationship' between Winston Churchill and President Roosevelt made itself felt.

Roosevelt was now a dying man. The great American war leader, whose voice and actions had brought hope to millions of Europeans in their dark hours, now seemed strangely different. At Yalta his attitudes towards his chief allies seemed to change. The famous American democrat, the sup-

'. . . a powerful military force which had already succeeded in liberating large areas . . .' Marshal Tito at a partisan HQ in 1942

porter of European freedom, appeared to think that the dictator Stalin would be a better collaborator in building a democratic world order after the war than Churchill. When Roosevelt and Churchill had met at Placentia Bay in 1941 and proclaimed the war aims of democracy in the Atlantic Charter, they had asserted 'the right of all peoples to choose the form of government under which they will live'. But now, in 1945, it seemed that Churchill had become the personification of British and European imperialism, which in Roosevelt's belief were very bad things. And so, ironically, he seemed to see the postwar threat to human rights and fundamental freedoms coming, not from Stalin, who had never believed in them, but from Churchill, who had been their champion. It was a sad change – with depressing implications for Europe.

Even more depressing were the implications for the British Empire, which was now staging a remarkable recovery, but obviously faced serious future difficulties. The British were now reversing (with powerful American support) the extraordinary run of Japanese victories over the European empires in the Far East in 1942. In that disastrous year, after the attack on the American Fleet at Pearl Harbor on 7 December 1941, the Japanese had wiped out the British and Dutch empires in South-east Asia. Hong Kong, Malaya, Borneo and northern New Guinea were quickly overrun. In February 1942 the British base at Singapore fell, the greatest British disaster of the Second World War, the greatest in history. The Dutch lost Java, Sumatra and the rest of their East Indian empire. Next came the conquest of Burma, which was occupied right up to the frontiers of India and China by the middle of May. The Japanese seemed to be unbeatable.

It was the speed of it all that was so staggering: every news bulletin on the radio, every morning's newspaper seemed to have a fresh story of defeat in the Far East. What it amounted to was the extinction of mighty European empires in under six months – and what could be done about it? As far as the British planners were concerned, surveying the innumerable problems of the war in distant London, the answer was: 'very little'. Until Hitler was beaten, until American production could supply the necessary arms for new campaigns, the Far East had low priority. It was not without reason that British soldiers in the East called themselves a 'forgotten army'.

The other Europeans were in an even worse state. French Indo-China, a country three times the size of Britain, with thirty million inhabitants, was still in theory under French rule, but only on Japanese sufferance. In March 1945 even this ended and the Japanese took over Indo-China, lock, stock and barrel. As for the Dutch, with Holland herself defeated and occupied by the Germans, there was practically nothing they could do to

'The dead are knocking on the doors of Unter den Linden'.
A Soviet soldier raises a flag on the Reichstag, Berlin, in 1945

defend their empire or regain it. Everything, in fact, depended on victory in Europe and American help. Now, as 1945 advanced, victory in Europe was obviously coming very close. It was a bad time to be having misunderstandings with America about future policy; but after Yalta Churchill, for one, was uneasy in his mind. With obvious sorrow he wrote,

I could not measure the forces at work in the brain-centre of our closest Ally, though I was soon conscious of them. I could only feel the vast manifestation of Soviet and Russian imperialism rolling forward over helpless lands.[23]

In March 1945 Soviet forces entered Austria, and in April they captured Vienna; the second of the Habsburg capitals was now in their hands. Already the famous city bore livid scars of war, heavy damage inflicted by British and American bombing. The price of Austria's Anschluss with Germany, which had seemed so desirable (indeed, essential) to many Austrians in 1938, had already been high, and the full bill had yet to be presented. With the capture of Vienna, the Soviet Union now firmly gripped the greater part of Central Europe.

Already the Red Army was in Germany. In its advance it had passed the Nazi concentration camps of Poland and the East: Auschwitz, where between 10,000 and 12,000 people were herded into the gas chambers every day, where medical experiments were carried out on living persons; Maidanek, where the Nazis murdered 1,380,000 people; Treblinka; and many more. The mood of the Red Army, entering Germany, was savage, and propaganda helped to keep it so. Posters were put up, saying: 'Red Army soldier! You are now on German soil; the hour of revenge has struck!'[118] Hard times for the Germans: the Soviet armies deliberately destroyed towns and villages; civilians were shot without remorse; looting was universal; rape was universal. The famous Soviet propagandist, Ilya Ehrenburg, wrote in his articles: 'We are in Germany. German towns are burning, I am happy. . . . We shall forget nothing. . . . A German is a German everywhere. The Germans have been punished, but not enough.'[118]

On 20 April the Soviet forces reached Berlin, and Ehrenburg said: 'The dead are knocking on the doors of the Joachimsthaler Strasse, of the Kaiserallee, of Unter den Linden and all the other cursed streets of that cursed city. . . . We shall put up gallows in Berlin . . .'[118]

The German capital was already a battlefield, pulverised by Allied bombing. Now there was tank fighting in the streets, and artillery fire at point-blank range: a final spasm of utter destruction, as the Red Army smashed, one by one, the last redoubts of Nazism. On 28 April Hitler's ally, Benito Mussolini, was caught and shot by Italian partisans. His body, beside that of his mistress, was hung upside down for all to see and mock. Adolf Hitler was spared such insults. Trapped in the Führerbunker under the Reich Chancellery, dreaming mad dreams of power and destruction to the last, he committed suicide on 30 April, and his body was burned.

Hard times for Germany; hard times without sympathy in the world that Hitler had brutalised. But the end was now very close. On 7 May 1945 the Third Reich capitulated to the Western Allies. General Eisenhower, the Supreme Allied Commander, took the capitulation formally at his headquarters in Rheims. The next day was celebrated as VE-Day, 'Victory in Europe Day', in the Western countries.

VE-Day was, without question, the greatest day that Western Europe has lived through in this century. In Britain it did not mean the same thing as it did in countries which had known the Nazi tyranny at first hand. Yet it did mean a liberation – liberation from the war itself, which was something that people had dreamed about for years. A great spontaneous rapture pulled the London crowds to certain magnetic areas on that day: to Whitehall, where Winston Churchill delivered fresh fitting phrases from a balcony; to Piccadilly, where Londoners and their guests habitually cavort; to Buckingham Palace, obeying that singular British wish for contact with the Crown in moments of mass emotion. For all these people in London and throughout the country, the sense of release was enormous. Release from air raids and sirens, from flying bombs which they jokingly called 'doodlebugs', but which were nevertheless quite terrifying, release from V-2 rockets, which arrived out of nowhere with deafening destruction; release from the blackout, that soul-corroding institution; release, they hoped (but alas!), from rationing, shortages, horrible substitutes – dried eggs, dried milk, spam, spam, and substances far worse than spam. By 1945 the British people had had just about enough. They would never have dreamed of giving in, but they did want it all to stop. 'London can take it!' said the propagandists, but there is a limit to how much you can take; a limit to how much of being ordered about and exhorted: 'Is your journey really necessary?' 'Careless talk costs lives.' 'Dig for victory.' Even the best cartoon humour begins to flag after five years; even the most inspiring leaders and causes begin to lose some magic.

There is not much magic left, in the fifth year of a war; everything looks shabby, the flavour of life is sour. On VE-Day the people of Britain were cheering their goodbyes to all that with heartfelt satisfaction. They were cheering about something else, too: they knew, privately, that they had done rather well, through all that danger and fear and discomfort. By not giving in in 1940, by fighting on alone against all the odds, they had kept the flame of European freedom alive. It is doubtful if they would have

'The greatest day that Western Europe has lived through in this century'. VE Day, London, 1945

understood, and improbable that they would have been flattered if told it, but the truth was that they had been very good Europeans.

And now it was possible to start thinking again about the future, to try to evolve a future which would justify all that the world had gone through during the last five-and-a-half years. This time, unlike 1918, the statesmen considered the problem *before* the war was over. In April 1945 a conference of forty-six nations convened in San Francisco to draw up the Charter of a new world organisation. This Charter spoke hopefully of restoring 'fundamental human rights' and 'fundamental freedoms' everywhere. Its language bravely echoed and amplified that of the Atlantic Charter of 1941.

When the war ended, however, one of the two authors of the Atlantic Charter was dead. President Franklin Delano Roosevelt had died less than a month before the surrender of Germany, with all his personal war aims and ideals unfulfilled. With his death the first significant change in world leadership took place. When the Allied leaders met for the next and last time at Potsdam in July 1945, America would be represented by President Harry S. Truman, an unknown quantity. Would he, as Roosevelt had seemed recently to do, smile more benignly on Stalin than on his West European allies? Time would show; meanwhile there was still Japan to be defeated.

It was at Potsdam that President Truman informed Churchill that final tests of an atomic bomb had been successful, and the decision was taken to drop such a bomb on Japan. Churchill commented: 'Here then was a speedy end to the Second World War, and perhaps to much else besides.'[23] In the event, two bombs were dropped: one on Hiroshima, on 6 August, a second on Nagasaki on 9 August, and on 14 August Japan surrendered.

On 2 September 1945 General Douglas MacArthur took the formal Japanese surrender in Tokyo Bay, in the presence of Allied representatives. Ten days later the Supreme Allied Commander, South-east Asia, Admiral Lord Mountbatten, took another surrender with equal formality in Singapore. This act had particular significance, over and above the capitulation of nearly 700,000 Japanese: it marked the beginning of the confrontation between the European empires and a new force in world affairs – Asian nationalism, which now demanded not merely liberation from Japan, but also liberty.

Lord Mountbatten was a member of the British royal family, a cousin of King George VI; did his presence in Singapore mean a return of the British Raj in South-east Asia? Did it imply the return of Britain's allies, the Dutch, to the East Indies? Would the French now rule again in Indo-China? Would the Europeans try to put the clock back, in other words? The answers to these questions were anxiously awaited, and would naturally vary according to the situation of each of the imperial powers.

It was Britain, of course, with her huge overseas empire, that would be most affected by the new force of Asian nationalism – but a new Britain. Winston Churchill had symbolised the British will to fight in 1940 and in the succeeding years. But there were other wills, other determinations, to do with peace, not war, and the kind of world they wanted to live in after the war, which had now crystallised in the minds of the British people. British attitudes had changed deeply during the war, and this was duly reflected in the General Election of 1945. Despite all his tremendous war-time services, and the enormous affection which the bulk of the nation still felt for him, Churchill was swept out of office. That other towering figure, General de Gaulle, remarked: 'His nature, identified with magnificent enterprises, his countenance, etched by the fires and frosts of great events, had become inappropriate in the era of mediocrity.'[32]

Certainly that is one way of putting it: another would be to say that it was the Conservative Party and old Conservative policies that were swept out in 1945, and Churchill had to go with them. In any case, Labour, under the premiership of Clement Attlee, came in. The whole atmosphere was very different from the postwar scene of 1918 and the notorious 'Khaki Election' of that year. Then people had wanted to return to what many thought of as 'the good old days'. In 1945 they wanted to turn their backs on 'the bad times' (the well-remembered period of the Depression and mass unemployment) and grasp a better future. Labour seemed to chime better with this wish than the Conservatives, many of whose very faces were reminders of the gloomy thirties. The British people were thinking of a future with no unemployment, more opportunity for all, much less social inequality, better education, and where ill health would not be penalised; all these prospects were envisaged in the Labour programme.

It was one of history's many ironies that these desires should be fulfilled at the very moment when Britain could least afford them. The inevitable impoverishment produced by the war led straight to the economic crises of peace, and these in turn soon produced the Age of Austerity. Those who lived through it will never hear the word without thinking of the stern face of the Chancellor of the Exchequer, Sir Stafford Cripps, often wearing a smile like a crevasse in a glacier. Indeed, austerity did seem a poor reward for so much effort, so much endurance, but there was no escaping it. In 1945 the British people collected a Welfare State and austerity in the same package, and they have been trying to make the best of the bargain ever since.

Amid much confusion one thing was clear about Britain in 1945: there was absolutely no disposition to attempt to hold on to imperial possessions by force, against the wishes of the native peoples. The British conscripts scattered across the globe wanted only to come home; the idea of sending more of them out to fight distant campaigns of repression was simply appalling. But in any case such a thing was quite contrary to Labour Party policies; in the case of India, for instance, there were specific Labour pledges to bring about her independence at the earliest possible moment.

This pledge, and the manner of its fulfilment, were the controls of much wider policies. India was the key to all Asia, partly because of its size and its 400 million people, and partly because the bulk of the British forces in the East were Indian. Two million Indians had volunteered to fight beside the British on many fronts during the Second World War, but they had not volunteered to hold other Asians in subjection to Europeans, in Burma, for instance, or Indo-China, or the East Indies.

By a happy conjunction, uncommon in history, the wishes of the British people, the aspirations of Indian nationalists and the policy of Mr Attlee's Government all coincided – and found a sympathetic and qualified executor. In 1947 Lord Mountbatten became the last Viceroy of India. His policy had always been to make Asian nationalists the friends of Britain, not enemies; now his task was to bring about the greatest triumph of Asian nationalism with British consent: Indian independence. Despite all the difficulties – the apparently insoluble disagreements between the Indians themselves – the job was done in only five months; on 15 August the subcontinent of India gained independence. There was a price to pay, of course; there always is. In this case the price was partition, with much bloodshed, and the long-drawn-out feud between India and Pakistan. But nothing could diminish the miracle of this transfer of power from the British Raj to its subjects without any conflict between the two – with, on the contrary, such immense good will. And so, in the earliest days of peace, the British began divesting themselves of empire. The question was, who else was interested in this process? Was anyone?

Certainly the Soviet Union was not interested. By 1948, the year in which Burma and Ceylon followed India into independence, certain things were becoming clear in Europe. In all the countries of Eastern Europe Soviet tanks and Soviet soldiers made certain that the Moscow version of Communist ideology should prevail. One by one the various coalition regimes, more or less democratic, which had masked Soviet domination, disappeared. In Poland Communist puppets of Moscow were already in power before the war ended – bitter fruit of the failure of the Warsaw Rising and the Yalta Conference. In Rumania King Michael, who had been a Soviet hero in 1945, was compelled to abdicate in 1947, and the sovietis-

'A man who had already become one of the nation's legends'. General de Gaulle in Chartres, 1945 (Robert Capa)

ation of his country followed rapidly. Bulgaria went the same way. In 1948 Hungary fell under full Communist subjection. All these were consequences of the agreements reached at Yalta.

With Eastern Europe, a large part of Germany and half of Austria firmly in the Soviet grip, almost the only area of hope was Czechoslovakia. Under President Beneš, a founder of free Czechoslovakia in 1919, a famous democrat, a famous internationalist, there seemed to be a reasonable possibility that the old democratic tradition of the Czech state might be revived. But this was not to be; the Communist Party of Czechoslovakia was strong and ruthless, and took its orders unhesitatingly from Stalin. In 1948 President Beneš was forced to form a communist government. Western opinion was shocked by this display of power politics, but there was a deeper, more personal shock to come. Jan Masaryk, Foreign Minister of Czechoslovakia, son of the Republic's first president, Thomas Masaryk, and himself a well-respected figure in many countries, was found dead under a window of his office. Was it suicide? Or had he been murdered by the Communists? Democrats everywhere feared the worst; in any case the fate of Czechoslovakia was sealed. Soon Beneš resigned, and a few months later died; Czechoslovakia began its experience of what would later be known as 'the years of deformation'. And so, behind bristling frontiers, human rights and fundamental freedoms were being extinguished over a large part of Europe; with Nazi imperialism still a recent nightmare, Soviet imperialism had moved in to take its place.

In other parts of the world imperialism continued to recede; empires do not sit easily on defeated nations. The Dutch Empire supplied a perfect example of this. Holland is only a small nation, but she has played a great part in European history, and above all in the history of European overseas discovery and colonisation. New York, we may remind ourselves, began life as New Amsterdam; Tasmania was first called Van Dieman's Land; there were Dutch colonies in the Caribbean; the first European colony in South Africa, at the Cape of Good Hope, was founded by a Dutchman, Jan van Riebeeck. Above all there was the work of the Dutch East India Company, founded in 1601, which opened up the East Indies, the fabled Spice Islands, whose riches poured into Holland for over 300 years.

All this, however, was set at nought when Holland herself was defeated and occupied in 1940. Liberation seemed a long time coming, but in 1945 it was a fact: liberation for Holland, that is to say – but what about the East Indies? What was going to happen to *their* human rights and fundamental freedoms? The nationalists had set up a Republic of Indonesia shortly before Japan surrendered; Holland refused to recognise the new status. The Dutch, in a sad hour, decided to try to suppress Asian nationalism in their empire by force; of course, they simply did not possess the force needed to fight an imperialist war on the other side of the globe in 1945. And nobody was going to help them. Yet fighting dragged on in the East Indies until 1949, when Holland at last accepted defeat and Indonesia gained her independence – and the right to manufacture her problems for herself.

In France liberation had begun in June 1944; when the war ended she was ruled by a man who had already become one of the nation's legends – and who knew it. General de Gaulle's triumphant walk down the Champs Elysées in August 1944, to the applause of two million Parisians, only twenty-four hours after the departure of the Germans was part of the legend. His arrival at Notre Dame, his almost regal entry into the cathedral, how he was shot at inside the cathedral itself, how everybody (except General Koenig) threw themselves flat, leaving the tall, unmistakable figure of de Gaulle continuing, at his normal unhurried pace, down the nave – it is all part of the legend.

And France certainly needed a legend in 1945. Her material condition was lamentable, worse in many ways than it had been in 1919. Half a million buildings had been destroyed. Communications all over the country were wrecked, partly by battle, partly by bombing, partly by Resistance sabotage. Less than 3000 locomotives were left out of 12,000 in 1940; 3000 bridges were blown up; rail communications between Paris and the large provincial centres such as Lyons, Marseilles or Bordeaux were completely cut. There were only 300,000 motor vehicles left out of three million, and in any case there was an acute petrol famine. Harbours were choked with wreckage. Canals were blocked. It was ruin on an indescribable scale, yet far outweighed by the human and psychological damage which France also suffered.

It was not merely that the war had cost France twice as many lives as it had cost Britain – a fact often forgotten. At least the dead were united: all victims of a common enemy. The survivors were by no means united, and it was de Gaulle's most urgent task to close the rifts between his countrymen after liberation. There were three groups to be reconciled, three factions in almost open hostility to each other. There were de Gaulle's own followers, the 'Free French' who had never acquiesced in the surrender of 1940 but had gone abroad to continue the fight, and were now home again. There was the Resistance Movement, which had risen against the Germans in 1944 – but the Resistance was dominated by the Communist Party, which had contributed greatly to the collapse in 1940, and in any case was the enemy of de Gaulle. And there were the collaborators of varying degrees, those whose attitudes ranged from mere passivity to positively

'Rough justice was indeed done'. A French collaborator (Robert Capa)

helping the Nazis in occupied France or supporting the now execrated Vichy regime of Marshal Pétain and Pierre Laval.

Some 200,000 French people had died in captivity in Germany during the war, mostly in concentration camps. What was detestable was that many of them had been rounded up by other Frenchmen, chiefly the militia and officials of Vichy. Such things could never be forgiven or forgotten, and so after liberation came 'purification' ('épuration'), a painful process, but, as de Gaulle said, necessary: 'To pass the sponge over so many crimes and abuses would have meant leaving a monstrous abscess to infect the country for ever. Justice must be done.'[32] Rough justice was indeed done – a bloody and nasty business. There were hasty trials, summary executions (sometimes without trial), public and private beatings; women collaborators had their heads shaved. The number of people put to death in this process of purification is still uncertain; figures range from 30,000 to over 100,000. What is not uncertain is that a lot of old scores were paid off.

Such was the France that de Gaulle was determined to make, once more, 'one of the greatest states'. And now the familiar question arose again: was the liberation of France compatible with liberty in the French Empire? What, for example, was going to become of Indo-China? Here, as in Indonesia, the nationalists (dominated by a Communist group led by Ho Chi Minh) had proclaimed independence; and here again early misunderstandings had tragic consequences. The French allowed themselves to be trapped into what looked like simple police actions, but turned out to be the beginning of a long, disastrous war for France, and an endless agony for Indo-China.

As the wretched drama unfolded the truth emerged that France, after all she had endured in the Second World War, had neither the will nor the power to defeat the nationalists in Indo-China, though there were brave if misguided soldiers willing to make the attempt. But the bulk of the French population was apathetic, hating the fresh bloodshed and grudging the expense of war. The Communists and the Left in general were always frankly opposed to the whole endeavour. And yet this futile conflict dragged on year after year, with varying fortunes. Under Marshal de Lattre de Tassigny the French for a time made considerable progress, but after his death their fortunes declined again. And then, in 1954, came the disaster at Dien Bien Phu, where 10,000 French troops were taken prisoner, and this at last put an end to a bad business.

Two months after Dien Bien Phu, a conference in Geneva brought the existence of French Indo-China formally to an end. In its place appeared the states of North and South Vietnam, Laos and Cambodia. None of them has yet been able to enjoy much in the way of human rights and fundamental freedoms. And France herself, in 1954, was firmly caught in the debilitating confusions of the Fourth Republic, with its merry-go-round of coalition governments. General de Gaulle had long since departed; his first administration lasted only until January 1946. After that his towering figure was to be seen in the wings, a disturbing spectator of the Fourth Republic's antics. De Gaulle brooded upon the lessons of liberation, of Indo-China and of party politics, and waited confidently for France to call him on stage again.

Holland, after the Indonesian fiasco, turned more and more towards her associates in Europe, Belgium and Luxembourg. During the war the three countries had joined for economic purposes to form the Benelux Union; this was a first step towards European unity, a subject which was going to become increasingly interesting. But now, plainly, the great power display of 1900 was reversed. The mighty European empires were fast vanishing from the scene, and half of Europe herself was again part of an empire. The mighty were fallen – fallen very low indeed.

'An end to a bad business'.
Dien Bien Phu, 1954

11   The Mighty fallen

Once we had a country and we thought it fair,
Look in the atlas and you'll find it there:
We cannot go there now, my dear, we cannot go there now.

In the village churchyard there grows an old yew,
Every spring it blossoms anew:
Old passports can't do that, my dear, old passports can't do that.

The consul banged the table and said:
'If you've got no passport you're officially dead':
But we are still alive, my dear, but we are still alive.

Went to a committee; they offered me a chair:
Asked me politely to return next year:
But where shall we go today, my dear, but where shall we go today?[4]

In 1945 a new category of Europeans came into existence, and a new
name had to be found for them: 'DPs' – Displaced Persons. They were
homeless, they belonged nowhere, they lived in camps administered by
international relief organisations, or they lived by the roadside, trudging
from one cold charity to the next. Some of the refugee camps still exist,
thirty years later, reminders of that very special punishment for the crime
of being European in 1945.

During the Second World War, millions of people were forcibly carried
off into Germany by the Nazis as slave labourers; about seven million of
them survived to the end of the war. Some, like the French, or Belgians, or
Dutch, could now make their way home; the road might be difficult, there
was no knowing what they might find when they arrived, but it was home
that they were going to. For others, East Europeans, things were different;
they knew only too well, in many cases, what their reception was likely to
be from the new Communist or Soviet-dominated governments of their
countries. They could not go home; and so they became Displaced
Persons.

A vast migration now took place: great streams of people flowing in
different directions, according to different necessities. There were the
Jews, chiefly survivors (by a miracle) of the extermination camps; they
would never feel safe again anywhere in Europe, but they still had no

'A new category
of Europeans'.
Refugees in Berlin,
1945

277

country of their own, their destinations were perilous and uncertain. All told, probably more than twenty million people were on the move: more than twenty million European nomads. Nothing like it had been seen since the great folk movements of the Dark Ages; nothing had ever been seen on such a scale. And most of these people possessed only what they could carry. All required to be fed – and food was hard to come by; many required clothing and fuel to survive the winter – also in short supply; they required medical attention, if they were not to be plague-carriers. They were a shifting tide of sheer human misery.

'How are the mighty fallen in the midst of the battle! . . . How are the mighty fallen, and the weapons of war perished!'

It is probable that nearly three times as many Europeans perished in the Second World War as in the First; and because the war was once more a total war, but fought with wider-ranging and more lethal weapons, a much larger number of the dead were civilians. The figures were terrible: in the Soviet Union, ten per cent of the population, about twenty million people; in Germany, also probably about ten per cent, six and a half million people; in Poland, one person in eight, 4,300,000; in Yugoslavia, also one in eight, 1,700,000; in all, perhaps something like thirty-five million European dead.[79]

Those who survived faced appalling tasks. Often they had only their bare hands and their indomitable courage and optimism to help them carry out the work of reconstruction which was clamouring to be done. Everywhere, great cities lay in absolute ruin: ninety per cent of Warsaw deliberately destroyed after the Rising in 1944; in the German-occupied zone of the Soviet Union six million homes destroyed; in some German cities ninety-three per cent of the houses made uninhabitable by strategic bombing. And everywhere palaces, theatres, churches and cathedrals, the fabric of European culture itself, lying wrecked.

The shadow of a new poverty lay right across the continent: poverty and famine at a level unknown since the Middle Ages. Europe's cereal crop production had fallen by almost half. In France, half the livestock had gone. Parts of Holland were submerged under the sea; parts of the Soviet Union were 'scorched earth'. Rationing was universal, and the rations were sparse. In 1945 something like 100 million Europeans were existing on what would normally be called a 'slimming diet', and sometimes even this was cut down.

Whole industries had been war targets. Now factories stood gutted, their productive machinery twisted into shapes of surrealist nightmare. Coal production in the continent had dropped to forty-two per cent of prewar level. Transportation was almost at a standstill: railways, rolling stock, bridges, canals and shipping reduced to rubble and junk.

And there was yet another shadow across Europe in 1945: the shadow of continuing tyranny. Peace, during the next decade, proved to be only a travesty of what millions had hoped and expected. Speaking at Fulton in America in March 1946, Winston Churchill used a phrase which was to become horribly familiar:

From Stettin on the Baltic to Trieste on the Adriatic an iron curtain has descended across the Continent. Behind that line lie all the capitals of the ancient States of Central and Eastern Europe – Warsaw, Berlin, Prague, Vienna, Budapest, Belgrade, Bucharest and Sofia. All these famous cities and the populations around them lie in the Soviet sphere, and all are subject in one form or another not only to Soviet influence but to a very high and increasing measure of control from Moscow.[59]

An 'iron curtain': what Churchill was also saying was that under a thin disguise of continuing cooperation the victorious wartime alliance of Britain, the Soviet Union and the United States was falling apart. The Western powers and the Soviet were now mostly at loggerheads. And behind the 'iron curtain' an Asiatic tyranny, the rule of Joseph Stalin, was supreme.

All in all, European prospects in 1945 and 1946 did not look good. Yet optimism remained, and curiously enough was once more given expression at Geneva. In April 1946 the League of Nations, the great hope of 1919, the great disappointment of 1939, held its last meeting in the Palace of the Nations. The purpose of the meeting was purely formal: to wind up the affairs of the League and transfer its headquarters, its archives and all its other possessions to its successor, the United Nations, the new hope of the world. 'We owe to the United Nations all our loyalties and all our services,' said the British delegate, and ancient champion of the League, Philip Noel-Baker.

The United Nations had been as close to the heart of America's wartime President, Roosevelt, as the League of Nations had been to the heart of its previous wartime President, Woodrow Wilson. And Roosevelt had paid attention to the hard lessons of Wilson's failure to convince the American people, and America's consequent fatal abstention from the League. It was not for nothing that the first meeting of the new United Nations Organisation, at which forty-six nations signed the Charter in 1945, took place in San Francisco. And it was no accident that the first UN Assembly, meeting in London the following year, decided that UNO's permanent home should be in New York. Partly, of course, this was a recognition of the extent to which the organisation leaned on America for all practical purposes (not least finance); partly also it expressed a determination that America should never be able to slide out, as she had done from the League; and partly it was an admission that power had now departed from Europe.

In the United Nations Europe has never been able to play the dominant part that she once played (with so little success) in the League. And UNO itself has steadily altered its character, with European influence declining at every stage. However, the real damage to the high ideals of UNO came right at the beginning. The constitution of the United Nations was based on the unity of five victorious powers: the Soviet Union, America, Britain, France and China (under Generalissimo Chiang Kai-shek). These five were permanent members of the Security Council, and each was given the right of veto, a device supposed to ensure Great-Power unity; in fact, it did the exact opposite. Soon the whole world found itself unwillingly understanding one disagreeable word of Russian, constantly repeated at the United Nations and at many other international conferences: 'Nyet' – 'No'. In the first ten years of UNO's existence the Soviet Union used the veto word seventy-seven times; by 1973 she had used it 107 times. In the early post-war days, when all humanity was reaching out for some hope to cling to, those frigid 'nyets', which paralysed UN action, were like buckets of cold water on a dream.

Thus Great-Power unity was soon seen to be a myth, and Great-Power confrontation once more became an ominous reality. On one side of the Iron Curtain, in Stalin's new empire, men's hopes dwindled of ever being able to enjoy the human rights and fundamental freedoms promised in the United Nations Charter. On the other side, fear grew of new Communist expansion. Only America possessed the forces to offset Soviet military strength in Europe; but neither the American forces themselves, nor the American people, nor America's new President, Harry S. Truman, wanted entanglement in European affairs. America wanted her 'boys' back home, and at this time President Truman could not see why not. It required two years of frustration in the attempts at international cooperation, and fresh signs of Communist aggression, to bring about a change of American policy – a change with enormous consequences for Europe.

In South-eastern Europe, only Greece and Turkey now remained outside the Iron Curtain. But the Greek Communists were in revolt, and democracy only survived by British aid. In 1946 there was an election, in which seventy per cent of Greeks voted for the return of the King, driven out by the Nazi invaders in 1941. The Communists responded to this expression of the general will by increased violence, helped by Greece's Communist neighbours. Greece appealed to the United Nations for help, but the Soviet veto conveniently blocked effective action from that quarter. Greece also asked for financial help from Britain – but at what an inopportune moment! Britain, in 1946, was fully in the grip of impoverishment and austerity, and could do no more to help. Only America could supply what Greece needed.

The American decision to assist the Greeks marked the beginning of a new policy, a decisive alteration of the postwar power balance. The new policy is known in history by the name of the American President who enunciated it: the Truman Doctrine. Speaking on 12 March 1947 to the two Houses of Congress in Washington, President Truman said:

I believe it must be the policy of the United States to support free peoples who are resisting attempted subjugation by armed minorities or by outside pressure. . . . If Greece should fall, confusion and disorder might well spread throughout the entire Middle East. The disappearance of Greece would have a profound effect upon those countries in Europe . . which have struggled so long against overwhelming odds. . . . The free peoples of the world look to us for support in maintaining their freedoms. If we falter in our leadership we may endanger the peace of the world.[37a]

The President demanded from Congress $400 million for aid to Greece and Turkey. It was a momentous speech indeed. Not only did the Truman Doctrine mean a final abandonment of the isolationism which, in 1919, had left Europe 'to scramble out of the world disaster as best she could' (see p. 174); it also meant that the leadership of Western civilisation, once the prerogative of the great European powers, had now passed to America, and would stay with her for a very long time.

The immediate aftermath of the war was a miserable time for Europeans. Few of those who lived through it will forget the winter of 1946–7, one of the continent's legendary bad winters (like 1916–17). In both cases the misfortune fell upon people whose resistance was low as a result of war. In 1947 there was a world shortage of wheat, which meant that in Paris the bread ration was reduced to 250 grammes; Britain, having escaped bread rationing all through the war, had been forced to accept it in 1946. All over Europe fuel was desperately short; industry, naturally, had priority for whatever fuel there was, which meant that homes and schools and even hospitals were icy places. There were gas and electricity cuts everywhere; in Britain newspapers were reduced to four pages because of the fuel crisis. The freezing winds, the deep snow which never melted, the everlasting frosts seemed to many Europeans as bad as the war itself; recovery, during that winter of 1946–7, seemed an impossible dream.

It was precisely at this frozen moment, with all Europe in the depths of depression, and when even the smallest luxury could be the subject of tough Black Market trading, that Paris became 'Gai Paris' again and reintroduced the world to luxurious glamour. It happened like a bombshell at 10.30 am on Wednesday 12 February 1947, at No. 30 Avenue Montaigne: M. Christian Dior made his first presentation of the New Look. A glamour-hungry throng of fashion writers, many of them wearing their smartest duffle-coats for the occasion, caught its breath at a vision of long skirts using yards and yards of material (ah, the coupons!), wasp waists, sloping shoulders, plunging necklines: actual femininity, after all the durable severities of wartime. The fashion magazines went into rhapsodies; the official- and petty-minded denounced the waste and frivolity at such a time. But it was Dior and the need for a frolic at last that won the day; the New Look swept France and Britain and America like a gust of spring air.

There was a touch of spring in the world of stage and film also. In France at this time Jean Cocteau and Jean-Paul Sartre were exciting the theatre, while Marcel Carné was directing *Les Portes de la Nuit*, René Clair *Le Silence est d'or*, Henri Clouzot the haunting *Quai des Orfèvres*, and Jean Cocteau again *La Belle et la Bête*. In Italy Vittorio de Sica was working on *Shoeshine*, and Roberto Rossellini on *Paisa*, following his *Rome, Open City* in the preceding year; the Italian cinema was about to enter a golden age. In Britain Terence Rattigan produced *The Winslow Boy*, Christopher Fry and Jean Anouilh *Ring Round the Moon*, Carol Reed offered *Odd Man Out* and David Lean a wonderful interpretation of *Great Expectations*.

It was in 1946 that the BBC inaugurated its famous Third Programme, a long-awaited adventure in sound radio: a network purely for cultural minorities, the most complete justification of Public Service Radio. The following year saw the inauguration of the Edinburgh Festival of the Arts. The winter of the meteorologists might continue to grip, but all over Europe the artistic scene was like the putting forth of green shoots at the change of seasons.

Even politically 1947 was a year of hope for the people of Western Europe, and memorable if for that reason alone, because there were not many hopeful years to come. In June, hot on the heels of the Truman Doctrine, the American Secretary of State, General George C. Marshall, outlined a plan to restore Europe's wrecked economies. The Marshall Plan was conceived on the grand scale: America offered massive aid in money, machinery and raw materials to countries which requested it. The condition was that Marshall Aid should not be received by the European countries individually on a competitive basis, but distributed according to needs evaluated by a permanent organisation. This was duly set up in April 1948; it was called the Organisation of European Economic Co-operation, and it marked another early step towards the economic and political unity of Europe for which many important figures were already working.

The Soviet Union and the East European countries were invited to benefit from the Marshall Plan (officially known as the European Recovery Programme) along with the West, but the Soviet Government, obviously fearing political implications, turned the offer down flat. Fourteen countries, however, did avail themselves of America's help. They received in all Marshall Aid to the value of twelve billion dollars, a tremendous infusion of new life into their economies. The result was a fifty per cent expansion of their industrial production in five years. This was the real beginning of Europe's recovery, and gratitude towards America was immense; yet there were a number of Europeans who, remembering how mighty their continent had once been, found it a bitter pill to have to accept this charity. There were some who even insisted that it was only another form of subjection.

Behind American generosity, American wealth and American political power, a shadow loomed not only over Europe, but over the whole world: the atomic bomb, whose mushroom clouds had told the doom of Hiroshima and Nagasaki in August 1945. French, Italian, German and British scientists had all made their contributions to the discovery of atomic energy and its applications. But it was the vast funds available for research in America, and the sophisticated equipment of American universities, which brought into existence the bombs of 1945. And now the bomb was an American possession; only America could afford it. In military terms in the postwar world, possession of the bomb enabled America to offset the Soviet Union's vast advantages in manpower. So the sanction of the bomb protected Western Europe in its days of powerlessness; but what a protection!

The immediate, overwhelming destructiveness of this new weapon had been demonstrated; it had brought even the fanatical Japanese to their knees in a matter of days. Its long-term effects on those who had been exposed to the radioactivity released in the explosion had not yet had time to reveal themselves, but were obviously likely to be terrible. The bomb, in fact, was the supreme destructor: if Europe were to become the next arena for its use, what sort of 'protection' would that be? The atomic bomb could easily bring the annihilation of the once-mighty continent. It did bring, in those early postwar years, great fear and a nagging guilt which undermined the self-confidence of those who were associated with this awful power.

The shadow of the bomb is the darkest of all those cast by the Second World War, and there remains an ominous prophetic quality in Winston Churchill's words at Fulton in 1946: 'The Dark Ages may return, the Stone Age may return on the gleaming wings of science, and what might now shower immeasurable material blessings upon mankind may even bring

'An iron curtain has descended across the continent'.
The Berlin Wall was not constructed until August 1961
but is nevertheless the most perfect expression of
the iron curtain (Cartier-Bresson)

about its total destruction.' In a peaceful world, even the problems posed by the Atomic Bomb and all its terrifying successors might have been controlled; but the postwar world has not been peaceful. It was only a very short time after the shooting stopped in 1945, when a new phrase, full of unpleasant significance, came into the European vocabulary: after 'Iron Curtain' came 'Cold War'. It was certainly better that hot war, but it was not what millions had hoped that peace was going to be.

At the root of the Cold War lay fear: the West feared further Communist expansion; the Soviet Union feared American possession of the bomb. Capitalist hostility to the socialist world was an old Communist doctrine, which had already been invoked to justify many repressions. In the years after 1945 the bomb lent it fresh colour. Andrey Zhdanov, Stalin's favourite lieutenant, gave a retort to the Truman Doctrine in September 1947, saying: 'The United States proclaimed a new, frankly predatory and expansionist course. The purpose of this new, frankly expansionist course is to establish the world supremacy of American imperialism.'[45] And there, in that stilted language like an incantation, lies the nub: this belief in expanding American imperialism based on the bomb now became the mandatory creed of the Communists and their friends everywhere. One side believing in American imperialism, the other pointing at Soviet imperialism, that was the Cold War, and very alarming it was.

Soon the Cold War divided Europe into blocs, all too reminiscent of the divisions of 1914 and 1939. In 1948 Czechoslovakia was snatched into the Soviet bloc by a Communist coup; but in the same year Marshal Tito broke with the USSR and Yugoslavia began to steer a precarious middle course between East and West. So the lines of power were drawn and remained fixed. They ran through Austria, where the Occupying Powers sat like 'four elephants in a canoe' (to quote a phrase of Dr Karl Renner, the head of the Austrian Provisional government in 1945), and through a Germany also divided into four zones of Occupation.

Nothing underlined the fall of the mighty so clearly as the state of Germany. Even her most implacable enemies were moved at what the war had cost her. General de Gaulle, who would never forget what Germany had twice done to France in his lifetime, nevertheless wrote after a visit to that country: 'Amid the ruins, mourning the humiliation which had submerged Germany in her turn, I felt my sense of distrust and severity fade within me.'[32]

Germany now became the epicentre of the Cold War. In 1948, in order to revive the still limping German economy (without whose contribution Europe herself could not revive), America, Britain and France put forward a proposal to fuse their three Occupation Zones, and in spite of violent

Soviet opposition the plan was adopted. Out of it would emerge the Federal Republic of West Germany, with its capital in Bonn, and the so-called German Democratic Republic in the East, with the Soviet sector of Berlin as its capital.

Precisely how undemocratic the Eastern regime was in reality was constantly revealed by a flow of people – two million between 1945 and 1952 – fleeing from Eastern Germany to the West. These people were not permitted human rights and fundamental freedoms in the 'Democratic Republic', and so, in Lenin's famous phrase of 1917, referring to the mass desertions of Russian soldiers in that year, they 'voted with their feet'. But the hardening of Germany's division, and the deep mutual antipathy of the two German governments, created new dangers for Europe. In 1948 these became horribly real, and their focus was Berlin.

The Berlin Blockade crisis, which started in June and lasted eleven months, was the worst of all in a year of crises; every single day it lasted some incident or accident could easily have started a real shooting war between the Soviet Union and the West. Berlin lies a hundred miles inside what was then still the Soviet Zone, and its division into four sectors, each controlled by an occupying power, made it a microcosm of occupied Germany. On 23 June 1948 the Soviet authorities stopped all land traffic into and out of the Western sectors of Berlin; this was the beginning of the Blockade.

What prompted this act? Partly, no doubt, it was an attempt by the Soviet Government to use Berlin as a bargaining counter against the setting up of the Federal Republic; partly, perhaps, the Soviet Government may have had the idea of forcing the Western Allies out of the old German capital altogether – their presence there could hardly fail to be irksome. In any case, whatever the Soviet motive, the Blockade created a situation in which peace hung on a thread. Fortunately, as it turned out, the Soviet leaders had miscalculated; but Europe was about to live through a remarkable drama, often nerve-racking, but ending in a wonderful success.

Two million people lived in West Berlin; only three years earlier they would have been two million enemies of the Western Allies, and the sound of American and British aircraft would have been a warning of another fearful episode in the Battle of Berlin. In 1948 they were two million people who needed food, fuel, clothing, raw materials: a total of 4000 tons of supplies every day. The only means of defeating the Blockade and taking these supplies into Berlin was by using American and British air-power; and so the Western Powers began the famous air-lift.

At Gatow, Tempelhof and Tegel airfields day after day the planes streamed in. At first the amounts they carried were small, and West Ber-

'A shadow was about to lift'.
The embalmed bodies of Lenin and Stalin in the Kremlin mausoleum

liners had to endure much hardship, a situation to which they were not unaccustomed. But in spite of everything – winter weather and continuous Soviet obstruction – the air-lift steadily built-up. There came a fantastic day in April 1949 when it reached its peak: 1383 aircraft, arriving at intervals of sixty-two seconds, landed no less than 13,215 tons of supplies. This spelt the failure of the Blockade, and shortly afterwards the Soviet Government ended it. Europe could breathe again.

The Cold War was not going well for the Soviet Union. Already Marshall Aid had caused the countries of Western Europe to take a step towards economic unity and recovery which was certainly not to the Soviet taste. Next came a step towards military unity: a fifty-year alliance against aggression was signed by Britain, France and the three Benelux countries, Belgium, Holland and Luxembourg. And in contrast to 1919, European cooperation would be supported by increasing American involvement. In April 1949 the North Atlantic Treaty Organisation came into being; America and Canada joined ten European countries in agreeing that 'an armed attack against one or more of them . . . shall be considered as an attack against them all'.

This was a turning-point, a deliberate return to the doctrine of the balance of power which had been rejected during the inter-war years. Now the NATO powers and the Soviet Bloc confronted each other just as the Triple Alliance and the Triple Entente had confronted each other before 1914. Many feared that the outcome would be the same as in 1914, and when news came that the Soviet Union had produced an atomic bomb that became a frightening thought indeed.

Equally disturbing to many at the time was the cost of this confrontation. It meant rearmament on a massive scale: Britain alone budgeted for £1000 million to be spent on Defence in 1951. Could economies still struggling to recover from the Second World War stand this strain? The answer, surprisingly, was that they could. The economic resilience of Europe has never been more strikingly displayed. Despite defence expenditure (because of it, perhaps) economic growth targets set for the 1960s were reached halfway through the fifties in Western Europe – an amazing feat. In West Germany, under the Chancellorship of Konrad Adenauer, the revival was so swift and so sweeping that it has been called 'the economic miracle' – a startling repetition of the upsurge which had made Germany the power-house of Europe at the beginning of the century.

Recovery was not confined to the West. In Eastern Europe a huge programme of industrialisation was taking place, linked with collectivisation of agriculture and a reorientation of trade, away from the West and towards the USSR. By 1952 industrial production in Poland and Czechoslovakia was double its prewar level. Steel production in Eastern Europe had doubled; the industrial labour force had increased by thirty-three per cent. But there was another side to this progress: workers were dragooned and underpaid; housing was always insufficient; small farmers, many of whose holdings were the result of the break-up of large estates after the First World War, bitterly resented being forced into collective farms on the depressing Soviet model. Everyone resented trade treaties which creamed off industrial production for the benefit of the Soviet Union.

There was much unrest in Stalin's empire as the fifties began, and this was scarcely surprising, because Stalinism was presenting its ugliest face again. Purges, similar to the notorious Soviet purges of the thirties, of all who showed any sign of independence of the USSR, were being carried out in all the Communist Parties of Eastern Europe. For many distinguished Communist leaders, 'purge' meant exactly what it had meant before, torture and death, or at the very least harsh imprisonment. In Hungary, Laszlo Rajk, Minister of the Interior and one-time International Brigader, was executed. So was Bulgaria's Deputy Prime Minister, Traicho Kostov. In Czechoslovakia the chief victims were Rudolph Slansky, ex-Secretary-General of the Party, and Vladimir Clementis, former Foreign Minister. In Rumania, the redoubtable Anna Pauker was imprisoned; Wladislaw Gomulka was arrested in Poland; Paul Merker was disgraced in East Germany. There were many others.

This was Stalinism at work. Once more the world was shocked by the spectacle of brutal repression, and nauseated by trials in which the accused made ridiculous and humiliating 'confessions'. Fear and anger — — always ingredients of conflict between nations — were much increased. The forties went out, the fifties came in, but Europe did not yet have much sense of peace.

Yet there were hopeful signs. In Britain the Austerity Age was departing at last. Those who lived through it will never hear the word without shuddering, without black memories of shortages, rations, points and coupons. Even Princess Elizabeth, the heir to the throne, had to have a special allocation of 100 clothing coupons for her wedding to Prince Philip Mountbatten in November 1947. The royal bridesmaids received twenty-three extra coupons each, and as the national allowance was only twenty coupons a year, it is not hard to imagine the outcry in certain quarters. But clothes rationing ended in 1949, and austerity itself drew to a welcome end.

Britain decided to celebrate. Looking back on the occasion, one does wonder how the British had the audacity to think of celebrating in 1951, but the fact remains that they did. The happy event was called the Festival

'Life began to look more hopeful'.
A dance in a workers' canteen, Moscow 1954 (Cartier-Bresson)

293

of Britain, and the centre of it all was beside the Thames, a site where ruins were cleared for astonishing constructions such as the Dome of Discovery, or the 'Skylon', and where today the Royal Festival Hall stands as a highly practical memorial of a cheerful moment. In retrospect there are a number of aspects of the Festival of Britain which may strike us as odd or naïve or merely silly. On the credit side, we have to remember that it introduced a somewhat stolid population to new shapes, new designs, new materials, new ways of using light and colour. Most of them have now either become clichés or been abandoned, but at the time they were exciting; they made people talk and laugh, and that was not a bad way to begin the fifties.

In the East, also, a shadow was about to lift: in March 1953 Joseph Stalin died, at the age of 73, and a link with a cruel and bloody past was broken. The departure of this cold, bigoted, suspicious and ruthless character did not mean that Communist oppression ceased, but it would never be quite the same. For a short time Stalin's lieutenants remained in power: Vyacheslav Molotov, whose countenance was for ever associated in the minds of millions of people with that veto word 'Nyet', and Lavrenty Beria, head of the Soviet Secret Police and executioner of untold thousands. But new faces now came forward, new men elbowed their way to front-rank power, and they did not all wear the old sullen look. Europe became more closely acquainted with Malenkov, Mikoyan, Bulganin and other less familiar names, and discovered that Soviet leaders could actually smile, though sometimes it was a smile like a razor. None smiled more broadly than the new Secretary-General of the Soviet Communist Party, Nikita Khrushchev: he was the coming man.

Under the Soviet Union's new rulers it was possible to detect a change — if only a very slight change, sometimes only perceptible to highly trained observers — in the climate of life in the Soviet empire. Certain blatant asperities of the police states disappeared; consumer goods made a belated appearance in the shops; life in many ways began to look more hopeful. The writer Ilya Ehrenburg, with his quick sense of prevailing moods, conveyed the feel of it in a novel which he significantly called *The Thaw*.

Extraordinary things were certainly happening at this time. Beria the executioner was himself executed, and Molotov was exiled. Then came a tremendous shock: in May 1955 Bulganin and Khrushchev flew to Belgrade and made peace with the arch-heretic of the Communist world, Marshal Tito. It was as though the Pope had paid a courtesy visit to John Calvin; orthodox Stalinists were badly shaken, but there were even profounder shocks to come. In February 1956, at the Twentieth Congress of the Soviet Communist Party, Khrushchev electrified the Communist and non-Communist worlds alike with his famous denunciation of Stalin. He called the dead hero a bloody tyrant, an incompetent war leader and a distorter of Communist ideology.

It is hard to think of any speech that has had such a deep effect; implicit in Khrushchev's words was a rethinking of fundamental tenets affecting hundreds of millions of people. It was not surprising if a perceptible tremor ran right through the Soviet empire. It was a psychological disturbance compounded of many emotions: relief that truth had at last been spoken; hope that it might continue to be spoken on many more subjects; resentment at all the lies that had gone before; loathing of the cruelties which had supported the lies. A new word now came into the vocabulary of Communist Eastern Europe: 'democratisation'. In Communist language 'democratisation' did not mean 'democracy'; it only meant less oppressive Communism. But even that was well worth having.

So 1956 was launched: one of history's decisive years. Its chances looked roughly even for good or ill. On the one hand, the power confrontation remained, dividing Germany, dividing Europe down the centre with the NATO powers facing the Warsaw Pact (the name of the military treaty of the Soviet Bloc), and with the power confrontation the menace of the bomb. On the other hand there was the good omen of Austrian independence, the four occupying powers having reached agreement to withdraw in 1955. And Stalin was dead; Stalinism was condemned officially by the Soviet Government. This was an amazing new fact; did it imply a real hope of healing the breach between East and West, an end of the Cold War? It was an exciting speculation.

12   A certain amount of violence

In 1956 there was an 18-year-old student in Warsaw whose name was Michael Bruk; he was in a state of dire perplexity. His brother had been killed by the Germans during the war, fighting for Poland's survival in the Home Army. His brother had been Michael's hero – but then the Communists told him that the Home Army were traitors. Like many Poles, Michael had strong religious feelings – but the Communists told him that religion was rubbish. He became a Communist, and refused to believe what others told him about Stalinist dictatorship and the rule of the secret police. But in 1956 Khrushchev denounced Stalin and Stalinism.

What was Michael Bruk to think now? What could thousands like him think? What could any young Pole think? Michael Bruk wrote to the magazine *Nowa Kultura*, and in the atmosphere of 'democratisation' of April 1956 the magazine printed his letter:

I am ashamed of all of you, and above all of myself because of my stupidity and credulity. I know no longer how to raise my head . . . for I have no foundation for believing anything. . . . Perhaps now will begin the genuine realisation of Communist ideas . . . but probably I will not be with you, because I have no reason to trust you. . . . I wish you all success, but please do not be surprised at us young people.[103]

There was disturbance in the air in Poland, excitement, anticipation of further advances towards real democracy, especially among the young; anything might happen. Poland and Hungary were countries where nationalism and religion had always been closely linked and deeply felt, and this remained true now that both lay within the Soviet empire. In 1956 there was stir in both countries like a call to arms.

Hope, for large numbers of Poles in 1956, centred around the personality of Wladislaw Gomulka, the Communist leader who had been imprisoned during the last Stalinist purge. Now Stalin was dead and Gomulka was out of prison. He gave his countrymen a new phrase, a new idea to fight for: 'the Polish road to socialism'.

It is a poor idea [he said] that socialism can be built only by Communists, only by people professing a materialistic social ideology. . . . Even a theory of socialism evolved in the best possible way at any given time, in any given conditions, can-

'Khrushchev had something else to think about'. Hungary 1956 (Erich Lessing)

not embrace all the details of life, which is richer than theory. What is immutable in socialism can be reduced to the abolition of the exploitation of man by man. The roads leading to this goal can be and are different. They are determined by various circumstances of time and place. The model of socialism can also vary. It can be such as that created in the Soviet Union, it can be shaped in the manner we observe in Yugoslavia, it can be different still.[103]

These were strange words, coming from a Communist Party leader: interesting, exciting words. October 1956 was to be a month of experiment in Poland; the Warsaw radio commentator Henryk Holland said in a broadcast: 'This is spring in October, the spring of awakened hopes and of awakened national pride, the spring of true international proletarianism and of determined will to mark out our own Polish way to socialism.'[103] But it was not going to be easy.

A vital meeting of the Polish Communist Party, which would decide the character of its future leadership, was taking place in Warsaw under disagreeable auspices. There were already strong indications of Soviet disapproval; there were rumours of Soviet troop movements towards the city and debates about how to resist them. Then suddenly, while the meeting was still taking place, without any prior warning, the Poles were told that they had visitors. A plane arrived from Moscow bringing a Soviet delegation of the very highest power: Nikita Khrushchev, First Secretary of the Soviet Communist Party, backed by Mikoyan, Kaganovich and Molotov. Their object was to halt the tide of 'democratisation' in Poland, which was now flowing far too swiftly for Soviet taste. The encounter between Russians and Poles was stormy; Khrushchev himself was in one of his famous furies. For a time there was a serious danger of a new Soviet conquest of Poland; yet 1956 was not like 1945, conquest was something the Soviet leaders would be glad to avoid, and Gomulka stood firm on his basic principle:

The road of democratisation is the only road leading to socialism in our conditions. From that road we shall not deviate, and we shall defend ourselves with all our might against any attempts to push us off it.[103]

In October 1956 the Soviet leaders accepted, with reservations and misgivings, this declaration by Gomulka. Poland's new tragedy came when, not long afterwards, Gomulka himself seemed to lose 'the road of democratisation'. Yet the signposts remained, as the marked differences between Poland and the USSR today bear witness. Meanwhile Khrushchev and his colleagues had something else to think about.

In Hungary also the pace of democratisation had been too hot for their liking. In July the Stalinist leader Mathias Rakosi had been deposed, to the

'The Red Army was forced to evacuate Budapest'. A dead Russian officer, Budapest, 1956 (Erich Lessing)

great relief of many Hungarians, not that they much admired his successor, Erno Gero. The leader they would have preferred was Imre Nagy, whose recent quarrel with the Stalinists had brought him expulsion from the Party. In October a famous purge victim was ceremoniously – though belatedly – rehabilitated: the body of Laszlo Rajk, the International Brigader of 1936, executed in 1949, was disinterred and given a state funeral. Imre Nagy was readmitted to the Party; the cry went up that he should now take power as the Hungarian Gomulka.

On 23 October a vast demonstration, with students prominent in it, assembled in Budapest in support of Poland. Outside the Radio Budapest building the demonstrators clashed with the detested Security Police, who opened fire. But the upsurge was too great to be contained. Amazing scenes now took place: in the city park a huge statue of Stalin was toppled down and dragged away by a refuse truck. Revolutionary committees were set up all over the country; the Hungarian army fraternised with the rebels. Imre Nagy was recalled and became Prime Minister; Gero just disappeared.

By now the revolt had gone beyond the Polish model which had inspired it: it had become anti-Communist, above all anti-Soviet. The Red Army liberators of 1945 had become the oppressors of 1956; Red Army garrisons in Hungary, claiming to be answering an appeal by the Hungarian Government, opened fire on the rebels and began carrying out arrests. The reaction was fierce: after five days the Red Army was forced to evacuate Budapest. This was a moment in history to make men catch their breath.

Now Imre Nagy, under popular pressure, formed a Coalition Government pledged to free elections and Hungarian independence outside the Soviet bloc. This was too much; on 4 November the Red Army returned to Hungary in massive force. Budapest was reoccupied after bloody fighting with much destruction; about 25,000 Hungarians were killed. Imre Nagy, having been promised impunity, was arrested by the Soviet forces and duly executed in the all-too-familiar Stalinist style. The Soviet victory was apparently complete, a depressing spectacle in November 1956; it is only now, nearly twenty years later, in the light of distinct social changes in Hungary, that one may doubt whether the oppressors were the victors after all.

Nearly 200,000 Hungarians fled abroad in the aftermath of the 1956 rising, bringing their sad stories to all parts of Europe. Their very existence was evidence of what the realities of Soviet power could be, and people in Western Europe were shocked at this new revelation. Television, on which the day-to-day progress of the Budapest Rising had been eagerly followed, brought a new sense of special involvement in these events. The West European peoples raised funds to help the Hungarian refugees and took great trouble to absorb them as painlessly as possible into their countries of exile. As regards the two great powers of Western Europe, Britain and France, that was about all they could do; they were in a dismal plight themselves.

It is a strange reflection that one of the most disruptive and transforming events in modern European history actually began simply as a great European engineering achievement. The Suez Canal, built by a Frenchman Ferdinand de Lesseps in 1869, was the realisation of dreams going back down many centuries: a link between the Mediterranean and the Indian and Pacific Oceans; a link between Europe and her empires in the East. The Canal was owned and operated by a Company whose headquarters were in Paris, but the controlling interest was held by the British Government. This was not surprising, in view of Britain's dependence on sea-borne trade: in 1955 just under a quarter of Britain's total imports passed through the Suez Canal, and a third of the ships that used it were British. The Canal, in fact, was generally considered to be vital to Britain's economy.

It thus came as a traumatic shock when, in July 1956, the newly-elected President of Egypt, Colonel Gamal Abdel Nasser, suddenly nationalised the Suez Canal in retaliation for the British and American refusal to finance a new dam at Aswan on the Nile. In France there was outraged anger against Egypt, already known to be supporting the rebel cause in Algeria. In Britain a mood developed which can only be called hysterical: suddenly, all over the country, in bars, in clubs, in office corridors, across dinner tables and in lunch breaks, people began talking politics – a thing the British almost never do. Not only did they talk politics, they shouted and bellowed politics in a most uncharacteristic fashion; the country was divided right down the middle.

On the one hand there were those, like the Prime Minister, Sir Anthony Eden, who sincerely believed that Colonel Nasser was a dictator similar to Hitler. Nasser, in Eden's view, was a megalomaniac:

It is important to reduce the stature of the megalomaniacal dictator at an early stage. A check to Hitler when he moved to reoccupy the Rhineland would not have destroyed him, but it would have made him pause. The world would then have had time to assess the truth, and the Germans occasion to question themselves. This process would have been altogether salutary. . . . Some say that Nasser is no Hitler or Mussolini. Allowing for a difference in scale, I am not so sure.[36a]

Against this there were those like the Leader of the Opposition, Hugh Gaitskell, who, while disapproving of Colonel Nasser's high-handed ac-

tion, were convinced that it was unthinkable to use force against him without the backing of Britain's chief ally, America, without the moral sanction of the United Nations, and without the approval of the Commonwealth, none of which conditions existed.

The division between the two points of view had very little to do with political parties; many middle-class, normally Conservative voters would have backed Gaitskell, many habitual Labour voters would have supported Eden. But the division was absolute, and became more so, with tempers rising on both sides as time went by. 'As time went by' – there lay the crux of the matter. Even the most ferocious of the fire-eaters had to accept that the use of force against Nasser meant a large-scale military operation, and that it was impossible to mount a major military operation at the far end of the Mediterranean at short notice. So Britain entered a period of long-drawn-out nightmare; the country was not at war, but war preparations were visibly being made – reservists were called up, World War II equipment was taken out of mothballs, troop movements were taking place. The 'feel' of the times was extraordinary, described by one historian as 'trying to prepare for a war that was not a "proper" war in an atmosphere that was not properly peace'.[7]

During all this time there were international conferences at which impeccable sentiments were expressed. A Suez Canal Users' Association was proposed by the American Secretary of State, John Foster Dulles, and duly set up; it proved useful as an outlet for the widespread sense of frustrated outrage, but for nothing else. The Prime Minister of Australia, Robert Menzies, tried direct negotiation with Colonel Nasser, but without result. And all the time there was a pervasive stench of prevarication. Accusations of secret Anglo-French collusion with Israel were brushed aside, but there were strange comings and goings which were never fully explained. And undisguised military preparations never ceased, until at last, when nerves were fully stretched, on 29 October Israeli troops invaded Egypt, British and French aircraft shortly afterwards bombed Egyptian airfields, and British and French paratroops descended on Port Said.

World opinion (chiefly American opinion, but also Scandinavian, Canadian and Indian) was appalled at what could not fail to look like a revival of the most brutal side of European imperialism. The whole episode was rendered the more shameful by the fact of it exactly coinciding with the Soviet aggression against Hungary which Britain and France were, of course, denouncing in lofty moral terms. However, resemblances between the erring democracies and the Soviet Union were only skin deep: in Hungary the Soviet Government made no mistake, whereas the British and

'. . . what could not fail to look like a revival of European imperialism . . .' British troops bound for Suez, 1956

French, under American pressure and faced with economic collapse, had to call off their attack on Egypt after only twenty-four hours. Soon afterwards their forces made a withdrawal which was not merely humiliating in itself, but had a symbolic significance greater than men knew.

The United Nations Organisation, where the whole Suez affair had caused much excitement and consternation, now sent in a Peace-keeping Force. This looked satisfactory, and in other circumstances might have suggested that UNO was performing a valuable function; but in the circumstances of November 1956 this action was something of a mockery. It was all very well for UNO to send a force to the Suez Canal; the Security Council was prevented from even discussing what was going on in Hungary — by the Soviet veto. UN relief was allowed to enter Hungary; UN observers were not allowed. And so it was proved once again, as the League of Nations had often proved before, that international organisations are generally powerless against aggressive and ruthless dictatorships, but sometimes effective against democracies. The credibility of UNO was undoubtedly one of the casualties of Suez.

Another casualty was the credibility of the North Atlantic Treaty Organisation. America, strongly disapproving of the British and French action at Suez (her own moral stature still uncontaminated by Vietnam), was disgusted at the thought of American arms supplied for NATO purposes being used for 'imperialist' purposes against Egypt. But worse than this recrimination was the obvious complete breakdown of communication between the two European powers and their American ally. The depth of anti-American feeling displayed in Europe at this period was frightening, and the unfortunate truth is that it continues to this day.

Indeed, to list all the consequences of that tragic autumn of 1956 would be an almost impossible task. One thing now seems clear: the most far-reaching consequences were neither political nor economic (though these were significant enough) but psychological; they were in the mind. Budapest and Suez played havoc with cherished beliefs. Communism was never the same; it was not only that every Communist Party outside the Soviet bloc suffered heavy loss of membership; it was the fall of the idol, the disgrace of the Socialist fatherland, that counted most. Western ideas and ideals were no less seriously jolted.

On both sides of the Iron Curtain there was shame and demoralisation, reflecting a world in which more and more people knew what they were against, but fewer and fewer knew what they were for. This perplexity was echoed in literature and the arts. Already people were becoming familiar with Existentialism, the doctrine preached by Jean-Paul Sartre at the Café Flore, the Deux Magots, and elsewhere on the Left Bank where

Paris had incubated so many disturbing thoughts and theories in times past. Man, said Sartre, exists because he exists; his being is without necessity, without reason, without cause. In the collapse of illusions of 1956, this proposition seemed far from ridiculous.

The strange, haunted imagery of Jean Cocteau's films also seemed very much in tune with a period of jangled nerves and discontented dreams. In Britain a new generation of writers arose who became collectively known as 'Angry Young Men': the Royal Court Theatre saw the birth of a new reputation with John Osborne's *Look Back in Anger*, and Colin Wilson's *The Outsider* was published in the same year. Already Kingsley Amis had written *Lucky Jim*, which showed that if not exactly angry, he was certainly not exactly pleased. Expressed with anger or with satire, there was an unusual degree of questioning and outright rejection of what used to be called 'accepted values'.

It can be argued, indeed, that whereas, before the Budapest/Suez trauma, society had generally managed in some fashion to assimilate most of its rebels to 'accepted values', after 1956 the very phrase 'accepted values' had less and less meaning. In the West, certainly, established society suffered a great loss of self-confidence, an acute demoralisation. In Britain a gesture appealing to much that survived of the robust spirit of 1939–45 had ended in failure and humiliation. But that was not all by any means: there was the sense of being let down by trusted friends – America, and a number of countries of the Commonwealth. Whom could one trust now? What could one believe in? The disbelief was palpable, the sense of disintegration of an old system, acceptance of change for the sake of change, the trend seen as an end in default of anything better. Inevitably, there was a new jargon to go with the new frames of mind: one heard of 'dropping out', 'pop culture', 'trips', a 'generation gap'. It was, of course, in some ways sadly familiar:

What are the roots that clutch, what branches grow
Out of this stony rubbish? Son of man,
You cannot say, or guess, for you know only
A heap of broken images . . .[37]

One aspect of the West's loss of self-confidence produced startling results. In the 1880s a number of European nations had unashamedly taken part in what was called 'the scramble for Africa', a very cynical game of grab for which all that was required was an outline map of the 'Dark Continent', a ruler, a pencil, some pots of paint, and a lot of avarice. In the late 1950s and early '60s the whole process was seen in reverse, a

scuttle from Africa which was in some ways just as cynical as the original scramble to get there.

It was not all cynical: France gave independence to Morocco and Tunisia before Suez, in accordance with long-standing promises; but after 1960 independence was handed out in wholesale fashion, an egalitarianism for Africans which was close to being insulting. Britain gave independence to the reasonably advanced Gold Coast, under the new name of Ghana, in 1957, but the large-scale independence programme (often known as 'the wind of change') came between 1960 and 1964, affecting ten countries with populations totalling seventy-five millions, at very different levels of development. The Belgians, who had scandalised the world with their corrupt administration of the Congo at the beginning of the century, shocked everyone again by their indecent haste to leave that country in 1960, abandoning that unhappy country to the chaos and savagery of civil war for the next five years.

The story of the Europeans in Africa has been a mixed one. It has some good aspects: the struggles against slavery and disease; some disappointing aspects: the failure to implant democratic ideas (but in the time given was that ever likely?); and some shocking aspects: harsh repressions of native peoples, commercial exploitation. The manner of the Europeans' going was by no means the prettiest part of the story. But there is little point in repining; they had lost their self-confidence; their imperial role irked and frightened them; they just wanted to cut their losses and be gone.

To this general rule there was one single, solemn exception: Algeria. Algeria, in 1956, was not a country; it was not a colony; what was it then? According to all orthodox French textbooks, Algeria was 'part of France', a French Department, and had been so since 1834, just as Brittany had been part of France since 1491, or Corsica since 1769, or Savoy since 1860. That was the theory; and there were over a million inhabitants of Algeria of assorted European extraction who warmly subscribed to it. There were about ten and a half million who did not: the Moslems, who did not and never would feel at all like Bretons, or Corsicans, or Savoyards. And so, in defence of an idea which, while in some ways laudable, had never had much reality and had now become an anachronism, France plunged into a new tragedy.

'I was determined to extricate her from the constraints of her empire'. De Gaulle in Algeria, 1958 (Tikhomiroff)

An Algerian nationalist revolt in 1954 caught France unawares and was permitted to grow into a war, just as the Asian nationalist revolt in Indo-China had done. It is almost unbelieveable that, in the year of Dien Bien Phu and outright defeat in Indo-China, France should make the same mistakes again. But Algeria was 'Algérie française', and in 1954 (perhaps in reaction to the Indo-China disaster) the French mood was that she would remain so, whether she liked it or not – whether, in the end, France liked it or not. And this stubbornness, this blindness to reality, would be the downfall of the Fourth Republic.

Steadily, year by year, the Algerian insurrection escalated, and became another running sore, even worse than Indo-China because of its nearness to Metropolitan France and because of the intransigent problem of the settlers, the 'colons'. It became more violent in the aftermath of Suez, with France struggling to avoid another humiliation by any means. The mood of both sides became more intractable, the weakness of the Fourth Republic more palpable. The war was carried from Algeria to France: Paris, only just recovering some of her pre-1939 glitter, became a battlefield. Algerian terrorists, the Front de Libération Nationale (FLN), and French counter-terrorists, the Organisation Armée Secrète (OAS), gave a new word to the vocabulary of terror: 'plastique', the plastic bombs whose explosions wrecked buildings in famous streets and upset the tourists. And certainly it *was* upsetting to see policemen on point duty in the middle of Paris standing in bullet-proof steel boxes; it was upsetting to see the doors and windows of police stations and public buildings sandbagged against blast once more. It was disconcerting to be returning to one's hotel, and have a tommy-gun rammed into one's stomach by a nervous policeman. It was unpleasant to watch the round-ups of suspects in the Algerian quarter after an 'incident'; it was very unpleasant indeed to speculate on the identity of the bodies which would from time to time be discovered floating down the Seine.

That was Paris during the years of the Algerian War – an hysterical Paris, covered with slogans, full of suspicion, ready to burst out at any moment into ritual war-cries and street violence. Even an ordinary traffic-jam would become a demonstration, with every horn blaring out the rhythm of 'Al – gér – ie franç – aise'. And in the midst of these uproars the Fourth Republic collapsed of sheer impotence, and France found salvation where she had found it once before.

On 29 May 1958 General de Gaulle formed a Government of National Safety; a few months later, by referendum, he became President of a Fifth Republic whose new constitution substantially enlarged the presidential authority. So de Gaulle returned, the most remarkable leader of the Second World War, one of the most remarkable in European history. This was the man who, almost unknown and without a scrap of power, had picked France up out of the dust in 1940, retaught her the manners of a great nation, placed her back among the victors in 1945, accepted the verdict of the French people against him in 1946; had gone into retirement, thought much, learned much, and now came back in 1958 by the overwhelming will of the people, but with more than a touch of majesty on the hem of his garment.

One lesson de Gaulle had thoroughly learned during his long wait in retirement at Colombey-les-deux-églises: the futility of imperialist wars in the twentieth century. He wrote:

On resuming the leadership of France, I was determined to extricate her from the constraints imposed upon her by her empire and no longer offset by any compensating advantages. As can be imagined, I did not undertake it lightly. For a man of my age and upbringing, it was bitterly cruel to become through my own choice the overseer of such a transformation.[32]

In a more astringent mood at the time, he summed up his attitude towards France's empire in a mordant phrase: 'L'Afrique est foutue, et l'Algérie avec.'[10] Politely, this might be translated as: 'Africa has had it, and Algeria likewise'. And it was possibly under the inspiration of this thought that de Gaulle handed out the wholesale independences of 1960; inspired similarly, he set about ending the Algerian War. For all his clarity of mind and determination, it took him until 1962 to bring the war to an end in a manner acceptable both to France and to independent Algeria. When at last he succeeded, all France's energy could be poured back into Europe.

'Into Europe': this was a phrase which was acquiring a new meaning because Europe was moving towards a new unity. The idea of European unity, of course, was anything but new; it had existed for centuries, partly as a folk memory of the Roman Empire, which really did unite Western Europe, and the Holy Roman Empire, which was intended to do the same thing, or Christendom, the collective word for all the Christian countries. It was an idea which attracted all sorts of conditions of men. In 1897, the year of Queen Victoria's Diamond Jubilee, a time when the British felt very separate and powerful, the Prime Minister, Lord Salisbury was saying: 'The Federation of Europe is the only hope we have.' Alas, seventeen years later Europe suffered the First World War instead. In 1930 the great internationalist, Aristide Briand, made another appeal for a United States of Europe. Once more the appeal fell on deaf ears, and nine years later came the Second World War.

In the aftermath of that war, the idea of unity was revived. In 1948 a 'Congress of Europe' was called at the Hague, to promote the cause of European Union. Winston Churchill gave the inaugural address on 7 May:

We shall only save ourselves from the perils which draw near by forgetting the hatreds of the past, by letting national rancours and revenges die, by progressively effacing frontiers and barriers . . . and by rejoicing together in that glori-

ous treasure of literature, of romance, of ethics, of thought and toleration belonging to all, which is the true inheritance of Europe . . . which by our quarrels, our follies, our fearful wars, and the cruel and awful deeds which spring from war and tyrants, we have almost cast away.

In 1953 a large practical step towards the unification of Europe was taken. It was inspired by two remarkable Frenchmen, Robert Schumann and Jean Monnet. Schumann was an Alsatian, and so he began life as a German citizen and fought in the German Army in the First World War. The Treaty of Versailles made him a Frenchman, and in the Second World War he fought against Nazi Germany in the French Resistance. Later he became Foreign Minister and Prime Minister of France. Schumann was determined to end the Franco-German feud which had twice torn the continent apart, and his solution, with the aid of that outstanding economic planner, Jean Monnet, was to internationalise the coal and steel which had provided the sinews of modern war for both countries. It was an astonishingly bold idea (and widely misunderstood, above all in Britain), but thanks in no small part to the enthusiasm of the German Chancellor, Konrad Adenauer, it worked, and so the European Coal and Steel Community (ECSC) came into being.

In 1957 the process was carried a stage further: France, Germany, Italy, Belgium, Holland and Luxembourg signed the Treaty of Rome, setting up the European Economic Community, EEC, the 'Common Market'. The effect of this coming together on the economies of the states involved was very striking: rapidly expanding production, a broad flow of consumer goods, an unmistakable whiff of new European wealth. The political implications of the new community were also impressive, and if realised could become a new factor in Europe. Not everyone liked those implications: in 1957, despite disappointments, Britain's Commonwealth links still seemed strong, there was still nostalgia for the 'special relationship' with America, and there was distrust of what looked like European 'supranationalism'. Britain turned her back on EEC, and attached herself instead to EFTA, the European Free Trade Association of Sweden, Norway, Denmark, Switzerland, Austria and Portugal.

Western Europe's economy was greatly changed by EEC; what did not change was the state of European power in a world where military force still counted above all. In 1962 a dramatic power confrontation underlined Europe's continuing feebleness. The Soviet government, largely inspired by Nikita Khrushchev, undertook to supply missiles to Cuba. The United States Government, now headed by President John Fitzgerald Kennedy, reacted violently to this unprecedented Soviet intrusion into the Western hemisphere. And public opinion in the United States was not to be calmed by reference to the ring of American bases which closely encircled the Soviet Union. A nerve-racking crisis quickly built up: as the Soviet vessels carrying the missiles to Cuba approached the line of the American blockade, the world watched its television sets and held its breath. Was it possible for either of the nuclear super-powers to climb down? If not, what would happen? Full-scale nuclear war? And if so, what would happen to Europe, right in the middle? In the event, nothing happened; seized by saner second thoughts, Khrushchev did climb down. But there is not a scrap of evidence that Europe exerted any influence on him to do so, nor on President Kennedy, on the other side of this terrifying poker game.

Soon afterwards there was another reminder, but in a different manner, that if European prosperity was reviving, European power was not. In January 1965 Sir Winston Churchill died, and it was scarcely possible to watch the passing of that great figure without speculations of some sort about the shifts of power. Churchill had served on the North-west Frontier of India, in the Sudan and in the South African War. The result of all these enterprises in which he had been involved was to add to the British Empire. He had once said: 'I have not become the King's First Minister in order to preside over the liquidation of the British Empire.'* But now the British Empire, and almost every other European empire, was in the process of liquidation.

In a moment of terrible danger in 1940, he said to the British people: 'Let us therefore brace ourselves to our duty and so bear ourselves that if the British Commonwealth and Empire lasts for a thousand years men will still say, "This was their finest hour".' On this note he had led the nation to victory; he had made it believe in its 'finest hour'. But twenty years after the war, that hour seemed a long way off, and there was nothing to match it, either for Britain or the rest of Europe.

A great patriot always, Churchill had ended his active life as a great European. But by the time of his death it was reasonable to ask whether his Europe even still existed. Was it not just an old story of bygone days? Were not the Churchillian attitudes about as relevant to modern Europe as the Crusades? The last decade of Churchill's life had seen changes which seemed utterly unconnected with previous human experience – and which underlined yet again how very far from mighty the continent of Europe had become. It was in 1957 that the Soviet Union launched the first two Sputniks, and the Space Race became a preoccupation. The difficulty of grasping the full meaning of the Soviet achievement is illustrated by the

*In a speech at the Mansion House, November 10th 1942.

demand of an inflamed American that the United States should shoot the Sputniks down! However, America was not far behind in the race: in the year that Churchill died, both Americans and Russians were walking in space – a concept smacking of the miraculous – and in 1969 the Americans actually landed on the Moon.

So this was goodbye to all lunar romanticism, goodbye to Diana,

Queen and Huntress, chaste and fair,
Now the sun is laid to sleep,
Seated in thy silver chair
State in wonted manner kccp:
Hesperus entreats thy light,
Goddess excellently bright.[58]

Goddess no longer, the Moon is now, thanks to remorseless technology, just another piece of ground for Man to march on, perhaps to turn into another battlefield – or be saved only by its sterility.

The only contributions that Europe could make to all this were some minor technical components and admiring crowd noises. Western Europe, even with reviving economies, simply could not afford the cost and diversion of resources required to compete in the Space Race. (Whether the Soviet Union can really afford her achievements either, in view of the condition of her peoples, is distinctly open to doubt.) Western technology, certainly, is fully stretched without such extravagance. The Concorde aeroplane was planned as far back as 1962 as a fine example of what could be done by technical cooperation between Britain and France. Ten years later it rose from the ground at a steep angle, but nothing like as steep as the rise in the project's cost: a price escalation of 500%. And now* the decisive question for Concorde's future is simply whether it would be more expensive to stop than to go on. It is a salutary reminder that the word cooperation does not automatically solve all problems.

However, there is no doubt that the fifties and sixties did witness an astonishing phenomenon in Europe, the fruit of the Marshall Plan. Statistically, it can be expressed like this: in the seventy years before 1955, Europe's industrial production doubled; in the ten years after 1955, it doubled again. What that sudden leap meant in human language was that an age of affluence had begun. Of course, the pace and extent of it varied; areas of poverty, reminders of that very acute, widespread poverty at the beginning of the century and the black days of the Depression in the 1930s, certainly remained. But nothing altered the fact that all over Europe, in Spain (whose poverty was once notorious), in Eastern Europe (despite the

*In June 1974.

straitjacket of Communism) and in Western Europe (through various forms of Welfare State), a vast redistribution of wealth was taking place.

Redistribution of wealth implies social revolution; that also was taking place. More and more people came to regard as normal the possession of property once regarded as the privilege of a few. Housing standards improved, and the everlasting shortage of housing reflected a mounting demand that could not have been uttered in earlier decades. With this improvement came a social equalisation. It was the same with cars, with television sets, now normal features of working-class life; with washing machines, spin-dryers and a whole range of household and kitchen gadgetry which have transformed the life of the housewife. It was the same with food: greater quantities, wider varieties, new tastes, the exotic available to many, not a few.

It was also the same with leisure: catering for the leisure of the masses became a profitable industry, or set of industries. At the beginning of the century the masses had no leisure, except Sundays and unemployment. And catering for the tastes of youth now became a profitable concern too – another revolution, made possible by the new spending power of youth. At the beginning of the century only the gilded youth of the aristocracy and the bourgeoisie had spending power. Now it jingled in the pockets of millions.

And so what every progressive, every revolutionary of the earlier part of the century had clamoured for was now happening: a levelling out of wealth and opportunity, a greater protection for the weak and needy than ever before. Whereas in the days of Europe's power there was much poverty in the midst of plenty, now there was plenty without power. In consequence, although divested of empire and no longer mighty in that manner, Europe remained an object of envy.

What was the result of this profound, revolutionary change inside the continent itself? Was it satisfaction, congratulation, happiness? Quite the contrary. This was the incubation period of the New Left, indissolubly linked to the new Avant-garde. All over Europe (though more covertly in the Communist states) the twin phenomena were observable: a proliferation of art-forms calculated to outrage – new iconoclasm, new surrealism, under the blanket title of 'pop culture' – and a proliferation of extremist political sects: Trotskyists, Maoists, Castroists, anarchists of a dozen varieties.

The New Left and the new Avant-garde were, above all, manifestations of youth, reflecting a sudden passionate concern with politics and social problems among the young; reflecting also the need of the young for a cause, an outlet for idealism. In the new conditions of the world, which to

314

thoughtful minds seemed to rob old slogans of their meaning, it was all somewhat puzzling, and to none more puzzling than to members of the Old Left. The New Left rejected the Old Left as part of the bourgeois scene; rejected it along with bourgeois music, bourgeois art, bourgeois morality and bourgeois politics. 'Nous avons une gauche préhistorique' (We have a prehistoric Left), said one wall slogan. Hurt and daunted, the Old Left tried to understand. The veteran Austrian Communist, Ernst Fischer, offered this explanation: 'Perhaps we are approaching total catastrophe. To confront this possibility, total revolution is chaotically preparing itself.'

Certainly the slogans and sayings of the New Left and its associates had a violent quality which matched its belligerent activities in the late sixties:

'Revolution is the festival of the oppressed,' wrote Germaine Greer, champion of Women's Liberation.

'People don't have a predisposition to order, they are educated to it . . . Our problem is to prove they are wrong,' said the revolutionary student Daniel Cohn-Bendit.

'Insurrectional activity is today the number one political activity,' wrote the professional revolutionary Régis Debray.

'That a certain amount of violence will take place is inevitable and unavoidable,' announced the perennial student activist Tariq Ali.

The sixties were a disturbing time; not least disturbing to some was the awareness that in all its aspects – explosions in the streets, explosions of sound, explosions on canvas – this agitation was an echo only. What was it that Michael Bakunin said in 1848? 'We must overthrow from top to bottom this effete social world which has become impotent and sterile!' (see p. 88). What could the 1960s add to that 120-year-old clarion call? Or to Filippo Marinetti's proclamation in 1909 (scc p. 105): 'We will have none of it, we, the young, the strong, and the living Futurists!'

Futurists indeed! The war-cries of the sixties had a depressingly familiar sound; also familiar, and more disconcerting for that reason, was the sense of imminent eruption.

A European idea

'Contestation permanente': 'unending dispute'; this was the new slogan of the 1960s, which was to swell into a war-cry. It meant dispute about all manner of things: a questioning, a doubting, a challenging of anything that smacked of 'official' or orthodox thought; a convulsion akin to the Renaissance, or the debates which preceded the American and French Revolutions.

... it is becoming more and more clear that the idea of revolution in the twentieth century is the political expression of a romantic temperament, and that it is a permanent struggle, against habit in oneself, tranquillity in one's surroundings and stability in one's government.[27]

This 'unending dispute' cuts across nationality, across race, and across class. It also cuts across age groups, though often it does not look as though it is doing so; the usual outward manifestation of it is a picture of burning youth confronting crabbed old age.

In the 1960s universities all over the world became the arenas of this confrontation. This was no cause for wonder; the disputation was, after all, fundamentally philosophical, even religious, and as such a natural preoccupation of intellectuals. In America, in West Germany, in Berlin, in Scandinavia, in Holland, in Britain, and ultimately with sensational results in France, millions of young people, chiefly students, questioned or rejected existing society, its manners, its methods, its goals. 'On ne compose pas avec une société en décomposition.' (One does not compromise with a society that is decomposing.)[105] This graffito on the wall of the large lecture hall of the Sorbonne expressed a very general attitude; it is again not surprising if youth in America and Germany, where opulence can be notably ostentatious, led the way in rejecting the grosser attributes of affluent capitalism, but other countries were not far behind. It was not surprising, after the fiasco of Suez in 1956, if patriotic nationalism in Western Europe now attracted the jeers and distrust of youth. It was not surprising, after what happened in Warsaw and Budapest in 1956, if Soviet-style Communism no longer seemed to offer satisfying alternatives. It was not surprising, in the age of triumphant technology, if old-fashioned

'A bad year for revolutions'. Russian tanks in Prague, 1968 (Marilyn Silverstone)

religious beliefs sounded more unconvincing than ever. 'Assez d'églises' (Enough of churches)[105] pronounced a wall on the Boulevard St Germain. Not everyone was quite so sure about this: 'Dieu, je vous soupçonne d'être un intellectuel de gauche' (God, I suspect you of being a Left-wing intellectual)[105] was the doubting message elsewhere.

In all countries youth flung its questions at old beliefs and values. If tobacco and alcohol, why not cannabis and heroin? 'Take a trip every day of your life.'[105] If old enough for conscription, why not old enough for copulation? If science is kind enough to invent a wide array of contraceptives, why not use them, not now and again, but Now, and Again, and again and again and again. 'Contestation. Mais con d'abord.'[105] There were not always simple, uplifting answers to these questions; and so the universities of the Western world became centres of doubt and discord which, in some cases, turned unending dispute into unending uproar.

In May and June 1968 the University of Paris, the Sorbonne, supplied the arena for dispute and confrontation at revolutionary level. It was curiously hard to grasp, until it happened, that revolution was coming to the boil inside that famous seat of learning. But the students of the Sorbonne, in 1968, were highly combustible material: the dead weight of bureaucracy, the French state education system, lay heavily upon them. 'Regarde ton travail, le néant et la torture y participent' (Look at your work; nullity and torture are its ingredients).[105]

Sheer numbers helped to make a stultifying system even more soulless: in 1946 France had 123,000 students, in 1961 202,000, in 1968 514,000. The expansion had been too swift: there were neither the teachers, nor the buildings nor the opportunities in society for so many. Hence frustration, and a rage turning into every possible extravagant political demonstration, but beginning exactly where it might be expected to begin, where frustration usually smites the young: beginning with sex. 'We want the Pill. We want a normal sex life at seventeen,' demanded the Comité d'action lycéen, an extreme Left movement of schoolboys and schoolgirls. It was, in the first place, a revolt against residential segregation of the sexes in the University that set off the student revolt in Paris in May 1968, and an element of sexual liberation permeated all the subsequent proceedings.

'Plus je fais l'amour, plus j'ai envie de faire la Révolution.
Plus je fais la révolution, plus j'ai envie de faire l'amour.'
(The more I make love, the more I want to make Revolution.
The more I make revolution, the more I want to make love.)[105]

'The revolution didn't look very much like love'. Barricades, Paris 1968

The Revolution itself did not look very much like love. For six weeks the Latin Quarter of Paris, the University area, became a battlefield where

students in their thousands fought the police and the CRS* with paving-stones, petrol bombs, clubs and burning cars. This was urban guerilla warfare, the dream-tactic of the New Left, spear-headed by the Trotsky-ists. It was a direct, savage onslaught on complacent, bourgeois France, and it caught the Fifth Republic unawares. President de Gaulle was pre-occupied at the time, as he frequently was, with the lofty destiny of the nation; the Prime Minister, M. Pompidou, was on a ten-day visit to Persia and Afghanistan. And in the meantime the Sorbonne students, under their tireless leaders Daniel Cohn-Bendit, Jacques Sauvageot, Alain Geismer and others, were shaking the state to its foundations. And then the work-ers came out on strike; by 20 May six million had stopped work, and the economic life of France faced paralysis.

This alliance of students and workers was another dream of the New Left – and it was the Old Left that shattered it. The French Trade Unions were dominated by the Communist Party, which now proved to be very conservative. The Communist Party simply refused to accept that a revolutionary situation had been created by the action of the students. The Communists preferred to bargain in the old style; the Socialists wavered; M. Pompidou returned, and took hold of affairs with capable hands; and General de Gaulle woke up. On 30 May he delivered a speech on television and radio: 'I have taken my decisions. In the present circum-stances I shall not resign. I have a mandate from the people. I shall fulfil it.'

Bourgeois France also woke up. A new slogan appeared on the walls: 'Assez de violence' (Enough of violence). The Champs Elysées, where crowds of mocking students had so recently been bidding de Gaulle 'good-bye', now filled with his supporters, about a million of them, marching under the tricolour and the Cross of Lorraine. These were the people who had seen surrender and Nazi Occupation, who had known the reign of the Gestapo, who had chosen Free France under de Gaulle, and under de Gaulle had experienced Liberation; this was their demonstration against those who only knew the inadequacies of the bourgeois state and who, in the act of destroying it, had nothing to offer instead.

The bourgeois state proved stronger than its enemies supposed. When it bases itself firmly on democracy, it gathers to itself the strength of demo-cracy. The secret, democratic ballots of the June election gave de Gaulle a massive majority; and that was the end of the French Revolution of 1968.

It was a bad year for revolutions, on both sides of a curtain which still gave out the ring of iron. It was now twenty years since Czechoslovakia had become a Communist state; they had not been pleasant years. Indeed, *Compagnies Républicaines de Sécurité, a Security force raised by the Fourth Republic during the Algerian War disturbances.

'A dream of the New Left'.
Students and workers at
the Renault works, 1968

there was little that was pleasant in Czechoslovakia's recent history. The Germans, during their Occupation from 1938 to 1945, had tried to divide Czechs from Slovaks to the disadvantage of the Czechs, and had not entirely failed. Then came liberation, and two years of democracy. And then, in 1948, there was the Communist coup, ushering in what were to be called 'the years of deformation' – deformation of human behaviour, deformation of the human spirit.

Now, in January 1968, a fresh wind was blowing. There was a new General Secretary of the Communist Party, Alexander Dubcek, a Slovak whose name was still unfamiliar in his own country; soon it would be known throughout the world. Under Dubcek's leadership 'democratisation', hastily attempted in Poland and Hungary in 1956, defeated but later more discreetly resumed, now began at last in Czechoslovakia. There was no question of overthrowing the Communist regime, no question of abandoning the Soviet alliance or the Warsaw Pact; there was just a desire, a deep, passionate, irrepressible desire for a little more freedom in literature and the arts, a little more honesty in public life, a little more efficiency, a little more decency. And Dubcek sympathised; he did not clamp down; he tried to help. That was all.

And yet that was too much. The East German Government, always neurotically suspicious of any softening of Communist doctrine, feared that the example of 'democratisation' in Czechoslovakia might lead to a repetition of the rising in Berlin in 1953, when the Red Army had had to be called in to suppress the German workers with tanks. The governments of Poland and Hungary remembered with horror their own similar experiences in 1956. The puppet governments communicated their fears to the Soviet leaders, Brezhnev and Kosygin; like Khrushchev in 1956, they decided to take no more risks of revolt or defection.

On the night of 20 August 1968 Soviet, Polish, Hungarian and German troops entered Czechoslovakia. Only Rumania, of the Warsaw Pact states, held herself explicitly and honourably aloof.* And the only concession to the sense of disgrace with which history might invest this whole episode was that the German divisions wore Red Army uniforms, not their own, because the German uniforms did rather hideously resemble those of 1938. Now Czech and Slovak cities, above all the capital, Prague, became in their turn arenas of confrontation – but confrontation of a very different quality from that which the world had watched in Paris three months earlier. Czechoslovak students and workers poured into the streets to oppose the invaders as best they could, but these were not policemen and

*Bulgaria did not take part in the invasion, but did not oppose it. Yugoslavia, of course, condemned it hotly.

riot squads: this was an army of 650,000 soldiers with thousands of tanks which they meant to use. It is difficult to conduct 'unending dispute' with a tank. The Czechs did their best; they tried mockery and they tried argument, both with some effect on the invaders' morale; and they encouraged each other with poetry and song.

You have tanks,
We have the truth,
And our finest hour.
You have only power
To beat and betray,
To beat and betray,
I only sing a song,
And this is what I say:
Go away, go away![20]

Of course, the Soviet forces did not go away; in the face of Czech hatred and the condemnation of world opinion they remained; short of a third world war, there was no way of shifting them. Bad times returned to Czechoslovakia: Dubcek was arrested, handed over to the Soviet Secret Police – but allowed to go, stripped of all power; Czechoslovakia was forced to abandon the 'democratisation' policy (though no doubt she will try to return to it, as other have done); it was agreed that Soviet forces would remain indefinitely. All in all, the 1968 invasion was a useful reminder that brute force is still very much a factor in European affairs, and a reminder, too, of what brute force can achieve when nothing hinders it.

Such reminders are not in short supply; Germany herself is one. The Berlin Wall, and the lethal fence which seals off East Germany's frontier with the West, are similar manifestations of brute force. The Wall has been there since August 1961, and the reasons for its existence are quite simple. By 1961, in the sixteen years that Germany had been divided, three and a half million people had left the 'Democratic Republic' and fled to the Federal Republic, a migration rate of 850 a day. This was not merely bad for the image of Communism, it was also desperately bad for the East German economy. In fact, if the migration had continued at that rate, the East German economy would probably have collapsed. In desperation, Walter Ulbricht's government decided to adopt the crudest possible expedient: to prevent their people escaping from their particular 'workers' paradise' by walling them in.

Unfortunately, they would keep trying to escape. There were awful scenes when the Wall was erected in Berlin, with people flinging themselves out of high windows and crashing to their deaths, one of them an 80-year-old woman who jumped from five stories up. All in all, the Wall

'It is difficult to conduct unending dispute with a tank'. Prague 1968

and the frontier fence together have now claimed over 170 known victims, whose memorials stand beside the hateful barrier. As recently as 1972 its effectiveness was 'improved' by the installation of a comprehensive booby-trap and automatic shrapnel-firing system, designed to give the refugee no chance of survival, while relieving the guards of the necessity of shooting him in full view. Within six weeks this sophistication had proved its worth.

The Wall and the sealed frontier tell us many things. First, as long as they are there we know that the Cold War is still with us. The frontier it marked out was at first far more absolute than the frontiers which had spelt so much danger to the mighty continent at the beginning of the century. The Iron Curtain (frontier of the Cold War) marked an ideological divide, a clash of cultures as clear to begin with as resistance to the Mongol invasions or the coming of the Turks. East Germany apart, the Iron Curtain is now, happily, far more penetrable in both directions. The irresistible force of modern tourism has to a considerable extent beaten down the obstacle, so that now it is even possible to drive one's car (on authorised routes) from end to end of the Soviet Union itself. And the value of the tourist trade is such that even Communist governments will not rashly discourage it.

Nevertheless, the Wall does also remind us that on one side of it (whether in East Germany, in Czechoslovakia, or in the USSR itself) there is still a distinct shortage of human rights. First proclaimed in the Atlantic Charter in 1941, and then embodied in the United Nations Declaration to which fifty-seven nations subscribed in 1945 (among them the Soviet Union) these include:

'the right of all peoples to choose the form of government under which they will live';
'freedom from fear and want';
'no territorial aggrandisement';
'no territorial changes except by the freely expressed wishes of the peoples concerned'.

Eastern Europe has still some distance to go, to live up to those ideals.

What is encouraging is that, just as we accept that the phrase 'the West' embraces a variety of living styles within the broad context of democracy, 'Eastern Europe' now also has to be regarded as the sum of distinctly different parts. Nearly twenty years after their ill-fated assertions of national identity in 1956, Poland and Hungary are visibly distinct not merely from the Soviet Union, their overlord, or East Germany, but also from each other, and from Rumania, the latest challenger of absolute

Soviet domination. This is a healthy sign, with indications that an increasingly Social-Democratic West may one day arrive at a genuine meeting with a decreasingly doctrinaire Communist East.

And it is with this encouragement in their minds that statesmen and others have spoken in recent years of a 'détente' between the West and the Warsaw Pact countries. The Ostpolitik associated with the name of Willy Brandt during his Chancellorship of the German Federal Republic was an interesting aspect of 'détente'; increasing trade with Eastern Europe and the USSR is another. Yet this thaw was perhaps a little premature, like an earlier one in the 1950s. Once more there was a reminder that great differences remain between the Communist idea of life and the democratic idea.

People in the West found themselves becoming familiar with new Russian names; many were writers – the poet Yuly Daniel, the novelist Lidia Chukovskaya, the novelist and critic Andrey Sinyavsky, the poet Yevgeny Yevtushenko, Andrey Amalrik. In 1970 Amalrik was imprisoned for three years for publishing a book called *Will the Soviet Union survive until 1984?* At the end of his sentence in 1973 he was imprisoned for another three years, without trial. Associated with these men (and many others like them) are the nuclear physicist, Academician Andrey Sakharov, Pyotr Grigorenko, a former Red Army major-general, Valery Panov and his wife Galina, Jewish dancers at the Kirov Ballet in Leningrad (in 1974 allowed to leave the USSR for Israel). These are dissidents: eminent people in many different walks of life who are opposed to the Soviet Government, and have dared to say so – to their cost.

No dissident is more famous (rightly or wrongly) than the novelist Alexander Solzhenitsyn. In 1945 Solzhenitsyn was sentenced to eight years' forced labour on a charge which was later admitted to be false. The experience, not unnaturally, coloured his life and work, with the result that his books, well known in the West, have been largely withheld from Soviet readers. By 1968 Solzhenitsyn and the Soviet authorities were on a collision course; he was accused of 'maliciously slandering the Soviet system' and warned to cease his 'anti-Soviet activities'. He refused to compromise, and deliberately made himself a test case, using the Press conference with Western journalists as a weapon. He told them:

In our country the lie has become not just a moral category, but a pillar of the State. . . . Everyone must decisively stop cooperating with the lie, everywhere he sees it himself: where they force him to speak, write, quote or sign, or even simply to vote or read . . .

Solzhenitsyn did not 'cooperate with the lie'. In February 1974 the confrontation came to a head; Solzhenitsyn was arrested, and the world watched with alarm. But 1974 was not 1949, or 1956, or even 1968: Solzhenitsyn was not imprisoned, he was exiled, and his family was shortly afterwards allowed to join him. The *Daily Telegraph* wrote (14 February 1974):

In depriving Alexander Solzhenitsyn of his citizenship and expelling him, the Soviet Government has in effect admitted that he posed a problem too big and too hot to handle. . . . For the West, the lesson is clear: a State as powerful as Russia which can deal with a world-famous author only in this way must be so unstable as to be really dangerous.

The Solzhenitsyn case (and the others like it) cast serious doubts upon 'détente', and lent new point to the reflection that at that time the forces of the Warsaw Pact outnumbered the forces of NATO by two to one in men, two to one in aircraft, and four to one in tanks.

It is with these mixed reflections that we have to look back across half a century, to 1925, when the German Foreign Minister, Gustav Stresemann, said: 'We have the right to speak of a European idea' (see p. 175). Have we forfeited that right? Are we any closer to exercising it? In 1957 the creation of the EEC looked like a definite step towards realisation of the 'European idea'. In the years that followed EEC appeared to be very much a going concern, conferring considerable material benefits on its members. This association of six Western states rapidly developed into the world's greatest trading entity, its biggest importer of raw materials and exporter of finished products. In its offices and commissions a new human specimen appeared, and was given a new name: the Eurocrat, habitually thinking and planning across national frontiers. The ever-increasing numbers of the Eurocrats even caused alarm in some circles, representing, as they did, an unfamiliar kind of 'group patriotism' instead of national patriotism. In other circles, this was regarded as an encouraging sign.

The weakness, of course, was that in its first form EEC was an association of only six countries, of which only three are large units. Britain, a major manufacturing and exporting country still, despite her recurring economic crises and endemic industrial disputes, stood outside. Then, in 1961, the Prime Minister, Harold Macmillan, came to an important decision. He told General de Gaulle:

Believe me, we are no longer the England of Queen Victoria, of Kipling, of the British Empire, of 'splendid isolation'. Many of our people, especially among the young, feel that it is time we opened a new chapter in our history. . . . Let us bring Europe together, my dear friend! There are three men who can do it: you, Adenauer and I. If, while the three of us are still alive and in power, we let this historic opportunity pass us by, God knows if, when and to whom it will ever present itself again.[32]

Macmillan, always at heart a believer in the 'European idea', announced in the House of Commons on 31 July 1961 that Britain would apply for membership of EEC, subject to certain 'satisfactory arrangements' concerning the Commonwealth and her European Free Trade Area partners. The application was welcomed by most members of the Community, and Mr Edward Heath accordingly opened negotiations in Brussels; he told the Commission: 'We desire to become full, whole-hearted and active members of the European Community in its widest sense.'

The negotiations dragged on for eighteen months, and General de Gaulle, at first sympathetic to Britain's entry, became more and more doubtful whether Britain really was ready, as he put it, to 'moor herself to the Continent'. On 14 January 1963 at a Press Conference he uttered the words which effectively vetoed the British application:

England, in effect, is insular, she is maritime, she is linked through her exchanges, her markets, her supply lines to the most diverse and often the most distant countries. . . . She has in all her doings very marked and very original habits and traditions. In short, the nature, the structure, the very situation that are England's differ profoundly from those of the continentals.

In other words, Britain did not truly belong, whatever Mr Macmillan and Mr Heath might say; there were many in Britain who profoundly agreed with de Gaulle, while stoutly disputing his right to say these things.

Four years later it was Labour's turn to reverse a policy; a new Prime Minister, Harold Wilson, made a second application for British membership of EEC. But de Gaulle was immovable; he now believed that if Britain joined she would seriously change the nature of the Community, that it would be impossible to prevent her 'from dragging the West into an Atlantic system which would be totally incompatible with a European Europe'.[32] And there, until his death, the matter had to rest.

General de Gaulle died in November 1970, a week short of his eightieth birthday, a compound of many qualities: an anachronism and a visionary; a legend, an enigma; a great man; a European extraordinary. Immediately Mr Heath, now returned as Prime Minister, raised the question of Britain's entry into EEC again. De Gaulle's successor, President Pompidou, and the German Chancellor, Willy Brandt, proved amenable. Despite considerable public reservations in Britain, including demands for a referendum, Parliament voted for British entry, and in January 1972 Mr Heath signed the Treaty which one year later would make this a fact. The Republic of Ireland and Denmark followed suit.

So, in January 1973, when the new members took their places in the European Parliament in Strasbourg and in the EEC Commissions in Brus-

'A salutary reminder that co-operation does not solve all problems'.
Concorde unveiled

sels, the Six became Nine, and an important fresh stage appeared to have been reached in the development of the 'European idea'. But the year 1973 had more to say. In October a new war flared up between Israel and her Arab neighbours. Mortified at missing a success that had seemed within their grasp, the Arabs blamed American aid to Israel and announced drastic cuts in oil production in retaliation. The effect on America was disagreeable; on Western Europe and the EEC it was disastrous. At one stage Europe was threatened with cuts in oil supplies of up to twenty per cent, creating an energy crisis which threatened to undermine all her economic gains (already menaced by a galloping inflation).

As the stark implications unfolded, there were distressing scenes in the EEC, a marked absence of 'Community' spirit or activity. There was little or no disposition for the better placed countries to help the worse off; on the contrary, on all sides there was unilateral negotiation for special terms with the Arabs. An *Evening Standard* headline for 9 November, over an article by the Paris correspondent, Sam White, read: 'Europe – Impotent and Humiliated'. Sam White reported French opinion as saying:

What is the use of champing at the bit at the prospects of becoming a US satellite, if you end up as a satellite of the Sheikdoms? It is pointed out, for example, that the choice of Holland as the first victim of Arab blackmail over oil was not the result of any action by the Dutch Government, but purely an expression of resentment at the high level of public sympathy for Israel in that country. In those circumstances, every West European country is vulnerable . . .

The immediate energy crisis died away in 1974, but the damage to the EEC was not easily repaired. The British, in particular, were disappointed by the results of an entry which had already deeply affected their way of life. By May 1974, with Pompidou dead, Heath and Brandt out of office, and a new British government, officially opposed to EEC, some British delegates at Strasbourg were openly saying that the EEC was in danger of collapse: a depressing setback for the 'European idea'.

At the centre of Europe's story in the twentieth century, the undoing of the mighty continent, very nearly the death of the 'European idea', there are the two catastrophes, the two attempts at suicide which almost succeeded. Twice in this century aggressive nationalism in Europe has proved stronger than the system of international security. Twice the powers of Europe went to war, once in a mood of innocent enthusiasm based on ignorance, the second time without the enthusiasm, but with no less savagery. In the process, twice the mighty continent tore itself to pieces. The great productive power which, at the beginning of the century, had been a dominating fact of the world economy, was largely smashed. The communications network, the most elaborate system of roads and railways, canals and harbours, in the world, was rendered useless. Twice the most sophisticated agriculture in the world was wrecked.

Worst of all was the human loss. The great static battles of the First World War, Verdun, the Isonzo, the Somme, Ypres, took a toll of human life beyond anything previously experienced. In the Second World War improved weapons, mass bombing from the air, and policies of racial extermination probably trebled the loss. The astronomical mortality figures still do not tell the full truth. It is not just the bodies of hundreds of thousands of Europeans that lie in the War Cemeteries; it is a generation twice over, two age-groups, the pick of the active males between eighteen and thirty-five, twice running. In both wars it was the men with courage, dedication and initiative who were the first and most numerous casualties. The War Cemeteries are the graveyards of Europe's leaders and Europe's leadership.

In 1918 the old empires of Europe vanished, rubbed out by the First World War. The departure of the Habsburgs, the Romanovs and the Hohenzollerns is a major fact of this century in Europe. All their empires had been founded on varying degrees of social inequality, with wealth in the hands of a few and often much poverty at the base of the pyramid. Their disappearance seemed to be a necessary part of progress. No one dreamed of the darker empires that would succeed them.

First in Russia, then in Italy, but most dramatically in Germany, new tyrannies sprang up between the wars which put the injustices and inequalities of the old empires in the shade. Lenin paved the way for the abominable Stalin; the abominable Mussolini charted his own course, and with it the course of the most abominable Hitler. Hitler and the Nazi regime marked not only the lowest ebb of European civilisation in this century, but one of its lowest ebbs in history. Invoking the romantic idealism, particularly of youth, that has inspired so many European achievements, Hitler turned it into courses of pure evil. This indeed, was his ultimate crime: the corruption of virtues. He brutalised patriotism, he prostituted labour, he perverted sacrifice. His hideous memorials are the concentration camps in which perhaps six million Jews and who knows how many others were done to death amid trappings of sadism and torture unknown even in the Middle Ages. The Nazi empire has been dead for thirty years; the shame of it will never die in Europe's memory; and we have to remember that the death of Nazism was not the death of tyranny.

The sense of shock and outrage, when the reckonings of the war of the old empires and the war of the new empires were presented, was in each case enormous. And in each case there was a sense of the need for sweeping remedies, bold experiments. After the First World War there was the

League of Nations, with its headquarters in Geneva, ostensibly a world organisation but, in the absence of the United States and the Soviet Union, actually dominated by Europe. This was the last time that Europeans would dominate a world political arena.

The League, of course, was a failure; it failed even to control the feuds of Europe, chiefly because, recoiling from the horrors of the First World War, the men who most believed in the League found it hardest to believe that force was still present in the world, and that the League itself might need force. 'The League of Nations is enormously strong,' said Professor Gilbert Murray, one of its most devoted supporters, famous internationalist and pacifist (see p. 199); 'such weakness as it shows is the weakness of timidity, not lack of strength.' That was in 1935, the year in which Italy attacked Abyssinia and wrecked the League.

With the League of Nations shown to be helpless, the old method of balance of power by alliances still discredited, totalitarianism on the march and a maniacal dictator in power in Germany, there was no real obstacle to the second catastrophe. When it was over, and the new reckoning was presented, once more men put their faith in a world organisation, the United Nations. The UN has now existed for thirty years; it has consumed and continues to consume a great deal of time and a great deal of money – a lot of it spent on very good works. The United Nations Relief and Rehabilitation Administration, UNRRA, in the years immediately after the Second World War helped millions of refugees and Displaced Persons. The World Health Organisation conducts the battle against disease as an international enterprise. The Food and Agriculture Organisation tries to resolve the world's urgent food problems; that is a battle in which defeat does not bear thinking of. UNESCO, the United Nations Educational, Scientific and Cultural Organisation, tries to spread knowledge and diminish prejudice. These are just a few of the United Nations Agencies which are working to improve Man's lot, and it is hard to grudge the money spent on them.

The work of the Agencies does not, however, conceal the harsh fact that the UN (despite some early successes, such as Korea and the Congo) has increasingly failed in its main political purpose: peace-keeping and preventing aggression. During the thirty years of the UN's existence, war has continued almost without interruption in Vietnam, and the UN has been able to do nothing about it. The state of Israel, a fragment of Europe transplanted to the Middle East, is a creation of the United Nations. This, however, has not prevented intermittent wars between Israel and her Arab neighbours, notably in 1956, 1967 and 1973. The UN was unable to prevent the Suez invasion, and in Europe itself it has been powerless against the aggressions of 1956 in Hungary or of 1968 in Czechoslovakia.

The truth is, of course, that the UN was founded upon the supposition of Great-Power unity; when that crumbled, it lost its strength. Now, with a vast influx of new states, its very character has changed: it has become a system of lobbies, a propaganda forum. This is sad; it is sad also to see the decline of European influence in the United Nations (although the advent of affluence brought a corresponding demand for Europe's money). So the UN, like the League, is a disappointment; but it is hard to resist the conclusion that a world without it would be an even more unpleasant and dangerous place.

The failure of the United Nations to bring security inevitably resulted in a return to a balance of power: the long, unlovely confrontation between the Soviet bloc and a Western Europe which leaned heavily on American military support. It was in 1947 that President Harry Truman told the American Congress (see p. 281): 'The free peoples of the world look to us for support in maintaining their freedoms. If we falter in our leadership we may endanger the peace of the world.' For twenty-five years this doctrine lay at the heart of American policy, and at the heart of European security. But in 1973 another President, Richard Nixon, said in his second inaugural address:

We shall do our share in defending peace and freedom in the world. But we shall expect others to do their share. The time has passed when America will make every other nation's conflict our own, or make every other nation's future our responsibility, or presume to tell the people of other nations how to manage their affairs.

Western Europe has been reluctant to grasp the significance of President Nixon's message; she has lost the military habit. Western Europe has also been reluctant to see the further significance of an unexpected and untoward event: the Watergate scandal, which has not merely undermined the reputation of President Nixon, but has undermined the morale and authority of America herself, with potential grave effects upon the balance of power. The implications are entirely unpalatable; but Western Europe will have to grasp the problem of self-defence, along with the problem of economic inflation which seems equally intractable, and the problem of energy supplies, which may be overcome for a while by timely discoveries in the North Sea.

The Europe of tomorrow is arising today. In every country the tall crane and the bulldozer are at work, with their messages of change for better or worse. First they cleared away the rubble and ruins of war; then they became more ambitious: they began to clear away old Europe itself. A phrase was coined for anything built before 1939: 'primitive construc-

'It would certainly not be true to say that
all the ancient feuds of Europe have died away'.
Cyprus 1964 (Don McCullin)

tion'. The new Europe would not like to be thought primitive, and so we have seen, in a very short time, familiar skylines change, familiar landmarks suddenly juxtaposed with novelties. Inevitably, this abrupt alteration of landscapes, urban and rural, brings to many a sense of loss at least as great as the enrichment it brings to others. The new Europe has been looking for a style, but so far has only succeeded in evolving a plethora of styles which often lie unhappily together and with the remains of old Europe around them.

As with buildings, so with their contents: today's offering is a polished, refulgent, aseptic world of plastic furnishings and metallic vegetation where comfort is not for creatures, and to be human must certainly be to err. But nothing can be bright for ever, clean for ever; nothing lasts for ever. Even the most dazzling of metal flowers must fade and – somehow – die. And meanwhile, whether one welcomes all its manifestations or not, there is no doubt that this new Europe does proclaim a recovery from a mighty fall, that it proclaims an equalisation of society, a changed concept of social justice. The question remains, whether European man can fit himself into the scene he is creating.

And now we may ask ourselves: how stands the 'European idea' after three quarters of a century? What are the chief changes that we see? In one respect, a hasty glance might tell us that the continent has gone back two thousand years. In the days when a large part of Europe was united under the Roman empire, its frontier was in many places indicated by a great wall, which marked the separation of civilisation from the barbarians. And today, as we have seen, there is again a wall, but we have also seen that it no longer separates to the extent that was first intended. And it is worth noting, too, that on either side of it lesser separations have died away.

At the beginning of the century Europe was full of feuds: France's feud with Germany; Russia's feud with Germany and Austria; Austria's feud with Italy; the Slav feud with the Turks; the Greek feud with the Turks and Italians; almost everybody's feud with England. All these were plants with deep roots (see p. 76).

It would certainly not be true to say that all the ancient feuds of Europe have died away. A very old feud indeed, part-racial, part-religious, in the province of Ulster brought Britain to the edge of civil war in 1914, and has done untold damage in Ulster, as well as in England and the Republic of Eire, since it flared up again in 1969. Fanaticism on both sides has made this feud more intractable than ever. The old Greek-Turkish feud still from time to time gives Cyprus its place in the headlines. In Belgium the Walloons and the Flemings can still fly at each others' throats. The Croats have not forgotten their quarrel with the Serbs.

We may, nevertheless, take some comfort from the fact that these feuds are now, by and large, internal matters. Britain and Eire cooperate against terrorism; Greece and Turkey have been close to war again, but thought better of it; Belgium seeks no dispute with France; Yugoslavia threatens no neighbour with retaliation. Indeed, national wars, like the Franco-Prussian War of 1870, the Italo-Turkish War in 1911, or the Balkan Wars of 1912-13, no longer seem to be real prospects. Following the fall of empires there has been an unquestionable decline of nationalism in Europe. Or rather, in some parts of Europe; and that qualification makes what ought to be a sign of hope also, to some extent, a sign of danger.

If nationalism and the patriotic instincts to which it made appeal have receded, so also has religion – Christianity. That is not to say that the Christian religion does not remain a powerful force in many places: a pillar of the state (with reservations) in Spain, an inspiration of resistance to the state in Poland or Hungary, an aspect of nationalism itself in Cyprus, a social corrosive in Ulster. Those are all places where forms of Christianity remain strong; elsewhere, in Britain and France and Scandinavia, churches are becoming emptier, the sound of church bells is becoming unfamiliar. We even see churches being pulled down, or sold for non-religious uses, while churchmen no longer emphasise the apartness of their calling. But Man has to believe in something, and so we also see a host of ideological demons rushing in on the heels of the departing angels.

The twentieth century has amply fulfilled its promise in one respect: its seventy-five years have been an unparalleled Age of Technology. The ramifications of technological progress are vast, but one or two aspects of it may be taken as symbolic. It is hard to recollect, in Western countries (and increasingly so in Eastern Europe also) that in 1900 Europe's chief motive power was still the horse. As the poet Laurie Lee told us (see p. 25), the horse's eight miles an hour 'was the limit of our movements, as it had been since the days of the Romans'. Here, definitely, a link with the distant past has been snapped; the motive power of the continent for thousands of years has almost vanished in this century. The transition from horses to horsepower is practically complete; and the internal combustion engine is a true symbol of the twentieth century.

So is electricity. In 1900 the Paris Exhibition boastfully displayed the Palace of Electricity, 'already', said the prospectus, 'an almighty sovereign'. The telephone had arrived, television was on its way. Europe said good-bye to oil lamps (like the horse, dating back to Roman days and beyond) and goodbye to gaslight. Grasping the significance of the new power source, Lenin stated in the early twenties: 'Communism equals

Soviet power plus electrification.' The progress of a country was measured by its electrification programme. To those who remember the much darker Europe of the thirties and forties, the electrification of the continent is one of the most striking symbols of technological change in the twentieth century.

Another symbolic fact is undoubtedly the shrinkage of the mighty continent due to modern technology. We must admit that it was the Romans who started this; it was they who drove long straight roads across Europe, flinging majestic viaducts across wide valleys, bridging great rivers, and all leading to Rome. The Romans began it, indeed; but the Roman legions, even on paved roads, could only manage twenty miles a day. Napoleon I imitated Rome with his Routes Nationales, and bewildered Europe with some prodigious marching; but the speed of his armies remained, in the end, the speed at which a man's legs can carry him. It was left to the twentieth century, the age of the railroad, the autobahn, the motorway, to devour the distances of the continent, and roll it into a ball. And what the railways and roads began, the flightpaths have continued; by air, the shrinkage becomes absurd: London to Moscow in three hours and thirty minutes; Athens to Brussels in two hours and ten minutes; Madrid to Paris in one hour and forty-five minutes. The nations of Europe are now very close together; very close and very vulnerable.

The loss of might, the shaking of beliefs and the accompanying technological progress stand out as the major happenings in Europe in this century. They are the stuff of Europe's history. And history does not pretend to read the future; all too soon the future becomes history. What we have seen, in seventy-five years, is a continent at first possessing almost unbelievable power, wealth and prestige, twice inflicting terrible wounds upon herself, and rising again nevertheless; helpless, impoverished, divided, but rising again. History only traces the curve as far as it goes; history notes that the curve is at present upward; history warns that satisfaction should be tempered. The mighty continent has many adjustments to make.

'That a certain amount of violence will take place is inevitable'.
Belfast, 1971
(Giles Peress)

References

Numbers in the text refer to those in this list.

1   Aldington, Richard, *Death of a hero,* Chatto & Windus, 1929; C. Chivers, reprint 1968.

2   Alexander of Tunis, Field-Marshal Earl, *Memoirs, 1940–1945,* Cassell, 1962.

3   Amery, Julian, *Approach March,* Hutchinson, 1973.

4   Auden, W. H., 'Spain 1937' and 'Refugee Blues' in *Another Time,* Faber, 1951.

5   Balfour, Michael, *The Kaiser and his Times,* Cresset Press, 1964.

6   Baring, Maurice, *The Puppet Show of Memory,* Heinemann, 1922.

7   Barker, A. J., *Suez: the Seven Day War,* Faber, 1964.

8   Barnett, Correlli, *The Collapse of British Power,* Eyre Methuen, 1972.

9   Barnett, Correlli, *The Swordbearers,* Eyre & Spottiswoode, 1963.

10   Behr, Edward, *The Algerian Problem,* Hodder & Stoughton and Penguin Books, 1961.

11   Binding, Rudolph, *A Fatalist at War,* Allen & Unwin, 1929.

12   Bond, Brian, 'The Austro-Prussian War, 1866' in *History Today,* August 1966.

13   Bonsal, Stephen, *Unfinished Business,* Michael Joseph, 1944.

14   Briggs, Asa, *They saw it happen; 1897–1940,* Basil Blackwell, 1960; n.e. 1973.

15   Briscoe, W. A. and H. R. Stannard, *Captain Ball, VC,* Herbert Jenkins, 1918.

16   Brooke, Rupert, *Poetical Works,* Faber, 2nd rev. ed. 1970.

17   Carlyle, Thomas, Letter to *The Times,* 18 November, 1870.

18   Carrington, C. E., *The British Overseas,* Cambridge University Press, 2nd ed. 1968.

19   Carrington, C. E. (as 'Charles Edmonds'), *A Subaltern's War,* Peter Davies, 1929; C. Chivers, reprint 1969.

20   Chapman, Colin, *August 21st: the Rape of Czechoslovakia,* Cassell, 1968.

21   Chastenet, Jacques, 'La Semaine Sanglante de la Commune' in *Historia,* June 1966.

22   Churchill, Sir Winston, *The World Crisis 1911–18,* Thornton Butterworth, 2 vols 1923; New American Library, n.e. 1968.

23   Churchill, Sir Winston, *The Second World War,* Cassell, 6 vols 1948–54.

24   Conrad, Joseph, *Under Western Eyes,* Methuen, 1911; Dent (Everyman), 1972; Penguin Books 1969.

25   Cooper, R. W., *The Nuremberg Trials,* Penguin Books, 1947.

26   Crankshaw, Edward, *The Fall of the House of Hapsburg,* Longman, 1963; Sphere, n.e. 1970.

27   Cranston, Maurice, ed., *The New Left,* Bodley Head, 1971.

28   Crozier, Brian, *De Gaulle the Warrior,* Eyre Methuen, 1973.

29   Dangerfield, George, *The Strange Death of Liberal England,* MacGibbon & Kee, 1966; Paladin, n.e. 1970.

30   Day-Lewis, C., *Overtures to Death,* Jonathan Cape, 1938.

31   De Gaulle, C., *War Memoirs:* Vol. 1 *The Call to Honour, 1940–1942,* Collins, 1955.

32   De Gaulle, C., *Memoirs of Hope: Renewal 1958–62,* Weidenfeld & Nicolson, 1971.

33   Dempster, Derek, and Derek Wood, *The Narrow Margin,* Hutchinson, 1961; Arrow Books, n.e. 1969.

34 Desmond, S., *The Edwardian Story,* Rockliff Publications Corp., 1950.

35 Dimbleby, Richard, Despatch to BBC War Reporting Unit No. 7726, 19 April 1945.

36 Donaldson, Frances, *The Marconi Scandal,* Hart-Davis, 1962.

36a Eden, Sir Anthony (Lord Avon), *Memoirs,* Part 2 *1951–7 Full Circle,* Cassell, 1960.

37 Eliot, T. S., *Poems, 1909–1925,* Faber, 1925.

37a Elliott, B. J., *Western Europe after Hitler,* Longman, 1968.

38 Fishman, W. J., 'Louis Auguste Blanqui: Stormbird of Revolution' in *History Today,* June 1964.

39 Fulford, Roger, *Hanover to Windsor,* Batsford, 1960; Fontana, n.e. 1966.

40 Fuller, Major-General J. F. C., *The Decisive Battles of the Western World,* 3 vols, Eyre & Spottiswoode, 1954–6; Paladin, n.e. 1970–

41 Galland, Adolf, *The First and the Last,* Methuen, 1955.

42 Gedye, G. E. R., *Heirs to the Habsburgs,* Arrowsmith, 1932.

43 Gibbs, Sir Philip, *Realities of War,* Heinemann, 1920; C. Chivers, reprint 1970.

44 Gibbs, Sir Philip, *The Pageant of the Years,* Heinemann, 1946.

45 Gilbert, Felix, *The End of the European Era, 1890 to the present,* Weidenfeld & Nicolson, 1971.

46 Grant, A. J., and H. Temperley, *Europe in the Nineteenth and Twentieth Centuries 1789–1950,* Longman, 6th rev. ed. 1971.

47 Graves, Robert, *Goodbye to all that,* Cape 1929; Cassell, 1957; Penguin Books, 1969.

48 Grunberger, Richard, *Germany 1918–1945,* Batsford, 1964.

49 Gunther, John, *Inside Europe,* Hamish Hamilton, 1936.

50 Hagen, Louis (ed.), *The Schellenberg Memoirs,* André Deutsch, 1956.

51 Haldane, Viscount, *Before the War,* Cassell, 1920.

52 Hamilton, Mary Agnes, *Arthur Henderson,* Heinemann, 1938.

53 Hammerton, J. A., and H. W. Wilson, *The Great War: The standard history of the all-Europe conflict,* Amalgamated Press, 9 vols, 1914–18.

54 Harcave, Sidney, *First Blood: the Russian Revolution of 1905,* Bodley Head, 1964.

55 Hedin, Sven, *With the German Armies in the West,* John Lane the Bodley Head, 1915.

56 Horne, Alistair, *The Fall of Paris,* Macmillan, 1965, Pan Books, n.e. 1968.

57 Joll, James, *The Anarchists,* Eyre & Spottiswoode, 1964.

58 Jonson, Ben, 'Hymn to Diana' in *Works,* vol. 8 The Poems, Clarendon Press, 1947.

59 Keesing's *Contemporary Archives.*

60 King-Hall, Stephen, *Our Own Times, 1913–1938,* Nicholson & Watson, 1938.

61 Kipling, Rudyard, 'The Voortrekker' and 'Tommy' in *Verse,* Hodder & Stoughton, 1940.

62 Lawrence, D. H., *Kangaroo,* Secker, 1923; Heinemann, 1955; Penguin Books, 1950.

63 Lee, Laurie, *Cider with Rosie,* Hogarth Press, 1959; Penguin Books, 1970.

64 Legendre, Pierre, *Notre Épopée Coloniale,* Pan's: Librairie Charles Tallandier, 1901.

65 Liddell Hart, B. H., *History of the Second World War,* Cassell, 1970.

66 Lloyd George, David, *War Memoirs,* Nicolson, 6 vols, 1933–6; Odhams Press, 2 vols, 1938.

67 Ludendorff, F. W. E., *My War Memories 1914–1918,* Hutchinson, 1919.

68 Lyons, Eugene, *Assignment in Utopia,* Harrap, 1938.

69 MacDonald, Charles B., *The Mighty Endeavour,* New York; Oxford University Press, 1969.

70 MacNeice, Louis, *Autumn Journal,* Faber, 1939.

71 MacQueen Pope, W., *Give me Yesterday,* Hutchinson, 1957.

72 Majdalany, Fred, *Cassino: Portrait of a Battle,* Longman, 1957.

73   *Manifesto of Futurism,* first published in *Le Figaro,* Paris, 20 February 1909.

74   Marwick, Arthur, *The Deluge,* Bodley Head, 1965.

75   Marx, Karl, and Friedrich Engels, *Manifesto of the Communist Party,* 1888, Lawrence & Wishart, n.e. 1932; W. Reeves, n.e. of 1888 ed., 1964.

76   Masaryk, T. G., *The Making of a State,* Allen & Unwin, 1927.

77   Maurice, Sir Frederick, *Forty Days in 1914,* Constable, 1919.

78   Moorehead, Alan, *Gallipoli,* Hamish Hamilton, n.e. 1968.

79   Mordal, Jacques, 'Les Pertes Humaines dans les deux Guerres Mondiales' in *Miroir de l'Histoire,* September, 1961.

80   Morgan, Brigadier, J. H., *Assize of Arms,* Methuen, 1945.

81   Muggeridge, Malcolm, *The Thirties,* Hamish Hamilton, 1940; Collins, 1967.

82   Musil, Robert, *Man without Qualities,* Secker & Warburg, 3 vols, 1953–60; Panther, 3 vols, 1968.

83   Mussolini, Benito, *Scritti e Discorsi,* Rome: Hoepli, 1934; edizione definitiva, 1914–39.

84   Nicolson, Sir Harold, 'British Public Opinion and Foreign Policy', in *The Public Opinion Quarterly,* January 1937.

85   Nicolson, Sir Harold, *King George the Fifth,* Constable, 1952.

86   Nicolson, Sir Harold, *Peacemaking 1919,* Constable, 1933.

87   Nicolson, Sir Harold, *Small Talk,* Constable, 1937.

88   Nietsche, F, *Ecce Homo,* 1909; Vintage Books, n.e. 1973.

89   O'Ballance, Edgar, *The Story of the Foreign Legion,* Faber, 1961.

90   *Official Guide to the National Monument of the Santa Cruz del Valle de los Caidos,* Patrimonio Nacional, Madrid, 1972.

91   *Official Guide to the Paris Exhibition,* 1900.

92   Oliver, F. S., *Ordeal by Battle,* Macmillan, 1915.

93   Peacock, W., ed., *English Verse,* vol. 2, Oxford University Press, 1940.

94   Pethybridge, Roger, ed., *Witnesses to the Russian Revolution,* Allen & Unwin, 1964.

95   Rothel, Hans Konrad, *About the Blue Rider Group* (Brochure of the Blaue Reiter Exhibition, Villa Lenbach, Munich).

96   Schneckenburger, Max, *The Rhine Watch,* Germany, 1871.

97   Seale, F. and M. McConville, *French Revolution 1968,* Penguin Books, 1968.

98   Senger und Etterlin, F. M. von, *Neither Fear nor Hope,* Macdonald, 1963.

99   Shattuck, Roger, *The Banquet Years: The Originals of the Avant-garde in France, 1885 to World War I,* Faber, 1959; Cape, rev. ed. 1969.

100 Sitwell, Sir Osbert, *The Scarlet Tree,* Macmillan, 1946.

101 Solzhenitsyn, Alexander: *August 1914,* Bodley Head, 1972.

102 Steinberg, Jonathan, *Yesterday's Deterrent,* Macdonald, 1965.

103 Syrop, Konrad, *Spring in October,* Weidenfeld & Nicolson, 1957.

104 Taylor, A. J. P., *The Course of German History,* Hamish Hamilton, 1945; Methuen, 1961.

105 Tchou, Claude, ed., *Les murs ont la parole,* Paris, 1968.

106 Temperley, A. C., *The Whispering Gallery of Europe,* Collins, 1938.

107 Tennyson, Alfred, Lord, *Poems,* Henry Frowde, various eds.

108 Terraine, J. A., *Impacts of War, 1914 and 1918,* Hutchinson, 1970.

109 Terraine, J. A., *The Western Front,* Hutchinson, 1964; Arrow Books, n.e. 1970.

110 Thomas, Hugh, *The Spanish Civil War,* Eyre & Spottiswoode, 1961; Penguin Books, n.e.

111 *The Times History of the War,* 22 vols, 1914–1918.

112 Trevelyan, G. M., *Grey of Fallodon,* Longman, 1937.

113 Vansittart, Lord, *The Mist Procession,* Hutchinson, 1958.

114 Verity, William, 'The Rise of the Rothschilds' in *History Today,* April 1968.
115 Verrier, Anthony, *The Bomber Offensive,* Batsford, 1968.
116 Watt, D. C., et al., *A History of the World in the Twentieth Century,* Hodder & Stoughton, 1967; Pan Books, 3 vols, 1970.
117 Watt, R. M., *Dare Call it Treason,* Chatto & Windus, 1964.
118 Werth, Alexander, *Russia at War, 1941–1945,* Barrie and Jenkins, 1964.
119 Western, J. R., *The End of European Primacy, 1871–1945,* Blandford Press, 1965.
120 Wiskemann, Elizabeth, 'The Origins of Fascism' in *History Today,* December 1967.
121 Wrench, Sir Evelyn, *Struggle 1914–1920,* Nicholson & Watson, 1935.

Picture Credits

In page order: Title page, August Sander; page 10, Radio Times Hulton Picture Library, London; 12–13, J. E. Bulloz, Paris; 16, John Hillelson, London; 19, Caisse Nationale des Monuments Historiques, Paris; 22, August Sander; 24, Popperfoto, London; 26–7, Giraudon, Paris; 30–1, Popperfoto, London; 33 Süddeutscher Verlag, Munich; 35, Mansell Collection, London; 36, Roger Viollet, Paris; 38–9, Phaidon Press, London; 42, Mansell Collection, London; 45, Ullstein Bilderdienst, Berlin; 47, Roger Viollet, Paris; 50–1, Franz Hubmann; 53, Radio Times Hulton Picture Library, London; 54, Franz Hubmann; 58–9, Giraudon, Paris; 61, Staatsbibliothek, Berlin; 62, Süddeutscher Verlag, Munich; 66–7, Radio Times Hulton Picture Library, London; 71, Radio Times Hulton Picture Library, London; 74, Snark International, Paris; 77, Ullstein Bilderdienst, Berlin; 78, August Sander; 81, Süddeutscher Verlag, Munich; 82, Snark International, Paris; 86–7, Franz Hubmann; 93, Ullstein Bilderdienst, Berlin; 95, Staatsbibliothek, Berlin; 101, Tate Gallery, London (photo John Webb); 102–3, Giraudon, Paris; 106, Staatsbibliothek, Berlin; 110, Press Association, London; 113, British Broadcasting Corporation, London; 114–15, British Broadcasting Corporation, London; 120, National Maritime Museum, London; 126, Süddeutscher Verlag, Munich; 128–9, Radio Times Hulton Picture Library, London; 131, Ullstein Bilderdienst, Berlin; 134–5, Imperial War Museum, London (photo Eileen Tweedie); 137, Camera Press, London; 139, Author's collection; 140–1, Imperial War Museum, London; 143, Ullstein Bilderdienst, Berlin; 147, British Broadcasting Corporation, London; 148, Roger Viollet, Paris; 150–1, British Broadcasting Corporation, London; 154–5, Radio Times Hulton Picture Library; 156, National Portrait Gallery, London; 158, Syndication International, London; 162–3, Syndication International, London; 166, Novosti, London; 170–1, Süddeutscher Verlag, Munich; 173, Radio Times Hulton Picture Library; 176, Richard S. Zeisler, New York; 179, John Hillelson, London; 182, Radio Times Hulton Picture Library, London; 184, John Hillelson, London; 187, Roger Viollet, Paris; 191, August Sander; 192, Süddeutscher Verlag, Munich; 198, Radio Times Hulton Picture Library, London; 200, John Hillelson, London; 204–5, Radio Times Hulton Picture Library, London; 207, John Hillelson, London; 207–8, John Hillelson, London; 213, John Hillelson, London; 216–17, John Hillelson, London; 219, August Sander; 222–3, Süddeutscher Verlag, Munich; 225, Staatsgemäldesammlung, Munich (donation Gunther Franke); 226, Imperial War Museum (photo Eileen Tweedie); 229, Staatsbibliothek, Berlin; 232, Staatsbibliothek, Berlin; 235, John Hillelson, London; 239, Staatsbibliothek, Berlin; 241, Staatsbibliothek, Berlin; 243, Tate Gallery, London (photo John Webb); 244, Ullstein Bilderdienst, Berlin; 245, Staatsbibliothek, Berlin; 247, Popperfoto, London; 250, Ullstein Bilderdienst, Berlin; 253, Staatsbibliothek, Berlin; 257, British Broadcasting Corporation, London; 259, Staatsbibliothek, Berlin; 262, Radio Times Hulton Picture Library, London; 266–7, John Hillelson, London; 270–1, John Hillelson, London; 274–5, Radio Times Hulton Picture Library, London; 276, Staatsbibliothek, Berlin; 284–5, John Hillelson, London; 288–9, Camera Press, London; 292–3, John Hillelson, London; 296, John Hillelson, London; 299, John Hillelson, London; 302, Popperfoto, London; 306, John Hillelson, London; 310, Popperfoto, London; 316, John Hillelson, London; 319, Snark International, Paris; 321, Snark International, Paris; 324–5, John Hillelson, London; 330–1, Camera Press, London; 336–7, John Hillelson, London; 341, John Hillelson, London.

Index

(Figures in *italics* refer to illustrations)

Abbey theatre, 32
Abdul Hamid II, Sultan of Turkey, 56–7, 60, 117
Abyssinia, 75, 197–9, 334
Adenauer, Konrad, chancellor of W. Germany, 290, 311
Adler, Viktor, Austrian socialist, 55
Adowa, 75
Afghanistan, 320
Africa, 11, 72, 73, 109, 130, 305–7
Agadir, 122–3
agriculture, 23–5
Albania, 56, 186, 195, 221
Aldington, Richard, 201
Alençon, Emilienne d', 18
Alexander, King of Serbia, 118
Alexander I, King of Yugoslavia, 195–6
Alexander of Tunis, Earl, British field-marshal, 237, 238
Alfonso XIII, King of Spain, 195
Algeciras conference, 112
Algeria, 72–3, 130, 238, 301, 307–9
Ali, Tariq, 315
Allen, Lord, 197
Alma-Tadema, Sir Laurence, Anglo-Dutch painter, 21
Alsace-Lorraine, 169
Amalrik, Andrey, Russian writer, 327
Amis, Kingsley, British writer, 305
Amsterdam, 48
anarchism, 88–9, 100–4
Annam, 73
Anouilh, Jean, French writer, 282
Antwerp, 244
Apollinaire, Guillaume, French poet, 90, 104
Arab World, and Israel, 332, 334
army: Austro-Hungarian, *54*, 119–20; British, 25, 70–2, 119, 127, 193; French, 15, 119–20, 127, 149; German, 25, *30–1*, *36*, *63*, 65, 68, 111, 119–20, 127, 203; Russian, 25, *61*, 63 f., 119; tactics, 121
Arnhem, 244
arts, the, 18–23, 48–9, 104–5, 282, 304–5; in Austria, 41; in France, 18–21, 89–91; in Great Britain, 21
Asquith, H. H., Earl, British prime minister, 98, 145
Astor, Lady, 210

Aswan, 301
Athens, 340
Atlantic Charter, 263
atomic bomb, 263, 283–6
Attlee, Clement, Earl, British prime minister, 215, 264, 265
Auden, W. H., British poet, 218
Auschwitz, 246, 248, 260
Australia, 11, 69, 70, 127, 234, 303
Austria, 169, 172, 215, 286, 295, 311; and Germany, 203–6, 218; and Italy, 206; in World War 2, 260
Austria-Hungary, 11, 14, 49–56, 57, 63, 75, 79, 149, 159, 164, 165, 201 n., 251; Dual Monarchy, 52–5, 117 ff.; army of, *54*, 119–120; and the Balkans, 117 ff.; and Germany, 63 ff., 75, 112, 290; and Italy, 64, 76, 112; and Russia, 76
Axis, Rome–Berlin, *see under* Germany, Italy

Bakunin, Michael, Russian anarchist, 88, 315
Baldwin, Stanley, Earl, British prime minister, *178*
Balfour, A. J., Earl, British prime minister, 98, 99
Balkan States, 56–60, 116 *and see under* individual countries
Ball, Albert, British airman, 132
Barcelona, 80, 100–4
Barrès, Maurice, French writer, 21, 89
Bavaria, 167
BBC, 178–80, 282
Beardsley, Aubrey, British painter, 21
Beckmann, Max, German artist, *224*
Beethoven, Ludwig van, German composer, 41
Belfast, *340*
Belgium, 11, 73–5, 80, 88, 116, 127, 160, 169, 172, 188, 228, 240, 249, 273, 290, 307, 311, 338–9
Belgrade, 118, 238, 255, 279, 294
Bell, Dr, German statesman, 172
Belsen, 244–6
Benelux Union, 273
Beneš, Eduard, Czech president, 165, 268

Benz, Karl, 34
Berchtesgaden, 220
Beria, Lavrenty P., Soviet minister, 294
Berlin, 14, 23, 76, 80, *87*, 240, *258*, 260, 277, 279, 287; Blockade, 287–90; Wall, *285*, 232–6
Bernhardt, Sarah, French actress, 18–20
Bessarabia, 63
Bilbao, 100
Binding, Rudolph, 153
Birmingham, 76, 230
Bismarck, Prince Otto von, German chancellor, 34, 64–8, 84, 85, 97, 98
Black Hand Society, 124
Blanqui, Auguste, French revolutionary, 85
Blériot, Louis, French flyer, 18, 122
Blücher, G. L. von, Prussian marshal, 37
Blum, Léon, French prime minister, 91
Bobrikov, Russian governor-general, of Finland, 94
Boer War, 70–2, 312
Bogolyepov, Russian minister, 92
Bologna, 183
Bombay, 69
Bonar Law, A., British prime minister, 188
Bonn, 287
Bordeaux, 228, 269
Borneo, 73, 258
Bosnia, 118, 122, 233
Bouguereau, French painter, 90
Boxer rising, 76, 77
Brahms, Johannes, German composer, 41
Brandt, Willy, German chancellor, 215, 327, 329, 332
Braque, Georges, French painter, 104
Bratianu, Rumanian statesman, 165
Braunau, 203
Brazzaville, 72
Brest–Litovsk, 146
Brezhnev, Leonid I., Soviet leader, 322
Briand, Aristide, French prime minister, 17, 100, *171*, 175, 189, 190, 309
Britain, *see* Great Britain
British Union of Fascists, 206
Brockdorff-Rantzau, Count, German foreign minister, 172
Brooke, Rupert, British poet, 57, 136

Bruk, Michael, 297

Brunete, 215, 218

Brüning, Heinrich, German chancellor, *184*

Brusilov, Russian general, 144

Brussels, 92, 244, 329, 332, 340

Bucharest, 279

Buchenwald, 244

Budapest, 49, 52, 80, 117, 118, 256, 279, *298*, 300, 304, 317

Bukharin, Nikolay I., Soviet leader, 211

Bulganin, Nikolay A., Soviet prime minister, 294, *311*

Bulgaria, 56, 123, 153, 165, 168, 186, 195, 231, 255, 268, 291, 322 n.

Bülow, Karl von, German general and chancellor, 109

Burma, 11, 258, 265

Byron, Lord, British poet, 57

Caillaux, Joseph, French prime minister, 17

Calcutta, 69

Cambodia, 73, 272

Cameroons, 68, 130

Campbell-Bannerman, Sir Henry, British prime minister, 98

Canada, 69, 70, 127, 234, 237, 290

Caporetto, 152

Caribbean, 72

Carlyle, Thomas, British historian, 37

Carné, Marcel, French film director, 282

Carnot, Sadi, French president, assassination of, 88

Caserio, Santo, 88

Castellane, Bony de, 17

Caucasus, 63, 80

Cavalieri, Lina, 18

Cecil, Lord Robert, 178

Ceylon, 265

Cézanne, Paul, French painter, 20, 90

Chamberlain, Sir Austen, British foreign secretary, *171*, 175, 177, 189

Chamberlain, Joseph, British minister, 76

Chamberlain, Neville, British prime minister, 218, 220

Chavannes, Puvis de, 90

Chekhov, Anton, Russian writer, 23

Chetniks, 231

Chiang Kai-shek, Chinese nationalist leader, 280

China, 11, 63, 68, 76, 107, 196–7, 258

Chukovskaya, Lidia, Soviet writer, 327

Church, *see* religion

Churchill, Sir Winston, British prime minister, 98, 120, 133, 145, 157, 161, 164, 165, 174, 175, 190, *209*, 221, 230,

236, 254, 256–8, 260, 261, 263, 279, 283, 309, 312

cinema, 178

Clair, René, French film director, 282

class structure, 43 f.

Clemenceau, Georges, French prime minister, 17, 83, 145, *158*, 161–4, 186

Clementis, Vladimir, Czech foreign minister, 29

Clouzot, Henri, French film director, 282

Cocteau, Jean, French writer and film director, 282, 305

Cohn-Bendit, Daniel, 315, 320

Cold War, 286 ff.

Colette, French writer, 21

Cologne, 164, 238, 240

Colombey-les-deux-églises, 309

Comintern, 167, 214, 220

Commune, *see* Paris

communism, 46, 85, 167, 210–11, 304

concentration camps, 202–3, 244–8

Concorde, 313, *330*

Confederación Nacional de Trabajo, 104

Congo, 72, *74*, 75, 307, 334

Conrad, Joseph, Polish-British writer, 21, 57, 177

Constantinople, 57, 159

Corelli, Marie, British writer, 28

Coty, René, French president, 206

Court of International Justice, 195

Coventry, 230

Cripps, Sir Stafford, British minister, 264

Croatia, 198; *see also* Yugoslavia

Cuba, 73, 311–12

Cyprus, *336–7*, 338–9

Czechoslovakia, 52, 149, 165, 168, 174, 185, 186, 268, 286, 290–1; German invasion of, 218, 220–1, 222–3; 1968 Rising in, 320–3, 324

Daimler, Gottlieb, 34

Daniel, Yuly, Soviet writer, 327

D'Annunzio, Gabrielle, Italian poet and politician, 181, *182*

Danzig, 195, 221

Day-Lewis, Cecil, British poet, 214

D-Day, 240–2

Debray, Regis, 315

Debussy, Claude, French composer, 21

Degas, Edgar, French artist, *26–7*

Degrelle, Léon, Belgian fascist, 206

Delcassé, Théophile, French foreign minister, 72

Denmark, 49, 169, 228, 311, 329

Derain, André, French painter, 91

de Sica, Vittorio, Italian film director, 282

Detaille, Edouard, French painter, 15

Dicey, Edward, 109

Dien Bien Phu, *275*, 272, 307

Diesel, Rudolf, 34

Dietrich, Marlene, German actress, 20

Dimbleby, Richard, British broadcaster, 244

Dior, Christian, French couturier, 282

disarmament, 193 ff.; World Disarmament Conference, 196–7

Douglas, Lord Alfred, 17

Draga, queen of Serbia, 118

Dresden, 48, 104, *239*, 240

Dreyfus, Capt. Alfred, 15

Dual Monarchy, 52 ff., 117 ff.

Dubcek, Alexander, Czech leader, 322–3

Dublin, 32

Dulles, John Foster, US secretary of state, 303

Dumont, Santos, Brazilian flyer, 18

Dürer, Albrecht, *150*

Düsseldorf, 240

Ebert, Friedrich, German president, 169

Ebro, 218

economy, 107, 188, 190–3, 278–9, 281, 290–1, 313–14; *see also* under individual countries

Eden, Sir Anthony, earl of Avon, British prime minister, 177, 197, 301–3

Edinburgh, Festival, 282

Edward VII, King of Great Britain, 32, *42*, 44, 111

Egypt, 301 ff.

Ehrenburg, Ilya, Soviet writer, 260, 294

Eisenhower, Dwight D., US general and president, 242, 261

Elgar, Sir Edward, British composer, 21

Elizabeth, empress of Austria, 52, 89

Elizabeth II, queen of Great Britain, 291

Engels, Friedrich, German communist, 48, 80, 85, 88

Entente Cordiale, 111 ff.

Eritrea, 75

Esnault-Pelterie, French flyer, 18

Essen, 240

Estonia, 63, 167

Ethiopia, *see* Abyssinia

Eugene, Prince, Austrian general, 56

Europe, union of, 309 ff.

European Coal and Steel community (ECSC), 311

European Economic Community (EEC), 311 ff., 328 ff.

European Free Trade Association (EFTA), 311, 329

Farman, Henry, French flyer, 18, 122
fascism, 181–5, 206–10
Fashoda, 72, 111
Feisal, Emir of Arabia, 165
Ferber, Ferdinand, French flyer, 18
Ferry, Jules, French prime minister, 73
finance, 32, 46, 188
Finland, 63, 94, 167, 231
Fischer, Ernst, Austrian communist, 315
Fiume (Rijeka), 181
flying, early attempts at, 18; Schneider Trophy, 188; Zeppelin, 34–7
Foch, Ferdinand, French marshal, 168
Fonck, René, French airman, 132
Food and Agricultual Organisation (FAO), 334
Foreign Legion, 72–3
France, 11, 14–15, 23, 37, 43, 44, 49, 72–379, 83, 107, 127, 175, 181, 206, 221, 269, 290, 338; army of, 15, 119–20, 127, 149; economy and industry, 21, 269; population, 21; politics in, 100; student unrest in, 317–20; and Algeria, 307–9; and Germany, 64, 76, 111 ff., 186 ff., 228 ff.; and Great Britain, 72, 111 ff., 186; and Indo-China, 272–3; and Italy, 197–9, 206; and Russia, 111 ff.; and Spain, 214–15; and Suez, 301 ff.; and the EEC, 311; and the League, 186; and Versailles Peace Conference, 159, 161 ff.; in World War 1, Chapter 5 *passim;* in World War 2, Chapter 9 *passim*
Franco, Francisco, Spanish leader, 212–14, 220
Frankfurt, 46
Franz Ferdinand, Archduke of Austria, *53,* 124
Franz Josef II, emperor of Austria, 11, 49, 52, *53,* 60, 63, 64, 118, 124, 144
Freud, Sigmund, Austrian psychologist, 41
Friesz, Othon, German painter, 91
Front de Libération Nationale (FLN), 308
Fry, Christopher, British playwright, 282
Fullon, general Ivan, *92*
Fulton, *279,* 283

Gaitskell, Hugh, British politician, 301
Galland, German air force general, 238
Gallifet, Marquis de, French general, 83
Gapon, Father G., *92,* 94–6
Gaulle, Charles de, French general and president, 231, 244, 264, 269, 272–3, 286, *307,* 308 ff., 320, 328, 329
Geismer, Alain, 320

Geneva, 52, 89, 92, 177–8, 185, 195, 196, 272, 334
George II, King of the Hellenes, 280
George V, King of Great Britain, 98, 180 n.
George VI, King of Great Britain, 263
German Democratic Republic, 322–6
German East Africa, 130
Germany, 11, 14, 23, 44, 79, 80, 83, 84–5, 107, 168, 175, 197, 333, 334; air force of, 203, 230; army of, 25, *30–1, 36, 63,* 65, 68, 111, 119–20, 127, 204; division of, 286–7, 295; economy and industry, 21, 29, 34–7, 65, 186–9, 202, 290; Empire and colonies, 49, 63–6, 73, 307; navy of, 68 f., 111, 169, 194, 203; politics, 97 ff., 194 ff., 202; population of, 21, 64–5, 79–80; Weimar, 159, 169, 194; and Austria–Hungary, 63–4, 75, 112, 203–6, 218, 290; and Belgium, 228; and Denmark, 228; and France, 64, 76, 111 ff., 122–3, 186 ff., 228 ff.; and Great Britain, 37 ff., 68 ff., 122–3; and Holland, 228; and Italy, 64, 112, 206–10, 214; and Norway, 228; and Poland, 186, 195, 221 ff., 227–8; and Russia, 76, 111, 221, 233 ff.; and Spain, 214–15; and the EEC, 311; and the League, 190; and Versailles Peace Conf., 165, 169–72; in World War 1, Chapter 5 *passim;* in World War 2, Chapter 9 *passim,* 278
Gero, Erho, Hungarian leader, 300
Ghana, 307
Gibbs, Sir Philip, 180–1
Gide, André, French writer, 21, 210
Gladstone, W. E., British prime minister, 97
Glasgow, 189
Godesberg, 220
Goebbels, Josef, Nazi leader, 202
Goering, Hermann, Nazi leader, 203, 214
Gollancz, Victor, 210
Gomulka, Wladislaw, Polish leader, 291, 297–8
Goncourt, Edmond and Jules, French writers, 83
Gorky, Maxim, Russian writer, 23
Gottwald, Clement, Czech president, 215
Goulue, La, 20
Grable, Betty, American actress, 20
Grandi, Count Dino, Italian fascist leader, *184*
Graves, Robert, British poet, 153
Great Britain, 11, 14, 63, 76, 79, 83, 175, 181, 290; air force of, 193, 230; army of, 25, 70–2, 119, 127, 193; economy and industry, 29–37, 189,

190–3, 202, 281, 291; Empire, 69, 73, 263–4; festival of, 291–4; navy of, *66–7,* 69, 121–2, 193; politics, 97–100, 264; population of, 21, 29, 79–80; and EFTA, 311; and France, 72, 111 ff., 186; and Germany, 37 ff., 68 ff., 122–3; and Ireland, 99–100; and Italy, 197–9, 208; and Russia, 112 ff.; and Serbia, 124; and Spain, 214; and Suez, 301 ff.; and the EEC, 328 ff.; and the League, 186; and Versailles Peace Conf., 159; in World War 1, ch. 5 *passim,* 160; in World War 2, ch. 9 *passim,* 258 ff., 261–3
Greece, 44, 56, 195, 280–1; and Italy, 76; and Turkey, 76, 123, 165, 174, 338–9; in World War 2, 231
Greer, Germaine, 315
Grey, Sir Edward, Viscount, British foreign secretary, 125
Grigorenko, Pyotr, Soviet general, 327
Guadalajara, 218
Guilbert, Yvette, French music-hall star, 20
Gunther, John, 185
Guynemer, Georges, French airman, 132

Habsburg dynasty, 49–56, 63, 76, 153, 159, 333
Hague, The, 195, 309
Haile Selassie, Emperor of Abyssinia, 199
Haldane Reforms, 25
Hamburg, 34, 238–40
Hanoi, 73
Hanotaux, Gabriel, French historian and statesman, 83
Hardy, Thomas, British writer, 23
Hauptmann, Gerhart, German playwright, 240
Haussmann, Eugène-Georges, Baron, 17, 157
Haydn, Joseph, Austrian composer, 41
Heath, Edward, British prime minister, 329, 332
Hedin, Sven, 136
Henderson, Arthur, British foreign secretary, 177, 196
Herriot, Edouard, French prime minister, 189
Herzegovina, 118
Himmler, Heinrich, head of German Gestapo, 202, 248
Hindenburg, Paul von, German field-marshal and president, 144
Hiroshima, 263, 283
Hitler, Adolf, German Führer, 109, *192,* 194, 197, 202 ff., *204–5,* 212, 214, 218, 220 ff., 227 ff., *247,* 254, 261, 333
Ho Chi Minh, North Vietnam president, 272

Hofmannsthal, Hugo von, Austrian poet, 41
Hohenzollern dynasty, 64, 69, 76, 333
Holland, *see* Netherlands
Holland, Henryk, 297
Hong Kong, 69, 258
Horne, Alistair, 83 n.
Horthy, Admiral Nicholas, Hungarian leader, 174, 255
Höss, Rudolph, Auschwitz commander, 248
Hötzendorff, Conrad von, Austrian chief-of-staff, 118
Hugo, Victor, French writer, 85, 89
Humanité, L', 48
Hungary, 118, 165, 168, 174, 185, 186, 215, 231, 255–6, 268, 291, 326, 339; 1956 Rising, *297*, 298–301, 303–4, 322, 334; *see also* Austria–Hungary
Huxley, Prof. Julian, British scientist, 210

Ibarruri, Dolores, Spanish communist leader, 220
India, 11, 63, 69, 72, 109, 130, 234, 237, 258, 265, 312
Indo-China, 11, 72, 258, 263, 265, 272–3, 307
Indonesia, 268, 272
industry, 21, 29, 34, 91; *see also* economy
International Labour Organisation, 195
International Working Men's Association, 48, 88
Ireland, 23, 29, 99 ff., 174, 329, 338
iron curtain, 279
Isonzo river, 138, 333
Israel, 303, 327, 332, 334
Italian Somaliland, 75
Italy, 11, 52, 64, 75, 79, 88, 89, 168, 175, 186, 333, 334; and Abyssinia, 197–9; and Austria-Hungary, 64, 76, 112; and fascism, 181–5, 206–10; and France, 197–9, 206; and Germany, 64, 112, 208–10, 214; and Great Britain, 197–9, 206; and Greece, 78; and Spain, 212–15, 218; and the EEC, 311; and Turkey, 123; and Versailles Peace Conf., 159, 164; in World War 1, 138 ff., 149–52, 160; in World War 2, ch. 9 *passim*

Japan, 11, 37, 63, 130, 196–7; in World War 2, 234 ff., 258–63; war with Russia, 94, 107–9, *114*
Jaurès, Jean, French socialist leader, *46*, 48, 100
Java, 73, 258
Jawlensky, Alexei, Russian painter, 104

Jews, 60–3, 203, 248
John of Austria, 56

Kaganovich, Lazar M., Soviet leader, 298
Kamenev, Lev B., Soviet leader, 146, 211
Kandinsky, Vasily, Russian painter, 104
Karl, Emperor of Austria, *53*, 144, 153, 159
Katyn, 251
Kautsky, Karl, German socialist, 48
Kellogg Pact (1928), 190
Kemal Ataturk, Mustafa, Turkish leader, 174
Kennedy, John F., US president, 311–12
Khrushchev, Nikita S., Soviet leader, 294–5, 297, 298, 311–12, 322
Kiev, 233
Kipling, Rudyard, British writer, 119
Kippenberger, NZ general, 237
Kirchner, Ernst, German painter, 104
Kitchener, Herbert, earl, British field-marshal, 72, 136
Klimt, Gustav, Austrian painter, 41
Koblenz, 164
Koenig, Marie-Pierre, French general, 269
Koestler, Arthur, 215
Koner, Ivan S., Russian general, 214
Königgratz, battle of (1866), 63, 64
Korea, 334
Kostov, Traicho, Bulgarian leader, 291
Kosygin, Alexey N., Soviet prime minister, 322
Krupp, Alfred, *33, 81*
Krupskaya, Nadezhda, Lenin's wife, *166*
Kun, Bela, Hungarian leader, 174

Lansdowne, Marquess of, British statesman, 142
Laos, 73, 272
Lattre de Tassigny, French marshal, 272
Latvia, 63, 167
Laval, Pierre, French prime minister, 197, 272
Lawrence, D. H., British writer, 130
League of Nations, 153, 161, 164, 172–4, 177 ff., 185, 186, 189, 193, 195 ff., 210, 221, 279, 334
Lean, David, British film director, 282
Leclerc, French general, 244
Lee, Laurie, British poet, 25, 339
Lehar, Franz, Hungarian composer, 41
Lenin, Vladimir (Ulyanov), Soviet leader, 76, 92, 146, *166*, 177, 211, 287, *289*, 333, 339
Leningrad, 57, 76, *92*, 94–6, 100, 146, 233, 238, 327; siege of 233–4

Leopold II, King of Belgium, 75
Leopold of Prussia, prince, 246
Lepanto, battle of (1571), 56
Lerroux, Alejandro, 89
Lesseps, Ferdinand de, 301
Libya, *see* Tripoli
Liddell Hart, Sir Basil, 230
Lille, 80, *142*
Lissauer, Ernst, German poet, 138
Lithuania, 63, 167, 168, 186
Litvinov, Maxim, Soviet foreign minister, 210
Liverpool, 230
Lloyd George, David, earl, British prime minister, 98, 122–3, 145, 152, *158*, 161, 224
Lloyds of London, 32
Locarno, Treaties of, 174–5, 190
Lodz, 63
London, 14, 21, 23, 25, 29, 32, 46, 80, 85, 92, 189, 230, 238, 261, 279, 340; Treaty of, 116
Lorenzo, Anselmo, 100
Lorraine, 65, 169
Loti, Manon, 18
Loubet, Emile, French president, 17
Ludendorff, Erich von, German general, 144
Luxembourg, 273, 290, 311
Lyons, 269

MacArthur, Douglas, US general, 263
MacDonald, Ramsay, British prime minister, 98, 177–8, 189, 193, 196
Macedonia, 56
Macke, August, German painter, 104
McKinley, William, US president, 84; assassination of, 89
Macmillan, Harold, British prime minister, 328–9
MacNeice, Louis, British poet, 211, 214, 220, 224
Madrid, 25, 212, 218, 221, 340
Mahler, Gustav, Austrian composer, 41
Maidanek, 246, 260
Mainz, 164
Malaya, 11, 258
Malenkov, Georgy M., Soviet leader, 294
Malinovsky, Rodion Ya., Soviet marshal, 214, 256
Malraux, André, French writer, 218
Malta, 56
Manchuria, 94, 107, 196
Mannheim, 240
Mannock, Edward, British airman, 132
Marc, Franz, German painter, 104
Marchand, Jean B., French soldier, 72

Marinetti, Filippo, Italian writer and politician, 104, 181, 315
Marseilles, 80, 269
Marshall, George C., US general and secretary of state, 282; Marshall Plan, 282–3, 290, 313
Marty, André, French communist, 215
Marx, Karl, German communist, 48, 80, 85, 88, 133
Masaryk, Jan, Czech foreign minister, 268
Masaryk, Thomas, Czech president, 168, 268
Matisse, Henri, French painter, 90, 91
Maximilian, emperor of Mexico, 52
Mayerling, 52
Menzies, Sir Robert, Australian prime minister, 303
Merker, Paul, E. German leader, 291
Michael, King of Rumania, 255, 265
Mihailović, Draža, Yugoslav Chetnik leader, 231–3
Mikolajcyk, Stanislaw, Polish leader, 252
Mikoyan, Anastas I., Soviet leader, 294, 298
Milan, 23, 48, 80, 183
Mistinguett, French actress, 20
Molotov, Vyacheslav M., Soviet foreign minister, 294, 298
Monet, Claude, French painter, 20
Monnet, Jean, French statesman, 311
Monte Cassino, 236–8
Montenegro, 231
Moore, Henry, British artist and sculptor, 243
Morocco, 111–12, 122–3, 130, 212, 237, 307
Moscow, 61, 94, 108, 166, 211, 233, 256, 279, 292, 298, 340
Mosley, Sir Oswald, British politician, 206
Motor-car, 28–9, 34
Moulin Rouge, 10, 20
Mountbatten, Louis, earl, British admiral, 263, 265
Mozart, W. A., Austrian composer, 41
Muggeridge, Malcolm, 199, 220
Mukden, battle of (1905), 108
mulberry harbours, 242
Müller, Hermann, German chancellor, 172
Munich, 48, 194, 220, 221, 240, 256
Münter, Gabriele, German painter, 104
Murray, Prof. Gilbert, 186, 197, 334
music-hall, in Paris, 20
Mussolini, Benito, Italian fascist leader, 181–5, 194, 197, 206–10, 212, 214, 220, 221, 231, 236, 260–1, 333

Nagasaki, 263, 282
Nagy, Imre, Hungarian prime minister, 300
Naples, 46
Napoleon I, 121, 340
Napoleon III, emperor of France, 17, 119, 157, 201 n.
Nash, Paul, British artist, 134–5, 202, 227
Nasser, Gamal Abdul, Egyptian president, 301
Nazi party, 202 ff.
Nechaev, Sergey, Russian anarchist, 88
Nenni, Pietro, Italian socialist leader, 215
Netherlands, 73, 159, 228, 244, 249, 258, 268–9, 273, 311
Netherlands East Indies, 11, 73, 258, 263, 268
Neuville, Alfred de, French painter, 15
New Guinea, 11, 65, 68, 73, 258
New York, 73, 268, 279
New Zealand, 11, 69, 70, 127, 234, 238
newspapers, 63, 110, 112, 122, 138, 142, 190, 332
Nicholas II, tsar of Russia, 11, 44, 60, 63, 146, 159
Nicolson, Sir Harold, British diplomat, 32, 161, 165
Niemöller, Martin, German pastor, 246
Nietzsche, Friedrich, German philosopher, 40, 105
Nixon, Richard M., US president, 335
Noel-Baker, Philip, 279
North Atlantic Treaty Organisation (NATO), 290, 295, 304, 328
Norway, 44, 116, 228, 249, 311
Nowa Kultura, 297
Nuremburg, 204–5, 240

Omdurman, battle of, 72
Oradour-sur-Glane, 242
Orange Free State, 70
Organisation Armée Secrète (OAS), 308
Organisation of European Economic Co-operation (OEEC), 282
Orlando, Vittorio, Italian prime minister, 165
Orpen, Sir William, Irish artist, 157
Orwell, George, British writer, 218
Osborne, John, British playwright, 305

Paderewski, Jan, Polish prime minister, 165
painting, styles of: Academician, 20; art nouveau, 90; Blaue Reiter, 104; Brücke, 104; Classical, 20; Cubist, 104; Expressionist, 104; Fauvist, 91; Futurist, 104–5, 181; Impressionist,

20–1, 90; Neo-Impressionist, 90; Orphist, 104; Post-Impressionist, 90; Romantic, 20; Sezessionist, 41; Simultanist, 104
Pakistan, 265
Pankhurst, Mrs Emmeline, 99
Panov, Valery and Galina, Soviet dancers, 327
Paris, 14, 23, 46, 48, 80, 83–4, 88, 89–91, 111, 128–9, 148, 157, 165, 174, 215, 228, 244, 269, 281, 308, 318, 322, 322, 340; life in, 17 ff.; Paris Commune, 83–4, 85, 88, 100; Paris World Fair, 12–13, 14–15, 238
Pasič, Nicola, Serbian statesman, 165
Passchendaele, 152
Pauker, Anna, Rumanian leader, 291
Paulus, Friedrich von, German general, 255
Pavlovsk, 234
Pearl Harbor, 108, 258
peasants, 22–5, 79, 91 ff.
Péguy, Charles, French writer, 21
Peking, 76
Persia, 320
Pétain, Henri, French marshal, 272
Peterhof, 234
Phèdre, by Rawne, 20
Philip, Duke of Edinburgh, 291
Philippines, 73
Picasso, Pablo, Spanish painter, 90, 104
Pilsudski, Józef, Polish marshal, 195
Placentia Bay, 258
Plehve, V. K., Russian minister, 92
Plekhanov, George, Russian Marxist, 92
Pluto, 242
Poincaré, Raymond, French president, 17, 133, 186, 188
Polaire, 18
Poland, 49, 52, 63, 149, 164, 165, 167–8, 169, 174, 185–6, 195, 265, 290–1, 297–9, 322, 326, 339; in World War 2, 221–4, 227 ff., 251 ff., 256, 278
Polish Corridor, 168, 186, 218
Politics, theory of, 85, 314–15
Pompidou, Georges, French president, 320, 329, 332
Port Arthur, 107–8, 121
Port Said, 303
Portugal, 11, 73, 221, 311
Potsdam conference, 263
Pougy, Liane de, 18
Pradhan, R. G., 109
Prague, 41, 48, 49, 220, 221, 222–3, 279, 317, 322, 325
Primo de Rivera, Antonio, Spanish statesman, 195
Princip, Gavrilo, Serbian anachist, 124
Proust, Marcel, French writer, 21; Remembrance of Things Past, 21
Prussia, see Germany

Puccini, Giacomo, Italian composer, 21
  Tosca, 21
Puerto Rico, 73

Radek, Karl, Soviet leader, 211
radio, 178–80
Rajk, Laszlo, Hungarian communist leader, 215, 291, 300
Rakosi, Mathias, Hungarian leader, 215, 298
Rattigan, Sir Terence, British playwright, 282
Ravel, Maurice, French composer, 21
Reed, Sir Carol, British film director, 282
refugees, 277
religion, 25, 56, 79, 339
Remagen, 244
Renner, Karl, Austrian leader, 286
Renoir, Auguste, French painter, 20
reparations, 186 ff.
Resistance, French, in World War 2, 242–4
Rhine, crossing of, in World War 2, 244
Ribot, Alexandre, French politician, 17
Richthofen, Manfred von, German airman, 132
Rodin, Auguste, French sculptor, 21
Röhm, Ernst, Nazi SA leader, 248
Rokossovsky, Konstantin, Soviet marshal, 214, 254, 256
Rolls-Royce, 32
Romanov dynasty, 76, 159, 333
Rome, 14, 183; Treaty of, 311
Roosevelt, Franklin D., US president, 234, 254, 256–8, 263, 279
Roosevelt, Theodore, US president, 112
Roque, Col. de la, 206
Rossellini, Roberto, Italian film director, 282
Rostand, Edmond, French poet, 20, 21
Rothschild family, 46
Rotterdam, 228, 230, 238
Rouault, Georges, French painter, 91
Rousseau, Henri, Le Douanier, French painter, 91, *102*
Rudolf, Crown Prince of Austria, 52
Ruhr, 80, 188, 194, 240
Rumania, 44, 56, 118, 165, 168, 174, 185, 231, 254–5, 265–8, 291, 322, 326
Russell, Bertrand, Earl, British philosopher, 21
Russia, 11, 14, 23, 44, 56, 57–63, 64, 79, 80, 83, 118 ff., 165, 167, 174, *187*, 210, 283, 333; army of, 25, *61*, 63 f., 119; civil war in, 167; economy and industry, 91, 189, 211; Empire, 49; politics in, 92 ff.; purges in, 211, 291; revolution of 1905, 94–7; revolution of 1917, 145–6; social conditions in 91 ff.; and Austria-Hungary, 76; and cold war,

286 ff., 322 ff.; and Cuba, 311–12; and eastern Europe, 265; and France, 111 ff.; and Germany, 76, 111, 221, 233 ff.; and Great Britain, 112 ff.; and Hungary, 298 ff., 303–4; and Japan, 94, 107 ff., 121; and Poland, 168, 251 ff., 297–8; and Spain, 214; and the League, 180–1; in World War 1, ch. 5 *passim*; in World War 2, ch. 9 *passim*, 251 ff., 278

Saar, 195
Sadowa, 63
Saigon, 73
Saint-Exupéry, Antoine de, French writer, 215
St Petersburg, *see* Leningrad
Sakharov, Andrey, Soviet scientist, 327
Salisbury, Marquess of, British prime minister, 309
Salzburg Festival, 41
Samoa, 68
San Francisco, 279
Santander, 218
Sarajevo, 52, 124
Sargent, J. S., American painter, 21
Sartre, Jean-Paul, French writer, 282, 304
Sauvageot, Jacques, 320
Scandinavia, 116
Scheidemann, Philipp, German chancellor, 169
Schlieffen, Count Alfred von, Prussian marshal, 111; Schlieffen Plan, 111, 116
Schneider Trophy, 189
Schnitzler, Arthur, Austrian playwright, 41
Schoenberg, Arnold, Austrian composer, 41
Schumacher, Kurt, 246
Schumann, Robert, French foreign and prime minister, 311
Senegal, 130
Senger und Etterlin, general von, 237–8
Serbia, 56, 118 ff., 123 ff., 196; *see also* Yugoslavia
Sergey, Grand Duke, 94
Sert, José Maria, Catalan artist, 199
Severini, Gino, Italian artist, *177*
Shanghai, 196
Shaw, George Bernard, Irish playwright, 21, 210
Shipping, 32, 34
Shostakovich, Dmitri, Soviet composer, 234
Sibelius, Jan, Finnish composer, 21
Sicily, *235*, 236
Sickert, Walter, *100*

Sikorski, Wladyslaw, Polish prime minister, 252
Singapore, 69, 258, 263
Sinyavsky, Andrey, Soviet writer, 327
Sipyagin, D. S., Russian minister, 92
Sitwell, Sir Osbert, British writer, 25, 28–9, *38–9*
Slansky, Rudolph, Czech leader, 291
Slovakia, 52
Smith, F. E. (Lord Birkenhead), 98
Smolensk, 233, 251
society, structure of, 43 ff.; life in Paris, 17 ff.; in Vienna, 41
Sofia, 279
Solzhenitsyn, Alexander, Soviet writer, 327–8
Somme, battle of the, 136, 333
Sophie, wife of Franz Ferdinand, *53*, 124
Sorbonne, 317, 318
South Africa, 14, 65, 69, 70–2, 121, 127, 234
South America, 11, 73
South-West Africa, 68, 130
Soviet Union, *see* Russia
space research, 312–13
Spain, 11, 44, 73, 88, 100–4, 116, 195, 313, 339; Civil War, *200*, 211–21
Stalin, Joseph (Dzhugashvili), Soviet leader, 210, 214, 221, 251 ff., 263, 268, 279, 280, *289*, 291, 294–5, 297, 298, 333
Stalingrad, 240, 255, 256
Stanley, H. M., US explorer, 75
Stern, Lazar, Rumanian soldier, 215
Strasbourg, 244, 329, 332
Strauss, Johann, Austrian composer, 41
Stresemann, Gustav, German foreign minister, *171*, 175, 189, 194, 328
Strindberg, August, Swedish playwright, 23
Stuttgart, 240
Sudan, 72, 312
Suez, 301 ff., 317, 334
Suffragette movement, 99
Sumatra, 73, 258
Surinam, 73
Sweden, 116, 231, 311
Switzerland, 43, 89, 127, 146, 177, 231, 311

Tailhade, Laurent, French poet, 88
Tanganyika, 68
Tangier, 111–12
Tasmania, 268
Taylor, A. J. P., British historian, 69, 97
Tennyson, Alfred, Lord, British poet, 201
Teschen, 186
Thony, E., *112*
Tillett, Ben, 98

Tirpitz, Alfred von, German admiral, 68
Tito, Josip (Broz), Yugoslav president, 215, 231–3, 255, *256*, 286, 294
Todt Organisation, 240
Togoland, 68
Tolbukhin, Soviet marshal, 256
Toledo, 218
Tolstoy, Count Leo, Russian writer, 23, 92
Toulouse-Lautrec, Henri, French painter, 20
Trade Unions, 83, 100, 202
transport, 25 ff.
Transvaal, 70
Treblinka, 260
Treitschke, Heinrich von, German philosopher, 40
Trianon, Treaty of (1920), 185
Triple Alliance, 64, 75, 112, 290
Triple Entente, 112, 290
Tripoli, 123
Trotsky, Lev (Bronstein), Soviet leader, 97, 146, 211
Truman, Harry S., US president, 263, 280, 281, 282, 286, 335
Truman Doctrine, 281
Tsarskoye, Selo, 234
Tsing-tao, 68, 130
Tsushima Straits, 108
Tunisia, 75, 307
Turkey, 49, 56–7, 63, 76, 117, 149, 159, 164, 165, 174, 280, 281, 338–9; and the Balkans, 116–7, 123 ff.; in World War 1, 130, 138

Udet, Ernst, German airman, 132
Ukraine, 63, 168, 233
Ulbricht, Walter, East German leader, 215, 323
Ulster, 338, 339
Umberto I, King of Italy, 89
United Nations, 279 ff., 303, 304, 326, 334–5
United Nations Educational, Scientific and cultural Organisation (UNESCO), 334
United Nations Relief and Rehabilitation Administration (UNRRA), 334
United States of America, 37, 73, 83, 88, 89, 130, 282–3, 290, 311–12; economy of, 29, 234–6; isolationism of, 146–9, 172–4; and Spain, 215; and Suez, 301 ff.; and the League, 180; and the UN, 279–80; and Versailles Peace Conf., 159 ff., 165–7; in World War 1, 147–9; in World War 2, ch. 9 *passim*, 258 ff.
universities, unrest in, 317

Van Gogh, Vincent, Dutch painter, *58–9*
Vansittart, Robert, 41
Vasilchikov, Prince, 96
Vasilevsky, Alexander M., Soviet marshal, 256
Vatican, 79, 183
Vatutin, Nikolay, Russian general, 256
Venizelos, Eleutherios, Greek prime minister, 165, 174
Verdun, 133, 136, 333
Versailles, Treaty of, 169 ff., 177, 188, 193, 194, 203, 206, 251, 311; Peace Conference, 157 ff.
Vichy, 272
Victoria, Queen of England, 11, 32, *42*, 44, 69, 76, 309
Vienna, 14, 23, 41, 46, 48, 49, *50–1*, 52, 56, 64, 76, 169, 220, 260, 279; life in, 41
Vietnam, 272, 334
Vilna, 186
Vlaminck, Maurice de, French painter, 91
Voisin, Charles and Gabriel, French flyers, 18

Waldeck-Rousseau, René, French prime minister, 17
Warsaw, 63, 174, 221, 228, 230, 238, 252, *253*, 278, 279, 297, 317; Rising in, 252–4, 265
Warsaw Pact, 295, 328
Washington Naval Conference, 193
Webb, Sydney and Beatrice, British economists, 210
Weimar, *see under* Germany
Wellington, Duke of, 37
Werth, Alexander, 234, 254

White, Sam, 332
Wilhelm I, Emperor of Germany, 64
Wilhelm II, Emperor of Germany, 11, *42*, 44, 63, 68, *106*, 109–11, 112, 153, 159
Wilson, Colin, British writer, 305
Wilson, Harold, British prime minister, 329
Wilson, Woodrow, US president, 149, 152–3, 157, *158*, 161–4, 165–7, 172–4, 180, 279
Wittelsbach family, 52, 64
Workers Educational Association (WEA), 32
World Health Organisation (WHO), 334
World War 1, 127–55, 227, 333; causes of, 124–5; casualties in, 136 f., 144, 149, 157–9; tactics in, 121, 149
World War 2, 227–73, 333; causes of, 218 ff.; casualties in, 230, 233, 234, 238–40, 278
Wright, Wilbur and Orville, US flyers, 18

Yalta conference, 256, 260, 265, 268
Yellow Book, The, London magazine, 21
Yevtushenko, Yevgeny, Soviet poet, 327
Ypres, *141*, *147*, 152, 160, 333
Yugoslavia, 56, 118, 165, 168, 181, 185, 186, 195–6, 215, 286, 322 n., 338–9; in World War 2, 231–3, 249, 255, 278; *see also* Croatia, Serbia

Zeiss, 34
Zeppelin, Ferdinand von, 34–7, *139*
Zhdanov, Andrey, A., Soviet leader, 286
Zhukov, Georgy K., Soviet marshal, 256
Zinoviev, Gregory E., Soviet leader, 146, 211
Zita of Bourbon-Parma, Empress of Austria, *53*
Zola, Emile, French writer, 21